1,000

COMMON DELUSIONS

1,000

COMMON DELUSIONS

and the real facts behind them

Christa Pöppelmann

FIREFLY BOOKS

A FIREFLY BOOK

Published by Firefly Books Ltd. 2006

English translation © 2006 Firefly Books Ltd. All rights reserved.
English translation by Storm Dunlop. Additional English language material provided by Charis Cotter, Anna Simmons and Francoise Vulpe.

Title of the original German edition: Christa Poppelmann. 1,000 Irrtumer der
Allgemeinbildung © 2005 by Compact Verlag GmbH, Munchen.

First printing

Publisher Cataloging-in-Publication Data (U.S.)

Pöppelmann, Christa.
    1,000 common delusions : and the real facts behind them / Christa
Pöppelmann.
[320] p. :   cm.
Includes index.
Summary: Debunking myths that are accepted as absolute truths on topics
including: history, politics, natural sciences, technology, society and everyday
life.
ISBN-13: 978-1-55407-174-6 (pbk.)
ISBN-10: 1-55407-174-7 (pbk.)
1. Common fallacies. I. Title.
001.9/6 dc22   AZ999.P688 2006

Library and Archives Canada Cataloguing in Publication

Pöppelmann, Christa
    1,000 common delusions : and the real facts behind them / Christa
Pöppelmann.

Includes index.
ISBN-13: 978-1-55407-174-6
ISBN-10: 1-55407-174-7

    1. Common fallacies. I. Title. II. Title: One thousand common
delusions.

AZ999.P66 2006   001.9'6   C2006-903531-8

Published in the United States by
Firefly Books (U.S.) Inc.
P.O. Box 1338, Ellicott Station
Buffalo, New York 14205

Published in Canada by
Firefly Books Ltd.
66 Leek Crescent
Richmond Hill, Ontario L4B 1H1

Fact checking by Francoise Vulpe
Design by Interrobang Graphic Design Inc.
Jacket photo of Neanderthal by Time Life Pictures/Mansell/Time Life
Pictures/Getty Images

Printed in Canada

Contents

DID WE LIVE IN CAVES OR TREES?

Stone Age humans lived in caves

They lived in huts and tents. The caves that they painted with hunting scenes and representations of animals served only as rooms for ritual ceremonies. However, it is true that they often built their quarters beneath overhanging cliffs at the entrances of caves. Sheltered sites on southern slopes were particularly favored, where people enjoyed plenty of sunshine and had a good view over the landscape.

The Neanderthals died out

This question is still not fully resolved. The Neanderthals (*Homo neanderthalensis*) belonged to the same genus as *Homo sapiens sapiens*, and lived between approximately 150,000 and 28,000 years BP (Before Present) in Europe, where *Homo sapiens sapiens* appeared about 40,000 years BP. Formerly it was assumed that the more evolved *Homo sapiens* displaced the Neanderthals. More recently, many researchers think that it is most likely that the Neanderthals also continued to evolve and interbred with the new arrivals. Very recently, scientists have begun genetic studies, but as yet the information obtained in this way is extremely sparse.

Africa was the cradle of humanity

Scientists believed that they had discovered that all humans originated in East Africa, because it was only there that the early primates appear to have evolved into early anthropoids. Admittedly, there have also been primate finds in Asia, some of which are even older than the African ones. But the Asian representatives do not appear to have evolved any further. Recently, however, younger fossils have been found in Pakistan that are "only" 30 million to 23 million years old, and which, in contrast to previous discoveries, could well have evolved toward anthropoids.

The art of early humans was primitive

Not at all: When a Spanish amateur archaeologist discovered the Altamira cave paintings in 1879, all the experts declared that the paintings were modern fakes. According to them, Stone Age people would not have been capable of producing such works of art. This view has long since been revised. Art historians even distinguish between different styles of cave painting. With their complex hunting scenes, the Altamira pictures (10,000 to 6,000 years BP) in Spain belong to the so-called "Levantine" style, while the older paintings at the Lascaux grotto (30,000 years BP) in France are considered to belong to the "Large Animal" style.

Our ancestors did not live in trees

It has often been stressed that humans are not descended from apes, but do share common ancestors with them. These ancestors, however, include small mammals that lived in trees, where they fed on insects. Experts believe that a crucial evolutionary step did actually occur in trees. This habitat offered relatively good shelter and was technically demanding, causing flexible hands and climbing skills to develop. Whereas our human ancestors gave up their arboreal existence, some types of apes live more or less exclusively in the treetops.

WHEELS, WORK AND TATTOOS

The most important discovery was the wheel

The decisive discovery for humans was the hand-axe. However primitive it may have been, it was the first tool manufactured by humans. This was a catalyst. Rather than using accidentally encountered objects as tools, people began to create tools and utensils deliberately. Many cultures managed to get on very well without the wheel, but it is not possible to find any culture without toolmakers.

Agriculture and animal husbandry developed where the conditions were particularly favorable

Agriculture and animal husbandry developed where living conditions were unsuitable for hunter-gatherers. No society that was able to obtain sufficient food by hunting and gathering wild plants took the pains to start agriculture. What appears to us with hindsight as an advance was simply born of necessity. In the Near East, where the first farming was done, the hunter-gatherers' sources of food fell into short supply around 10,000 BC because of the detrimental climate changes that occurred at the end of the Ice Age.

The first metal to be worked was bronze

The first metal works of art were made from copper. As early as 12,000 years ago it was worked by beating, and from about 3500 BC it was also smelted. However, copper is too soft to be used for weapons or tools. This is why there is no Copper Age. The secret of bronze production was probably discovered by chance during the smelting of copper. Otherwise it would not be at all obvious that a mixture of two soft metals such as copper and tin produces a much harder one.

The art of tattooing came from the South Seas

"Ötzi the Iceman" (ca. 3300 BC), a frozen man found in the Alps in 1991, had tattoos. Tattoos that are almost 4,000 years old are also known from Egypt. There the pharaohs adorned their bodies with an ivy-leaf pattern. Representations of animals were also popular. The Pictish tribes in Scotland adopted tattooing to such an extent that their whole bodies were blue. There is also an old tradition for tattooing in Japan. The art of imprinting the skin with colored materials was developed independently by many cultures around the world. In recent times, however, European sailors brought the tradition from the South Pacific. The word "tattoo" is from the Tahitian *tatau*, meaning "to mark."

9

STONEHENGE AND DRUIDS

Stonehenge was a Celtic shrine

Even though so many modern druids assemble at Stonehenge for their esoteric meetings, the sacred site was built long before Celtic times. The earliest sections were created about 3100 BC, and the two large stone circles were erected between 2150 and 2000 BC. The stones were rearranged into the horseshoe and circle that we see today in about 1500 BC — and thus about 1,000 years before the Celts first arrived in the British Isles.

Stonehenge was built by the Druids

Stonehenge predates the Druids by more than 1,000 years. The misconception originated in 1740 when writer John Aubrey declared that Stonehenge was built by the Druids. Antiquary William Stukeley later confirmed this theory, and many people believe it to this day.

The Druids were Celtic magicians

There were three classes of Druids. The most respected were the priests. Then came the soothsayers and then the bards. Each class had its own secret form of training, which, in the case of the priests, lasted 20 years, but for the bards lasted just seven years. Among the Celts, the Druids were the sole authority higher than the tribes. As such, they functioned as judges and mediators in political conflicts.

THE INDO-EUROPEANS

The Indo-Europeans were one people

The Indo-Europeans can only be considered as a linguistic group. It is possible that there was one population that spoke the original Indo-European language. Candidates for this might be the nomadic Kurgan people of southern Russia. The Indo-European language and culture spread out from this region toward Europe and India in the third century BC. But it is not known whether this occurred through actual migration of the original Indo-Europeans or whether only the language and culture were passed on.

The Indo-Europeans conquered Europe

Predatory, seminomadic tribes appeared in Central Europe around 2000 BC, bringing with them an Indo-European speech and culture, including patriarchal gods and a hierarchical structure to society. They probably pushed forward as far as the Rhine River. How much of this was conquest and how much peaceful infiltration is unknown. The new arrivals did, admittedly, stamp their language on the earlier inhabitants, but in return adopted their settled way of life. Western Europe was first "Indo-Europeanized" by the spread of the Celts from about 500 BC.

Apart from Finnish and Hungarian, all European languages are Indo-European. There are a few additional exceptions: Estonian, which is related to Finnish; Basque, which is definitely a relict from pre-Indo-European times; Maltese, a Semitic language; and Turkish.

BABYLONIAN KINGS AND WORKERS

The Sumerian city-states were subjugated by Semitic invaders

The rulers of the Sumerian city-state in the third century BC endeavored to get as many of the neighboring Semitic nomads to settle down as possible in order to strengthen their state by increasing the labor force and the number of available soldiers. In addition, there was the constant danger of attacks on the cities by the nomads. Over the course of time, the Semitic proportion of the population grew to such an extent that their language was adopted. Culturally, however, there was no major change.

King Hammurabi enacted a revolutionary code of laws

The codex of the Babylonian king Hammurabi (1810–1750 BC), which is engraved on a black basalt column, is the most comprehensive collection of laws of early historical times, and contains an impressively precise code of laws. Criminal law based on the principle of "An eye for an eye, a tooth for a tooth," however, was by no means an advance, as was believed for a long time. We have since discovered the code of laws laid down by King Urnammu of Ur, which was created around 2050 BC. This punishes injuries with fines, and calls for the death penalty far more infrequently than Hammurabi's code.

Belshazzar was King of Babylon

The Book of Daniel in the Old Testament impressively recounts how the ruler of Babylon saw a threatening message appear on a wall, beginning with the words "*Mene Tekel*," and that predicted his rapid demise. In fact, in 539 BC, Babylon was captured by the Persian king Cyrus (reigned 559–529 BC), who was welcomed by the inhabitants with palm fronds and rejoicing. Belshazzar was killed, probably by his own people. He was, in any case, not the king of Babylon, but only governed it in the name of his father, Nabonidus (reigned 555–539 BC), who was so unpopular that he was not seen in his capital city for a period of 11 years.

Nebuchadnezzar II conquered Israel

The Babylonian king conquered the kingdom of Judea in 587 BC, and bore the inhabitants into "Babylonian exile." After the death of the Israelite king Solomon (ca. 965–926 BC), his realm was divided. The northern region retained the name of Israel, while the smaller region with its capital Jerusalem was called Judea, because it contained most of the area held by the tribe of Judah. By the time of Nebuchadnezzar's regency (reigned 605–562 BC), Israel itself no longer existed. It was destroyed by the Assyrians in 732 BC.

Temple prostitution was a typically Babylonian practice

There was temple prostitution in other cultures as well: Greece, for example. The Aphrodite temple at Corinth may have had as many as 1,000 prostitutes. The proceeds went to the benefit of the temple. However, the temple prostitutes in Greece were slaves. In Babylon, by contrast, as Herodotus (485–425 BC) states indignantly, every woman had to sleep with a stranger at the Ishtar temple once in her life, and donate the proceeds to the temple. The Greeks and the Jews regarded this as the height of immorality.

Social welfare was introduced in recent times

It was practiced in early history. In the Persian kings' workshops in the second half of the first century BC, for example, both male and female workers continued to receive their wages in the case of illness and women were given maternity leave as well as support from state-employed midwives. Men and women received equal pay, and this applied to simple workers as well as to those at management level.

PYRAMIDS AND PHARAOHS

Ancient Egyptian kings were called pharaohs

Each of the Egyptian kings had many titles, but pharaoh was not one of them. Not until the 14th century BC did ordinary people begin to describe the royal palace, the capital and the king himself with the term *"Par-o"* (Great House) — rather like the way the Pope and his whole power structure are known as the "Holy See." At that time the captive Israelites adopted the name of "pharaoh" for the king, and employed it in their literature as the king's title. In 950 BC "pharaoh" became the official title for the Egyptian ruler.

Khufu was buried in the Pyramid of Khufu

The Great Pyramid of Giza actually contains two burial chambers. One lies beneath the structure, as is customary with other pyramids. The second is located at a height of about 138 feet (42 meters), and is accompanied by numerous small chambers and shafts that have still not been fully explored. In the upper chamber investigators found a heavy, unfinished sarcophagus of pink granite that had never contained anyone's mortal remains. Whether Khufu (reigned ca. 2551–2528 BC, and also known by his Greek name, Cheops) was buried in an even more secret spot, or whether he died in such a way that his body was lost, we do not know.

The pyramids were built by slaves

The construction of the pyramids drew on the general Egyptian population. Each summer from July to October, when the fields were flooded by the Nile, that is how the farmers earned their living. In return for their work, they obtained free accommodation and food, and probably also a small wage. In addition, building the tomb of the pharaoh counted as service to the gods. Experts estimate that there were a few tens of thousands of such unskilled workers on a pyramid's building site during the building season. There were also a couple of thousand craftsmen.

The pyramids appear just as they did 4,500 years ago

Ancient Egyptians would consider the present state of the pyramids quite shabby. Originally the pyramids were faced with polished white limestone slabs. Ancient eyewitnesses reported rapturously that they glowed in the moonlight as if they were made of crystal, illuminated from within. In addition, the summit was covered with gold. When a ray of sunlight fell on the golden pinnacle, it was viewed as a direct link between Heaven and Earth; between the Sun God and the king. The obelisks had similar golden summits.

The tombs of the pharaohs in the Valley of the Kings were well hidden

Because the tombs in the giant pyramids fell victim to tomb robbers despite trapdoors and secret passageways, in the 16th century BC the pharaohs transferred their tombs to the narrow, winding Valley of the Kings. Initially they tried to keep their locations secret. The tombs were cut into the cliff at a height of about 100 feet (30 meters). But the rulers soon decided to lay out the tombs at ground level and to protect them by having the magnificently decorated entrances continually guarded. Ultimately neither of these tactics helped against tomb robbers.

Tutankhamen had a particularly magnificent tomb

The young (and not particularly influential) ruler Tutankhamen (reigned ca. 1332–1323 BC) lay in the only pharaoh's tomb that had not been plundered. The small, modest tomb remained unnoticed because the splendid entrance of the burial place of King Ramses VI (reigned ca. 1142–1132 BC) was built on top of it. From this we can conclude that other tombs were even more sumptuous.

MUMMIES AND HIEROGLYPHICS

In mummification the brain was extracted through the nose

Only with the rich. The well-known method of mummification where not only the brain, but also all other inner organs were carefully removed, was so expensive that only the upper classes were able to afford it. With those who had less money to spend, cedar oil was squirted into all the natural openings in the body, which dissolved the inner organs. The bodies of the poor, however, were simply laid in a bath containing a solution of salt or natron (soda) to dry out.

The Sphinx is female

The Egyptian Sphinx is the

representation of a pharaoh

with the body of a

lion — probably

Khafra (reigned

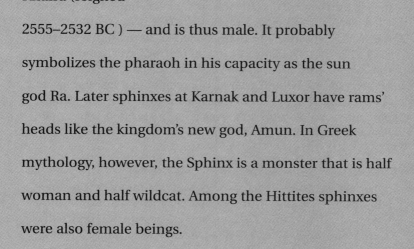

2555–2532 BC) — and is thus male. It probably

symbolizes the pharaoh in his capacity as the sun

god Ra. Later sphinxes at Karnak and Luxor have rams'

heads like the kingdom's new god, Amun. In Greek

mythology, however, the Sphinx is a monster that is half

woman and half wildcat. Among the Hittites sphinxes

were also female beings.

The Egyptians wrote in hieroglyphics

The word "hieroglyphics" means "Holy Signs." The complicated hieroglyphic script was used only for ritual purposes and official inscriptions. For daily use, from about 1500 BC there was an abstract, simpler script known as hieratic. About 700 BC, a second basic script, demotic, was employed, which was probably suited to the daily speech current at that time. Both scripts were written with a brush on papyrus.

UNUSUAL PHARAOHS

Hatshepsut was the only queen pharaoh

There were a few other queens who ruled Egypt. For example, there is a theory that the pharaoh at the end of the 6th Dynasty was a female, Nitokris (reigned ca. 2184–2181 BC), and at the end of the 12th Dynasty, Sobeknefru reigned from approximately 1790–1782 BC. Cleopatra VII (ca. 69–30 BC) was another. But Hatshepsut (reigned ca. 1494–82 BC) was the most famous, because she left behind a wonderful temple, and many works of art depicting her reign. She does seem to be the only female pharaoh who adopted the insignia associated with male pharaohs, including a Vandyke beard.

Hatshepsut was murdered by her successor

Originally, Hatshepsut acted as regent for her underage nephew and stepson Thutmose III (reigned ca. 1504–1450 BC). After a few years, however, she had herself crowned. Admittedly, Thutmose was co-ruler, but she overshadowed him. For a long time historians could not imagine how an energetic young man could allow this to happen. Because virtually all images of Hatshepsut's were destroyed, it was assumed that Thutmose must have had his stepmother killed. It has now been established that the images were broken up many years after Hatshepsut's death, and there is no firm evidence found to date that proves murder.

Akhenaten provoked a religious and cultural revolution

Under Amenhotep IV, who called himself Akhenaten (reigned ca. 1351–1334 BC) , quite a number of things changed in Egypt: out of all the gods, only Aten was to be worshipped. The power of the priests of the old official god, Amun, was destroyed and his images were smashed. Akhenaten built a new capital city and introduced an almost surrealistic style in art. Yet the superficial nature of this "revolution" may be seen from the fact that immediately after Akhenaten's death the old conditions were reestablished. In any case, the general population primarily worshipped regional gods, regardless of which one was the kingdom's official god.

CATS AND COSMETICS

The Egyptians worshipped cats and crocodiles

The ancient Egyptians worshipped humanlike gods that had developed from old totem animals and were represented with animal heads. It was only in the seventh century BC, after the foreign domination by the Assyrians, that an extreme fixation on supposedly ancient Egyptian traditions developed. Suddenly ancient titles and costumes were reintroduced. At the same time, people began — in the mistaken belief that this was typically Egyptian — to worship holy animals and to mummify them after their death. In the eyes of the Romans and Greeks, this made them fairly ridiculous.

Cosmetics were used primarily for beauty care

The oldest finds of cosmetics come from Egypt 5,000 years ago. The primary purpose of the ointments and oils was to protect the skin against the intense sunlight, particularly around the eyes. It did not take long, however, before people began to add colors and scents to the creams to increase the body's attractiveness. In Greece, by contrast, until about 700 BC, the body was only rubbed with olive oil or butter. Scents were denounced as effeminate.

CLEOPATRA: HER NOSE AND HER NEEDLES

The Egyptian rulers preferred to marry their sisters

Marriage to a half-sister happened time and again, and primarily served to legitimize heirs apparent who were the offspring of a secondary marriage by the old king. In fact, there appears to have been no major disputes over the succession in Egypt for almost 2,000 years. Marriage between full siblings was introduced by Arsinoe II (316–270 BC), who married her rather spiritual brother Ptolemy II (308–246 BC) and carried out government business on his behalf.

Cleopatra had a beautiful nose

The statements of ancient authors testify to the contrary: Cleopatra was not particularly beautiful and had a very distinctive long, bent nose. Historians went into raptures, however, about her charm and her seductiveness. Her intelligence was also highly praised. She not only understood more than a little about politics and finance, but also spoke eight languages — including, for the first time among the Ptolemaic rulers, Egyptian. The portrayal of Cleopatra as a pleasure-seeking schemer originates from her political opponent, Octavius, who later became Emperor Augustus (63 BC – AD 14).

Cleopatra was an Egyptian

Cleopatra VII (reigned 51–30 BC) came from the family of the Ptolemies, who were of Greek origin and had ruled Egypt since 367 BC. The Ptolemies developed Alexandria as both the most important mercantile center in the world and the hub of scientific discovery. They did indeed adopt some Egyptian traditions, but in reality the land was divided. All important positions were held by Greeks. The Egyptians were primarily farmers and producers of wheat, which Egypt depended on for export.

Cleopatra's Needles were built to honor Cleopatra

The three famous obelisks (now located in London, Paris and New York City) were not constructed during the reign of any of the Egyptian queens known as Cleopatra. Thutmose III had them built in about 1450 BC in the city of Heliopolis. The 68-foot (21 meter) red granite pillars, each inscribed with hieroglyphics, were moved to Alexandria by the Romans in 12 BC and erected in a temple in honor of Mark Anthony. Later they fell over, and in the 19th century they were presented to England, France and the United States by the Egyptian government.

EGYPTIANS, EXODUS AND SEA PEOPLES

Ancient Egypt was a major superpower

The Egyptian pharaohs were proud to be depicted in chariots or killing enemies, but for a long time their expeditions were limited to campaigns against the Libyan nomads or the militarily inferior Kushites from present-day Sudan. Only after 1500 BC did an expansionist policy begin. But the Egyptians did not really become a superpower, as their defeat by the Hittites at Kadesh in 1274 BC shows. To a nomadic people like the Israelites, however, the pharaoh with his horses and chariots must have appeared extremely powerful.

The exodus of the Israelites from Egypt is a legend

True, no pharaoh during the period in question was drowned in the Red Sea. The embalmed corpses of all of them have been discovered. However, there are records from the time of the reign of the pharaoh Ramses II (reigned ca. 1279–1213 BC) that indicate that Asiatics — as the Egyptians called any tribe from beyond Sinai — were used as workers in the construction of two great warehouse complexes. Possibly some Israelite nomadic tribes were actually driven into Egypt by a drought, and returned to Canaan around 1250 BC.

The Sea Peoples arrived by sea

In the 12th century BC, Egypt was attacked by a hitherto unknown people who arrived in ships from across the Mediterranean. The attackers were only part of a migration that probably began in the 11th century BC in the Balkans. It caused the displacement of many different tribes in the eastern Mediterranean. They were generally all referred to together by the Egyptians as the "Sea Peoples," although the Phrygians and Mysians, who destroyed the Hittite kingdom, did this without getting their feet wet. The best-known members of the "Sea Peoples" were the biblical Philistines.

TROY: FACT OR FICTION?

The Trojan War never really happened

The legendary city at the southern end of the Dardanelles was inhabited by the Luwians, an Anatolian people related to the Hittites. In 1280 BC their ruler, Alaksandu, concluded a vassal treaty with the Hittites. This safeguarded his throne (and that of his grandson, Warmu) against his enemies. Excavations show that Troy was destroyed at the beginning of the 12th century BC. Unfortunately, the Hittite kingdom came to an end shortly before that, so there are no more records. It seems logical, however, that the powerful Mycenaeans should have attacked the rich city of Troy after the Hittites were no longer able to protect it.

Troy was attacked by the Greeks

Many details in Homer's *Iliad* clearly show that the original tale of the Trojan War dates from pre-Greek times. Examples of this are that eating did not take place reclining, but sitting, and that ships could not sail against headwinds. These details indicate that Troy was attacked by the Mycenaeans. The Mycenaean princes lived in heavily fortified towns on the Peleponnese. They became rich by carrying out raids for plunder and dominated Mediterranean trade from the 16th century BC. About 1100 BC, however, invasions by Greek peoples brought an end to their great culture.

A LABYRINTH, A TOMB AND A SCARY GOD

The ruins of Knossos are a palace

When the British archaeologist Sir Arthur Evans (1851–1941) excavated a building complex on Crete measuring 215,000 square feet (20,000 square meters), with innumerable rooms and corridors, he was convinced that he had discovered the legendary labyrinth of the Minotaur and, at the same time, the palace of the Cretan king. Even now many experts hold this view. But there are inconsistencies. For example, the most magnificent rooms are deep in the cellars; storage jars are walled up and inaccessible; and what appear to be bathtubs are unusable. So another interpretation is that the "palace" was actually a magnificent burial place.

Schliemann found Agamemnon's tomb

"I have found Agamemnon's grave." This was the message that the German amateur archaeologist Heinrich Schliemann (1822–90) telegraphed, full of enthusiasm, to the Greek king on December 6, 1876. In several shaft graves on the castle mound at Mycenae he had come across 15 skeletons laden with gold and jewelry. One of the most beautiful pieces, a gold death mask, is still described as the "Mask of Agamemnon." In fact, however, the finds date from about 1600 BC, whereas King Agamemnon — if he actually existed — must have lived more than 400 years later.

The Phoenicians sacrificed to Moloch

At many points in the Old Testament there are warnings that one's children should not (following the example of the Phoenicians) be "sacrificed to Moloch" or "let them enter the fire for Moloch." But there is no evidence of a god called Moloch, although "*molk*" means sacrifice. The descriptions by ancient authors of some sort of automaton that shoveled the sacrificial children into its glowing innards with metal hands are undoubtedly scaremongering propaganda. Child sacrifice was, however, common. In the ruins of the Phoenician colony of Carthage, thousands of burnt bones have been found.

SLAVES AND TYRANTS

In the ancient Middle East women were suppressed

Everywhere — whether in Babylon or Egypt, or among the Persians and Hittites — women were able to possess money and to carry out business, even if they did not have quite as many rights as men. In Greece and Rome, in contrast, women did not have that legal standing. Whereas in Rome their actual position was not as drastic as the Civil Code laid down, in Greece respectable women were only permitted to bear children. In Sparta, however, which differed in many respects from the rest of Greece, men were forbidden to work or to conduct business. They were completely dependent economically on their wives.

A tyrant was a despot

The Greek word *turannos* meant autocratic rule, and indicated that the ruler had unlimited powers. Initially it was used as a neutral term. Only when more and more tyrants misused their powers did it acquire its negative connotation. In Rome there was the concept of a "good dictator," who would rule his people with a very high degree of efficiency in a time of crisis, but then step down when the crisis was over.

Slaves had to do the work that no one else would do

Slaves were always employed where they were cheaper and more productive than free workers. Or, to be precise: nearly always. For this reason, in all slave-owning societies — whether it was ancient Rome or the southern United States — there was a free lower class who had hardly any chance of obtaining paid work and who became so impoverished that their material living standards were even lower than those of many slaves.

Draco enacted draconian laws

The Greek law scribe Draco (born ca. 650 BC) codified oral Athenian laws in about 624 BC. He didn't make up the laws — neither did he have the power to enforce them — but in transcribing them he did apply his own penalties, which were extremely harsh — hence the meaning of "draconian." Death seemed to be the punishment for just about everything, from stealing a cabbage to homicide. Some of his laws were progressive, in that he differentiated between murder and manslaughter, and he was concerned that murder should be dealt with by the courts, not by angry relatives (as in the customary practice of the blood feud).

The administration of justice in early historical times was very cruel

That was not true everywhere. In the Hittites' legal system, for example, almost everything was settled by the payment of fines. The main focus was not punishment, but restitution. Anyone who killed or maimed a man had to ensure that the victim's family were compensated in a material sense — if necessary by serving as a slave to the family and taking on his victim's work. The death penalty itself was applied to very few crimes, and the mutilations that were so widespread among other societies were unknown. Among the Teutonic and Celtic tribes many matters were settled with "blood money," and degrading punishments such as public beatings were unknown.

A HORN, A HERO AND HIPPOCRATES

The Greeks drank out of horns

The Greeks have left many drinking vessels in the shape of curved horns, which end with an animal head. These were called rhytons, and originated in Persia. But nothing was drunk from them. Instead, wine was allowed to flow from a small hole into a shallow drinking bowl.

Leonidas saved Sparta

According to the popular legend, the Spartan king, Leonidas, died a hero's death alongside his loyal guard during the fight against the Persian hordes at the Pass of Thermopylae in 480 BC. However, military experts (beginning with Napoleon) have found that Leonidas' self-sacrifice was stupid rather than heroic. This is because the Persians had found another way across the mountains much earlier. So it would have been wiser for Leonidas to abandon the pass, and instead support the main Spartan and Athenian army.

Hippocrates introduced the Hippocratic Oath

The oath attributed to Hippocrates (ca. 460–375 BC) only arose after the famous Greek physician's death. But because the doctor from Kos was already a legend, the saying was attributed to him to lend it greater weight. In 1948, certain parts of the oath, such as confidentiality and duty of care, were incorporated into the Geneva Physicians' Code. Other sections, such as the observance of secrecy about the art of medicine, were excluded.

OLYMPIC TRADITIONS

The first Olympiad took place in 776 BC

The first Olympic Games were held in this year. But "Olympiad" referred to the interval of four years between Olympic Games. The Greek system of dating began with these games in 776 BC. At that time the sole sporting discipline in the competition was a foot race over the length of the stadium, barely 220 yards (200 meters). All free Greeks, with no criminal convictions, were permitted to take part, provided they had trained for the competition for nine months at home, and for 30 days at Olympia.

In antiquity women could not become Olympic champions

The first woman to win at Olympia was called Kyniska, the daughter of a Spartan king, who won a chariot race. In fact, the owner and breeder of the horses were chosen as winners, not the charioteer, who was generally a slave. Following Kyniska, other women also won at Olympia, although they were not allowed to watch "their" wins. The first woman who truly, actively won her medal was Charlotte Cooper (1871–1967) of England, who won at tennis in Paris in 1900.

The ancient Olympic Games were always fair

The first known case of Olympic corruption comes from the year 388 BC. A boxer by the name of Eupolos won by bribing his three competitors. The fraud was exposed, but under the rules at the time, Eupolos could not be forced to give up the winner's olive branch. As atonement, however, he had to pay a fine of six bronze statues of Zeus. His statues were the first to be placed on the road to the stadium, but were soon to followed by many others, all "donated" by cheating athletes.

Olympic champion was the highest sporting honor in antiquity

The games at Olympia were certainly the most important competition, but there was a title that was valued even more: that of Periodonike. A person became a Periodonike when, within an Olympiad (four years) they had won the four most important competitions: the Olympic Games, the Pythian Games at Delphi, the Nemean Games in Argolis and the Isthmian Games at Corinth. The wrestler Milo of Croton became Periodonike six times (from 540 BC).

TWO TALL BUILDINGS AND A GYM

The Acropolis is in Athens

The word *acropolis* means "top of the city," referring to fortified, elevated areas that were found in many ancient Greek cities. Originally they were places of safety where the first settlements were established. Little by little, they lost their role as refuges. Instead palaces and temples were built upon them. But "the" Acropolis is in Athens. No other acropolis could compare with the collection of buildings that Pericles (ca. 493–429 BC) built there during Greece's classical period.

Professionals were first allowed to take part in the Olympic Games in 1988

The competitors in antiquity were by no means amateurs. By the fourth century BC, professional sportsmen  were finally accepted. Officially, as Olympic winners they gained only the traditional olive branch, but their home cities offered juicy prizes. More than a few changed their place of abode as a result. Apart from this, an Olympic winner could demand high entry fees for other competitions.

Alexander the Great had the first lighthouse built

When Alexander (356–323 BC) founded the Egyptian city of Alexandria, he ordered a tower to be built on the offshore island of Pharos, to show mariners the way into the new harbor. But construction was delayed, and Alexandria had long become a boom town before the 426-foot (130 meter) tower was finally built at the beginning of the third century BC. Meanwhile, the harbor had become so busy that ships had to sail in by night. Someone hit upon the idea of installing a beacon on the tower, which is now regarded as one of the Seven Wonders of the World. By the 14th century it was in ruin, destroyed by earthquakes.

"Gymnasium" is the Greek name for a college

The translation of the word "gymnasium" means "place where people are naked" (from the Greek *gymnos* = naked) and denoted a practice area for sport, which at the time was conducted naked. Formal gymnasia were set up in Greece in the fourth century BC as training centers for young athletes. Philosophical lectures and education were eventually included in the programs provided by these ancient fitness clubs.

ETRUSCANS AND ROMANS AT HOME

The Etruscans had a gloomy culture

Etruscan tombs have survived, but none of their houses. The decorations found on the tombs suggest the work of painters in the Middle Ages, with depictions of Hell. In the work of ancient authors, however, the Etruscans appear as people with time on their hands, who enjoyed themselves with their wives in lavish banquets and displays of gluttony. Up until well into the fourth century BC, the Etruscans preferred to have their graves painted with festive scenes. It was only later that demons and depictions of violence predominated.

The Romans ate lying down

The tradition of feasting lying down was first adopted from Asia by the Greeks and then the Romans in sixth century BC. The Homeric heroes, for example, still ate when seated. Only men ate lying down at banquets. Women and children ate separately, and seated. In everyday life, most men satisfied their hunger at snack bars while out and about.

Family members are related to one another

Not in ancient Rome. There, the whole household, including all the slaves, was called "*familia*." Dependants also belonged to the family. These were men who were economically dependent on the head of the household and who therefore owed him their service.

The Baths of Caracalla were the largest in Rome

The ruins of the Roman Baths of Caracalla still produce a great impression with their giant structure, which was as much as 144 feet (44 meters) high and covered an area of 1,075,000 square feet (100,000 square meters). Yet they were exceeded by the baths of the Emperor Diocletianus (AD 243–316) at 1,205,000 square feet (112,000 square meters). However, not much of the latter remains to be seen. Anyone who wants to picture the size of the Baths of Caracalla must go from the church of San Maria degli Angeli, which was rebuilt from the former tepidarium — a moderately warm, transitional room between the hot and cold baths — to the church of San Bernardo, which was set in a rotunda on the outside wall of the baths.

Freed slaves did not have a high standing in Rome

It all depends. Many slaves, even before gaining their freedom, had considerable authority, often including the ability to carry out business on their own behalf. In addition, the standing of their former master played a part. Many freedmen were very rich and politically influential. It is true that in the eyes of the noble patricians they had the reputation for being "nouveau riche," but a rich freedman had more status than a poor plebeian.

CLASSICAL ROME

Latin was the first world language

By early historical times the Akkadian and Assyrian languages, which originated in Mesopotamia, were current over the whole of the Middle East. From 900 BC they were replaced by Aramaic, which became the language of trade and diplomacy for everyone between Greece and the Indus valley. Admittedly the Aramaeans were attacked and destroyed by the Assyrians, but their language, which had 22 consonants and was written on papyrus, was more practical than the Assyrian cuneiform script. At the beginning of the fifth century BC, Aramaic became the official language throughout the giant Persian empire.

Rome was built on seven hills

Rome was founded around the Palatine Hill. It is not known when Rome began to be called the "City of Seven Hills." The first mention of this appears in the fourth century. That lists the Palatine, Aventine, Caelian, Esquiline, Tarpeian, Vatican and Janiculan hills. Nowadays, instead of the last three, the Viminal, Quirinal and Capitoline hills are included in the classic seven hills of the Eternal City. So there are more than enough hills in Rome. The seven have a purely symbolical value.

The Forum was Rome's marketplace

Early in the city's history it definitely served that purpose. But then consuls and emperors encumbered the square with so many temples, official buildings and memorials, that with the best will in the world it was no longer possible to sell cabbages there. For that reason, in addition to the original "Forum Romanum," Julius Caesar as well as the emperors Augustus, Vespasian, Nerva and Trajan built additional fora. Part of Trajan's Forum was the Trajan Market, a six-story building with about 150 shops. Nowadays it would be described as a shopping center.

ROMAN ENTERTAINMENT

In ancient Rome, a thumbs-down gesture signaled death

For a very long time, people believed that when gladiators fought in the Colosseum, and the struggle came to the final death blow from the victor, they would look to the spectators for the decision: thumbs up for life and thumbs down for death. This misconception was perpetuated by a painting showing just this gesture as a death sentence. The painting was created in 1870 by Jean Gérôme, a French artist. But recent scholarship has revealed that probably almost the opposite was true: a thumb pointing upward and inward, like a dagger thrust, signaled death. The mistake probably arose as the result of a mistranslation of the Latin word for "turned in," which was translated as "turned down."

The Colosseum was named because of its size

The building is impres-
sive. With a capacity of
50,000 spectators, it
would be the envy of
many modern football
teams. The five-story

Colosseum building was built in

AD 80 by Vespasian (Emperor Flavius Vespasianus) and

named the Flavian Amphitheater. It was not referred to as

the Colosseum until the Middle Ages.

Emperor Nero fiddled while Rome burned

There is a popular legend that the slightly mad (or perhaps completely insane) Roman emperor, Nero (AD 37–68), had Rome set on fire so he could rebuild it the way he wanted to, and that he stood playing happily on his fiddle while the great city burned to the ground. Although Nero did love the theater, and wrote plays and operas that he compelled his courtiers to attend, he never played a fiddle, for the simple reason that it wasn't invented until about 400 years later. When the fire in Rome broke out (which he did not set), he did his best to organize the fight to save the city, and then helped the citizens left homeless with shelters and cheap grain.

Gladiatorial combats and animal hunts took place in the Roman Circus

The amphitheater, an arena surrounded by spectators' benches, was usually the place where exhibition fights and animal shows were staged. But even here it was not all bloodthirsty. Initially, exotic animals were far too expensive for them to be killed, and they were shown being trained. A circus, by contrast, was a long track for chariot racing, triumphal parades and processions. Whereas nearly every Roman city had an amphitheater, circuses were rather rare. The largest and most famous was the Circus Maximus in Rome.

During gladiatorial combats, women sat in the front row

Naturally, no director of a popular Roman epic would shoot a gladiatorial contest without a couple of passionate beauties sitting right up close to the edge of the arena. In reality, it was nothing like that. Women were allowed to view the spectacles, but had to take their seats on the uppermost tier, where, far from the action, they would not have been able to see the half-naked male bodies and the spurting blood at all clearly.

The Romans used chariots in warfare

There was nothing the Romans liked better than a fast-paced, exciting chariot race, but they didn't use them in battle. The Circus Maximus served as the racetrack for many chariot races, and the Romans also liked to use them in processions. Egyptians, Hittites, northern Europeans and ancient Britons probably all used chariots in warfare, but not the Romans.

CAESAR AND THE CAESARS

Julius Caesar was a Roman emperor

The first Roman emperor was Augustus, who became emperor after Caesar's death. Julius Caesar was a brilliant general and statesman who was appointed the dictator of Rome. The first five Roman emperors incorporated his name in their title as a sign of respect.

Caesar said, "The die is cast"

The historian Suetonius (ca. AD 69–140) reported that when Caesar (100–44 BC) crossed the Rubicon River (which divides Gaul from Italy) and marched against Rome in 49 BC, he said "*Iacta alea est*" ("The die is cast"). Caesar's exact words are in some dispute, and he himself made no mention of saying this when he wrote about his exploits. He may have been quoting a famous phrase from the popular Greek dramatist Menander: "Let the die be cast."

Caesar said, "*Et tu, Brute*"

These legendary words are supposed to have been used by Julius Caesar at the moment of his murder to express his shock on discovering that his close friend Marcus Junius Brutus (85–42 BC) was one of the participants. The Greek historian Plutarch (AD 46–127) had Caesar dying without speaking, although Suetonius had him saying "And thou, my son." It may have been Shakespeare who created the famous phrase "*Et tu, Brute*" in his play, *Julius Caesar*, written in about 1599.

Emperor Vespasian raised a tax on priggishness

Not even the Roman emperor, who was so resourceful at finding ways of collecting money, dared to do this. However, Vespasian (AD 9–79) did tax the sale of urine from public toilets to the fullers and tanners who needed the uric acid to treat their materials. To his son, Titus (AD 39–81), who found this practice offensive, the emperor responded with his famous dictum: "*Pecunia non olet*" ("Money doesn't smell").

HUNS AND VANDALS

The Huns were particularly cruel

Cruelty in warfare was perfectly normal at the end of the fourth century. The Huns, however, were frightening because of their exotic appearance and their ability, thanks to their stirrups, to fight on horseback. They set upon their enemies at a gallop and showered them with a hail of arrows. The Huns dominated eastern Europe for just about 80 years. During this time the Romans and the Germanic tribes not only fought them, but sometimes used them as valuable allies.

The Vandals devastated Rome

In AD 455, the Vandals, a Germanic people, captured Rome and plundered the city for 14 days. In the process it would seem that they burned down relatively few buildings, and did not instigate a great bloodbath. Later conquerors like the Normans (1084) or the troops of Charles V (1527) afflicted Rome with far greater destruction. The reason for the attack on Rome was the murder of the Vandals' ally, Valentinian III (AD 419–455).

THE SLAVS AND BYZANTINES

The description "Slavonic" derives from "slave"

It is rather the other way around. "Slav" is the Slavs' own description of themselves, which may perhaps derive from the word "*slovo*" ("word" or "speech") or from "*slava*" ("fame" or "hail"). The word "slave" is a creation of the Byzantines, who in the sixth century purchased many slaves that were Slavs, taken as prisoners of war.

Constantinople is an old name for Byzantium, nowadays called Istanbul

The name games concerning the city on the Bosporus are not easy to sort out. It was founded at the beginning of the seventh century BC as Byzantium. In AD 330, Constantine the Great (ca. AD 272–337) enlarged it and made it his new capital, calling it "Nova Roma" ("New Rome"). However, the name of the city rapidly became Constantinople, while the old name of Byzantium still remained in use. After it was conquered in 1453, the Turks renamed the city Istanbul, a name whose origins are uncertain. However, until the beginning of the 20th century, the city's official name was still Constantinople. Byzantium as a description of the Eastern Roman Empire (395–1453) is a modern invention.

FIEFS AND FREEDOM

Fiefdom was devised in the Middle Ages

There had been similar systems in earlier cultures. For example, the Chou Dynasty, which ruled China from 1050 BC, awarded land as fiefs to noble subjects, who in turn had it cultivated by rural forced laborers. Over time, however, the Chou armed the princes to defend the land against invaders to such an extent that the princes became stronger than the imperial house, and the dynasty eventually collapsed.

Running water was never available in the Middle Ages

In the Middle Ages, no — but definitely before that! The oldest town with a public sewer system that has yet been discovered was Mohenjo-Daro, one of the main cities of the Indus culture. It was built around 2600 BC. About 100,000 people lived there, with a water-supply system that many modern Indians can only dream about. The houses were connected to the public sewer system, and had baths, fountains and even toilets. Babylon, Hattusa and other early cities had functioning water-supply systems, and in Rome there were even taps that provided individual rooms with water.

Free farmers (yeomen) were better off than serfs

In the early Middle Ages it became a major problem when many free farmers voluntarily gave up their land to become serfs. This was because as freemen they were obliged to do military service. They had to pay for their equipment themselves, and during military campaigns (which were never-ending) they could not cultivate their land. As serfs, however, although they were obliged to provide work and duty to their master, the latter was obliged to provide for them.

There was no slavery in Europe in the Middle Ages

Both Celts and Germans had slaves, and even in Carolingian times (ca. AD 640–987) traces of slavery were still evident. However, the Church's prohibition of the enslavement of other Christians caused slavery to be slowly replaced with serfdom. During the Middle Ages there were many degrees of bondage in society. The conditions and hardships of bondage depended more on the specific master than on a person's actual status. The Vikings were great slave-traders who sometimes deliberately kidnapped people to sell them in the Middle East.

HEIGHT, LONGEVITY AND THE END OF THE WORLD

Formerly people were smaller and did not live as long

The nobles, who did not go hungry, reached similar body weights to those of people today, and some of the popes, who were spared any hard physical work, lived into their 90s. In contrast, the hungry and hard-working farmers were (on average) about 4 to 6 inches (10 to 15 centimeters) smaller than the upper classes. Their ages are more difficult to estimate, because the low average life expectancy of about 30 years is greatly distorted by high child mortality. Women tended to die earlier than men because they were doubly afflicted by repeated pregnancies and hard work in the fields.

People believed that the world would come to an end in the year 1000

Predictions of the end of the world were present throughout the Middle Ages, but there are no indications of any particular hysteria around the end of AD 999 and the beginning of 1000. Many people believed that 1,000 years after the death of Christ (not after his birth) was a far more likely time for the end of the world. Calculating the date from the birth of Christ had not been universally accepted, and large sections of the population did not have calendars and would not be aware of a particular date.

IRON MAIDENS AND CHASTITY BELTS

Torture was common in the Middle Ages

Until the middle of the 12th century, both capital punishment and torture were unusual in Central Europe. Crimes were generally punished by high fines, and uncertain cases often decided by "God's will" — which meant by ordeal or by single combat. But neither God's apparent judgment nor fines stemmed the number of crimes. This is why the law turned to deterrent punishments and unpleasant (and thus painful) interrogation. In torture, however, no lasting injury was to be inflicted, and anyone who withstood it without confessing was freed.

There was a *Droit de Seigneur*

The rights of a lord to spend the first night with any newly wedded woman among his servants is one of those greatly beloved legends about the Dark Ages. There is, however, not the slightest evidence that any such custom ever existed. Sexual exploitation of dependent women undoubtedly occurred to a large extent, but an institutionalized right to adultery is hardly conceivable, given the rigid sexual morals preached by the Church.

The "iron maiden" was a method of execution

It is the highlight of every torture chamber: the iron maiden, in which malefactors were locked up and slowly pierced by spikes. But this version of the iron maiden was a hoax invented in the 19th century, when it acquired its deadly spikes. In the Middle Ages the iron maiden was a coat of wood and tin that served simply as a "coat of shame." The convicted person would be forced to wear the cloak in public as a form of humiliation.

THE DOGES AND MARCO POLO

The doges ruled over Venice

The Doge of Venice was a representative of the Eastern Roman Emperor. But from the ninth century on, he acted independently. The doges had great authority at their disposal until the first half of the 12th century. But then the attempt by the Orseolo family to make the position a hereditary one led to the formation of the Grand Council. The committee became the Signoria, the highest legislative authority, and the doge was demoted to a form of puppet ruler.

Marco Polo was in China

He asserted this, but to this day it is not certain whether or not he should be believed. This is because the descriptions by Marco Polo (ca. 1254–1324) contain too little Chinese local color. For example, he never mentioned tea drinking, bound feet or the Great Wall of China. He may have only reached Karakorum, the old capital of his friend the Mongol overlord, Kublai Khan (1215–94). Many experts think that Marco Polo only traveled as far as Persia. However, many of the details of his journey ring true and were verified when British explorers followed his Silk Road route to China in the 19th century. Whether he gained his knowledge firsthand or from stories from other travelers, there is no doubt that Marco Polo was a wonderful story teller who awakened European interest in the East.

KNIGHTS

Knights were from the nobility

At first quite humble men, even serfs, could become knights by special services to their feudal lords. By the end of the 12th century, however, knights were considered members of the nobility. Many owned land, but some did not. They all owed allegiance to their feudal lord.

Knights were the strongest part of the army

The French found out how helpless the heavily armored knights could be during the first battles of the Hundred Years' War. At Crécy in 1346 and Maupertuis in 1356 their old-fashioned knights were crushingly defeated by the numerically far inferior English army, which had numerous archers at its disposal. It was Charles V of France who was the first to reject the arrogant assertion that the only honorable fight was a "knightly" one.

The Crusaders were knights

In the first Crusade in 1096, two armies of beggars set out alongside the French and Norman knights. One originated in southern France, and the other from the Rhineland and Flanders. Shortly before that time there had been famine in both regions. On their journey toward Palestine, the crusaders plundered many cities on the Rhine and in southern Germany, murdering their Jewish populations. The beggars never reached the Holy Land. They were captured by the Turks and sold into slavery.

POGROMS, THE PLAGUE AND THE HUNDRED YEARS' WAR

The origin of the pogroms against the Jews was the Christians' ban on interest payments

Bans on interest were first introduced in 1179 and 1215, but pogroms against the Jews started much earlier. The bans aggravated an explosive situation, but they were not the basic reasons for the hostility toward Jews in the Middle Ages. The tension between Christians and Jews was originally a by-product of the West's confrontation with Islam. The Jews were seen to be allied with the Muslims, because they were permitted to move freely within the Islamic countries. The first major pogrom in 1096 was carried out by the armies of beggars involved in the first Crusade, which had been initiated by the Pope to free Jerusalem from the hands of the "unbelievers."

Nothing depopulated Central Europe as much as the plague

Even worse was the Thirty Years' War. During the Great Plague, between 1347 and 1352, about one-third of the population of Europe died. But during the Thirty Years' War the proportion was rather more. The fewest died through direct warfare, but others died through famine, epidemics and attacks by mercenary soldiers.

The Hundred Years' War lasted one hundred years

In fact, the clash between France and England lasted 114 years. It began in 1339 with claim by Edward III (1312–77) of England to the French throne, because he was the nephew of the late, childless king Charles IV (1295–1328). The French had, however, chosen Charles' cousin, Philippe de Valois (1293–1350). The war ended in 1453 with the Battle of Castillon. England not only had to relinquish its claim to the throne, but also lost all of its territory in France, with the exception of Calais.

MEDIEVAL WOMEN OF SPIRIT

Lady Godiva rode naked through the streets of Coventry

According to the story, Lady Godiva, the wife of the lord of Coventry, struck a deal with her husband to lower people's taxes if she would ride through the streets of the town naked. People hid away inside and didn't look as a token of their respect for her. She was supposed to have very long, beautiful hair that concealed her private parts. But it is very doubtful that her naked ride ever took place, although it makes a great story. Lady Godiva was an actual woman living in 11th-century Coventry, but she probably ruled Coventry herself, and her famous ride may have been in her "shift" as a form of religious penance for the harsh taxes she herself had imposed. The story was recorded 170 years after her death by Roger Wendover who was not known for his meticulous adherence to facts.

Joan of Arc was French

Joan of Arc (1412–31) was born in Domrémy in the independent duchy of Lorraine. Lorraine did not become part of France until 1766.

Joan of Arc was a poor shepherdess

Joan of Arc grew up in a small castle. She was the daughter of a wealthy landed proprietor, who was also mayor of Domrémy.

PRINTING AND REVOLUTIONARY IDEAS

Printing was invented by Johannes Gutenberg

By the late Middle Ages, books were no longer always laboriously copied by monks, but were reproduced as quickly and cheaply as possible. The first printing of books existed before Gutenberg (1398–1468), but he improved the technology and invented printing with movable letters, as well as a new kind of printing press. The first goods to be printed were mass-produced books and pamphlets.

Luther nailed his 95 theses to the door of Wittenberg Castle

All reports about this event are either contradictory or arose after Luther's death. Martin Luther (1483–1546) himself confirmed that he had sent his theses to the Archbishop of Magdeburg and to the Elector of Saxony on October 31, 1517, so that they could express their opinion about them. Only afterward did he make them public. In addition, he had no intention of denouncing indulgences as such, but only the harmful consequences of the fact that forgiveness for sins no longer depended on the sinner's repentance, but only on their readiness to open their purse for the Church.

Luther said, "Here I stand. I can do no other."

Although it is a tradition that Luther uttered these words, it cannot be proved that he actually said them. What he did say, at the Diet of Worms in 1521, was that he would not retract his statements unless they were refuted by Holy Scripture. "For that reason, I can and will retract nothing, because to act contrary to conscience is arduous, not prudent and dangerous. God help me. Amen."

Copernicus remained silent from fear of the Church

Stimulated by ancient writings about the heliocentric universe of Aristarchus of Samos, the Ermland scholar and canon, Nicholas Copernicus (1473–1543), became convinced that the Earth actually moved around the Sun. He did not dare publish this discovery, for fear of being laughed at and ridiculed by other scientists, because his ideas were so revolutionary. The news leaked out, however. Of all things, it was a cardinal who urged Copernicus to publish his theory in 1543.

Galileo Galilei was incarcerated and mistreated

When Pope John Paul II (1920–2005) rehabilitated Galileo Galilei (1564–1642), a symbolic argument was brought to a close. But the Italian scholar was by no means so badly treated as is often claimed. The Church called him before the Inquisition in 1633, chiefly because of his assertion that the Earth was not the center of the Universe, but instead revolved around the Sun. At the time, this was considered heresy. However, Galilei was not forced to recant either by incarceration or by torture, but he must have thought of Giordano Bruno (1548–1600), who was burned at the stake 33 years earlier as a heretic. He was himself sentenced to house arrest, but was allowed to continue his research in private.

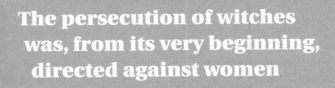

The persecution of witches was, from its very beginning, directed against women

The persecution of witches developed out of the persecution of heretics. According to the Church, a heretic was a person who demonstrably voiced heretical thoughts and persisted in these under questioning. But individual inquisitors, such as Conrad of Marburg (ca. 1180–1233), believed that they were on the track of esoteric satanic doctrines. In the 14th century, the French king Philip the Fair (1286–1314) used the Inquisition to destroy the rich order of the Knights Templar. Because the pious Templars did not behave heretically, he fabricated a devilish world conspiracy whose danger lay in that the children of Satan seemed outwardly to behave piously. The book *Hexenhammer* (*Hammer of Witches*), which so disastrously linked satanic rites with women and sex, first appeared in 1487.

WITCHES

The persecution of witches was a product of the Dark Ages

The persecution of witches took place at the beginning of modern times. The first known witch trial occurred in Lucerne in 1419. The real "witch mania" began around 1560. The peak of the hysteria was reached between 1590 and 1630. The last execution in Germany was in 1775, and the last in Europe, seven years later, in Switzerland. In total, about 300,000 to 500,000 people were killed as witches.

The witch mania had its roots in Catholic thought

The witch mania resulted from heathen ideas that persisted among the populace. For a long time it was not witchcraft, but the belief in witches that was a punishable offence in the Catholic church. At one point it was subject to the death penalty, and later it was punished by a year's penance. When in the 11th century, three women were burned publicly as witches in Freising, the Church declared that they were martyrs.

THE THIRTY YEARS' WAR AND DEFENESTRATION

The Thirty Years' War was triggered by the Defenestration of Prague

The notorious "Defenestration of Prague" refers to the fact that two of the emperor's representatives were thrown out of the windows of the castle in Prague. The bold action certainly contributed to the tension that led to the Thirty Years' War (1618–48), but it was not the true cause of the war. Emperor Ferdinand (1578–1637) would not have taken it kindly when his two envoys were thrown out of the Prague Castle and only escaped with their lives because the moat was filled with manure. But this action was just a symptom of the Bohemian unrest. They held the position that the Emperor should be deposed because of his merciless and illegal policy of forcibly reconverting people to Catholicism.

The Swedes were particularly brutal

Almost all the armies in the Thirty Years' War behaved with unbridled brutality, and the Swedes were no worse than any of the others. Basically, it made no difference whether an area was overrun by friend or foe, because every army ravaged the land in order to survive. Above all, it was Albrecht von Wallenstein (1583–1634) who used famine tactically. He restricted the freedom of movement of his opponents by allowing his soldiers to plunder the land so that the enemy armies would not find anything left to eat. Among the most brutal acts was the destruction of Magdeburg. Johann Tserclaes von Tilly (1559–1632) burned the town to the ground and murdered almost the whole population.

CHRISTOPHER COLUMBUS, THE FLAT EARTH AND AN EGG

Columbus' contemporaries still believed that the Earth was flat

No reasonably well-informed person and no seaman at the end of the 15th century still held that the Earth was flat. It was the size of the globe, not its shape, that fell into question. Christopher Columbus (1451–1506) believed he could reach the Indies by a western route because he made a mathematical mistake. Whereas the advisers to the Portuguese king Henry the Seafarer had a relatively realistic conception of the Earth's circumference as 24,900 miles (40,000 kilometers), Columbus underestimated the distances involved. He calculated the circumference of the Earth as 15,700 miles (25,255 kilometers). The government of Spain took a chance on his theories because they wanted to get the competitive edge on trade by discovering a Western route to Asia.

Christopher Columbus discovered America

Not even Columbus himself made this claim. He insisted that he had reached India, despite all evidence to the contrary. And he never did set foot in North America. His ships landed at islands in the Caribbean and in South America. The first Europeans to come to North America were Norwegian Vikings, in about AD 1000.

Henry Hudson discovered Hudson Bay and the Hudson River

Henry Hudson (1570–1611) was a great explorer who dedicated his life to finding the northwest passage to the Orient. He visited the Hudson River in 1609, but Europeans had made that trip before, most particularly a Portuguese explorer named Estevan Gomez in 1525. Likewise, Hudson explored the area now known  as Hudson Bay after other explorers had traveled there. Presumably he met his death in Hudson Bay — his crew mutinied against further dangerous exploration and left him, his son and some crew members there in 1611. Hudson Bay, Hudson Strait and the Hudson River were named after Henry Hudson to honor his memory.

Columbus stood an egg on end

The way the story goes, in 1421 the architect Filippo Brunelleschi (1377–1446) produced a bold design for the dome for Florence Cathedral. But his rivals maintained that his plan was not feasible. So Brunelleschi took an egg, tapped it lightly on one end to crack the bottom, and stood it upright on the table. His point was that once one knows the solution to a problem, then it is all very simple. Whether this anecdote is true is uncertain. What is certain, however, is that later the story was transferred to Columbus.

FAMOUS SAILORS

Henry the Navigator went to sea himself

The popular Portuguese Prince Henry (1394–1460) never under-took a single sea voyage. It is certain, however, that he gathered seafarers around him and financed expeditions to Madeira, the Azores and the Cape Verde Islands. Admittedly, he did not achieve major coups, such as, for example, the rounding of the Cape of Good Hope, but Henry was the first monarch to systematically support such voyages of discovery.

Hernando Cortés was the first European to look upon the Pacific Ocean

Many people believe that Cortés (1485–1587), the Spanish con-quistador who conquered the Aztecs in Mexico, was the first European to see the Pacific Ocean. John Keats wrote a beautiful poem with this surmise. But another Spaniard, Vasco Núñez de Balboa (1475–1519) first saw the Pacific on September 25, 1513. Cortés defeated the Aztecs in 1518.

POCAHONTAS, PILGRIMS AND ROCKS

In 1607 Pocahontas saved John Smith from being clubbed to death by her father

This myth collected numerous more inaccuracies when it entered popular culture with the 1995 Disney movie *Pocahontas*, in which she is portrayed as a young woman. In fact, she was a Powhatan girl of just 10 or 11, and her name was Matoaka. Pocahontas was a nick-name, meaning "the naughty one" or "spoiled child." John Smith was a soldier described as abrasive, ambitious and a self-promoter. The first time he told the story of Pocahontas using her body to shield him from her father's blow was 17 years after it was supposed to have happened. He also never mentioned it in his 1608 book, *A*

True Relation. The truth of Smith's tale will never be known, and since he was a consummate braggart, its veracity is doubtful. But the true story of Pocahontas ends sadly. In 1612, at the age of 17, the English took Pocahontas prisoner and held her hostage for over a year. As a condition of her release, she agreed to marry John Rolfe, a 28-year-old widow. Renamed Rebecca Rolfe, she bore him a son, Thomas. The couple traveled to London, England, where Pocahontas was used along with other Native North Americans to encourage settlers to come to the New World. She died in London from an unspecified disease at the age of 21 on March 21, 1617.

The first English emigrants reached America in the *Mayflower*

In 1620, when the Pilgrim Fathers landed the *Mayflower* on the coast of what is now Massachusetts, there were already many English settlements in North America. The oldest was Jamestown in Virginia. It was founded by about 100 British emigrants who arrived in America in 1606 on board the *Discovery*, *Godspeed* and *Susan Constant*. In the next few years the colony steadily grew.

Plymouth was the first English settlement in New England

Plymouth was settled in 1620, but in 1607 a colony was established named Popham, at the mouth of the Kennebec River in Maine. Led by George Popham, it only lasted a year. The harsh climate and Popham's death contributed to its failure.

The people who came on the *Mayflower* were Pilgrims

The religious dissidents who arrived in America on the *Mayflower* called themselves "Separatists," since they were members of the English Separatist Church. Later they were known as the "Forefathers," until in 1820 they were dubbed the "Pilgrim Fathers" at the bicentennial celebration of their arrival in America.

American Thanksgiving has been celebrated since the time of the Pilgrims

Although there is a record that the Pilgrims had a three-day celebration of Thanksgiving in 1621, American Thanksgiving was not an official holiday until 1863, when Abraham Lincoln established it as a national holiday that fell every year after the last Thursday in November. Thanksgiving was the result of a long campaign by Sarah Josepha Hale, who published a woman's magazine, *Godey's Lady's Book*.

The *Mayflower* landed at Plymouth, Massachusetts

Well, yes, eventually. But the popular image of the Pilgrim Fathers alighting from the *Mayflower* at Plymouth Rock isn't quite accurate. They reached America four weeks earlier, landing at Cape Cod harbor. They sent a small boat to scout around for a suitable site for their settlement, and it was this small, open boat that landed at Plymouth. The *Mayflower* came later, on December 20, once Plymouth was established as a good site. And no one writing about the Pilgrims' arrival in the New World said anything about a rock. Plymouth Rock became part of the legend about 120 years later.

THE SUN KING AND MADAME POMPADOUR

French kings were crowned in Notre Dame

That's right. But not in the famous Notre Dame Cathedral in Paris — instead in a cathedral with the same name in Rheims. Only Napoleon Bonaparte (1769–1821) and the English king Henry VI (1421–71) had themselves crowned in Paris. Architecturally, the churches of Notre Dame in Chartres and Rheims are both slightly more significant than the cathedral in Paris. The French rulers were likewise not buried in the capital, but in the Abbey of Saint-Denis.

There was a prisoner known as the "Man in the Iron Mask"

During the reign of Louis XIV (1638–1715) in France, there was a mysterious state prisoner who had to wear a black mask all the time. It was, however, not made from iron, but velvet. The most popular interpretation is that the Sun King was concealing his twin brother, who could have disputed his right to the throne. The prisoner had many privileges, but his warders were under orders to kill him if he made any attempt to reveal his identity. When there was a change of prison, priority was given to employing foreigners who spoke no French. The "Man in the Mask" died in 1703.

Madame Pompadour was an extravagant schemer

Jeanne Antoinette Poisson, the Marquise de Pompadour (1721–64) was the first bourgeois to become the official mistress of a French king. Her influence on Louis XV (1710–74) was extremely great, even when there was no longer any sexual relations between them. She promoted art and culture and advised the king in political matters. This aroused considerable mistrust at court and abroad, and gave rise to much malicious gossip. With hindsight, however, historians acknowledge that she used her privileged position extremely conscientiously.

Louis XIV told the president of his parliament: "L'État c'est moi"

The Sun King (1638–1715) is supposed to have uttered this famous saying, "I am the state," on April 13, 1655, to the President of the French Parliament, who had requested him to pay attention to affairs of state. However, nothing can be found in the files about this. It is possible that he did actually make the statement, but it may also have been attributed to him. Whatever the truth, it fits his arrogant reputation perfectly — which is why it has stuck.

SILENCE AND MARRIAGE

William the Silent was taciturn

William I of Orange-Nassau (1533–88), the first Stadtholder (governor) of the United Provinces of the Netherlands and titular hero of the Netherlands' national anthem, was anything but silent. He had, on the contrary, a talent for being frank, open and very communicative. The Spaniards described him, their great opponent, as "the Crafty," but among his compatriots he was known as "the Father of the Netherlands." Precisely when and by what means he became "the Silent" can no longer be determined. But ever since the 17th century this epithet has been stubbornly linked with his name.

"Left-handed marriage" was bigamy

A morganatic marriage was sometimes known as a "left-handed marriage" because the groom traditionally used his left hand rather than his right to take the hand of his bride during the ceremony. This was a type of marriage that was between people of unequal social rank, often royalty marrying commoners. Many princes entered into a left-handed marriage with their mistresses when their formal spouses died. It was a valid form of marriage, in which the children did not have full rights of inheritance, but were only entitled to their mother's property and position. In this fashion, mistresses and their children gained a semi-legal status, but did not obtain the rights of family members of equal social standing. Although there were rumors that princes or kings (such as the Prussian king Fredrick William II, 1744–97) contracted left-handed marriages with their lovers during the lifetime of their formal spouses, they cannot be confirmed.

THE FRENCH REVOLUTION

The storming of the Bastille started the French Revolution

The citizens of Paris are supposed to have stormed the Bastille, the notorious prison in Paris, on July 14, 1789, and this was the beginning of the French Revolution. However, the Bastille was by no means a sinister dungeon. For a long time, noble debtors were detained there in luxurious conditions. Moreover, it was never stormed. The attempts by the populace to force their way in were initially in vain. When soldiers eventually marched up to the Bastille, the governor surrendered immediately. He was killed, along with many members of the garrison.

Marie Antoinette told her subjects to eat cake

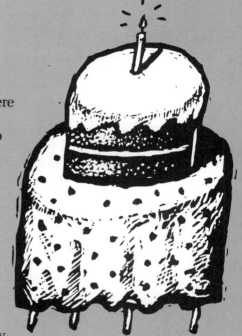

In 1760, in the book *Confessions* by Jean-Jacques Rousseau (1712–78), there appears an account of a princess who advised her starving subjects: "*S'il n'ont pas de pain, qu'ils mangent de la brioche*" ("if they have no bread, then let them eat brioches"). It is hardly likely that a decade later Marie Antoinette (1755–93) should say the same thing. The sentence was probably attributed to her because it agreed with the view of her that was generally held at the time.

The *Marseillaise* was written as a revolutionary anthem

Amateur composer Claude-Joseph Rouget de Lisle intended it to be a marching song, calling it *Marching Song for the Rhine Army*. But its rousing nature brought inspiration to the revolutionaries, who adopted it as their rallying cry. Rouget de Lisle was actually a royalist and was nearly guillotined for his beliefs. Later his song became the French national anthem.

Dr. Guillotin invented the guillotine

In October 1789, the doctor, Joseph Ignace Guillotin (1738–1814), a deputy to the French National Assembly, put forward the motion that the death penalty should, on humanitarian grounds, be carried out by a "head machine." Such devices had been used in ancient Persia, as well as in the Middle Ages in Germany, and in England in the 17th century. The National Assembly agreed to Guillotin's motion and had the "guillotine" built. The man who built it was a German craftsman.

NAPOLEON AND FRENCH FEET

Napoleon was short

This is a misconception that has persisted for many years. Napoleon was 5 foot 6½ inches (172 centimeters), a respectable height for his time. After all, the height requirement for a French soldier was 4 foot 11 inches (150 centimeters), and many were turned away for being too short. Because he measured 5 foot 2 inches using old French feet (*pieds de roi*), confusion arose as to his height in imperial measurements.

Napoleon said, "England is a nation of shopkeepers"

Well, yes he did say it, and it was a marvelous put-down. But he was quoting from Adam Smith's book, *Wealth of Nations*. Smith wrote, "To found a great empire for the sole purpose of raising up a people of customers, may at first sight appear a project, fit only for a nation of shopkeepers. It is, however, a project altogether unfit for a nation of shopkeepers; but extremely fit for a nation that is governed by shopkeepers."

Nowadays historians argue over whether Napoleon was a reformer or a conqueror

The contemporaries of Napoleon (1769–1821) also argued about this. In the occupied states, such as Germany, he was seen by some people as a brutal, foreign tyrant, whereas others rejoiced in the fact that he finally carried out reforms that their own princes had refused for many years. Only after Napoleon's continental blockade of England, which precipitated an economic crisis in Germany, and the catastrophic campaign against Russia in 1812, did public opinion turn to general disapproval.

Napoleon's Russian campaign failed because of the cold

"Our downfall was the winter; we are the victims of the climate," Napoleon asserted after he had lost 100,000 soldiers in Russia. In reality, the 1812 campaign had been badly prepared. Napoleon reckoned on a swift, decisive battle and was not prepared for the Russians to simply retreat. When he eventually began his retreat from Russia, he chose precisely the route where, during the advance, he had employed "scorched earth" tactics. It is no wonder that horses and soldiers died in their thousands — there were no crops to feed them on their way back. Climate records indicate that temperatures were actually fairly mild and his soldiers did not have to fight against endless snowstorms.

TEA AND REVOLUTION

The Boston Tea Party was a protest against British taxes on tea

Actually, the Tea Party was staged to protest the removal of tax on British tea. Most American tea at the time was smuggled in from Holland. The British tea companies ended up with a huge surplus of tea that they couldn't sell. An act of Parliament removed all the taxes on that tea, undercutting the Dutch tea price. In protest against what they saw as British interference with American business, about 60 men dressed up as Native Americans, boarded some British tea ships in Boston harbor, and dumped a whole load of tea overboard.

Paul Revere rode by himself through the night crying out, "The British are coming"

Paul Revere and two other men, Samuel Prescott, a doctor, and William Dawes, a cobbler, rode out to warn the citizens of Lexington and Concord that the British troops were on the move. However, Paul Revere was captured by the British troops after they rode through Lexington, while Prescott rode on to warn Concord and Dawes escaped back to Lexington. What Revere would have actually said as a warning would have been, "The regulars are out!" That is how the British regular troops were referred to at the time.

WHO FOUGHT WHERE?

The American Revolution was fought against the British

The American colonists were divided in their allegiance at the time of the American Revolution. It was estimated that about one-third supported the revolution, one-third were loyalists and one-third didn't care one way or the other. The battles were fought between American revolutionaries on one side, and loyalists, British soldiers and various mercenaries on the other. The numbers were almost equal on both sides. In some ways the American Revolution was a kind of civil war. After it ended, about 100,000 loyalists fled to Canada.

American colonists used Native American battle tactics to beat the British

Popular beliefs have the colonists defeating the British by using Native American strategies of surprise attacks and hidden ambushes. But the British were experienced in this kind of warfare and not about to be caught off guard. For the most part the battles of the Revolutionary War conformed to the conventional methods of warfare, with both sides resorting to guerrilla tactics when necessary.

The Battle of Bunker Hill took place on Bunker Hill

The first major battle of the Revolutionary War was supposed to take place on Bunker Hill, but Colonel William Prescott decided to fortify nearby Breeds Hill instead. That's where the battle was actually fought, and that's where you'll find an obelisk commemorating the battle.

The Battle of Bennington took place in Bennington

This significant battle of the Revolutionary War took place on August 16, 1777, near the Walloomsac River in New York. It pitted the American colonists, led by General John Stark, against a mixture of British, Loyalists, German mercenaries and Native American troops led by Lieutenant Colonel Friedrich Baum. The battle was fought over the control of the Bennington supply depot, about 4 miles (6 kilometers) from the battle site, across the border in Vermont. The battle drew its name from the supply depot, and a battle monument was subsequently erected in Bennington.

WASHINGTON, THE DELAWARE AND PATRICK HENRY

The painting "Washington Crossing the Delaware" accurately portrays this historical event

A 19th century painter, Emanuel Leutze, painted the picture in 1851 in Dusseldorf, Germany, using the Rhine River as a model for the Delaware. The flag in the middle of the picture has 13 stars and stripes — but this flag was not adopted until 1777, one year after Washington crossed the Delaware. Washington used boats 40 to 60 feet (12 to 18 meters) long to make his crossing, not the rather small boats depicted in the painting. And he probably wouldn't have stood in such a precarious yet imposing position in the boat. However, it is a wonderful, inspiring picture and there is such a thing as artistic license.

Patrick Henry said, "Give me liberty or give me death"

Patrick Henry (1736–99) was reported to have given a stirring speech to rouse his compatriots to revolutionary war in March 1775. It finished with the famous words: "Is life so dear or peace so sweet as to be purchased at the price of chains and slavery? Forbid it, Almighty God, I know not what course others may take, but as for me, give me liberty or give me death!" But no written record of his speech was ever made at the time. This version has filtered through three people. William Wirt wrote it based on the memories of two men who attended the speech. Wirt was known for his exaggerated and somewhat florid prose. The exact words of Patrick Henry's speech may never be known for sure, but whatever he said had the power to rouse his listeners to armed revolution.

The original Uncle Sam was Sam Wilson

There is some dispute to the origin of "Uncle Sam" as the personification of the United States. The 87th United States Congress believed that Sam Wilson was the source of the name, and on September 15, 1961, resolved to "salute Uncle Sam Wilson of Troy, New York, as the progenitor of America's national symbol of Uncle Sam." But the Sam Wilson story is unproven. Sam Wilson (1766–1854) worked as a subcontractor to one Elbert Anderson, who supplied rations to the military during the War of 1812. The initials "E.A.-U.S." were stamped on all goods shipped, and a joke began that the "U.S." stood for "Uncle Sam," meaning Sam Wilson. But another theory suggests that "Sam" is the Gaelic acronymn for *Stáit Aontaithe Mheiriceá*, meaning the United States of America, and Irish immigrants used this short form to refer to their new country. One thing is certain — Uncle Sam's appearance is purely an invention of political cartoonists. The most famous Uncle Sam is that seen on the "I Want You for U.S. Army" recruiting poster. It was drawn by James Montgomery Flagg (1877–1960), who used himself as a model.

PATRIOTIC FLAGS, SONGS AND BELLS

Americans fought under the Stars and Stripes during the American Revolutionary War

Many pictures that were painted of famous battles during the American Revolution feature the Stars and Stripes flying above the fighting men. Although a version of the flag was adopted by the newborn country in 1777, it did not come into general use for many years, and the first war to be fought under it was the Mexican-American War in 1846.

Betsy Ross sewed the first American flag

A family story passed down to Betsy Ross's grandson gradually became accepted as truth, but in fact, Betsy Ross did not sew the first American flag, or indeed have anything to do with it. In 1870, William Canby, her grandson, related the story at a meeting of the Historical Society of Pennsylvania. The way the story went, George Washington came to Betsy Ross and asked her to sew a flag for the new country. The story fell in nicely with the nationalistic fervor of the 1876 centennial celebrations, and soon everyone believed it to be true. It wasn't.

Francis Scott Key composed the tune and lyrics to *The Star-Spangled Banner*

Key wrote a poem on the back of an envelope after witnessing the British attack on Fort McHenry on September 13, 1814. Later he adapted the words to the tune of a drinking song popular at the time. The song became the American national anthem on March 3, 1931, but it was sung for many years before that as an unofficial anthem.

The Liberty Bell cracked while ringing on July 4, 1776

The famous bell did not ring, let alone crack, on this day. The initial Independence celebrations occurred a few days later. The bell had already cracked twice on the way across the ocean from England. It was repaired and hung in the Pennsylvania State House, where it rang out on many state occasions over the years. It cracked again in 1835, while tolling for a funeral for Chief Justice John Marshall. This crack worsened until the bell was put out of service in 1846.

The Declaration of Independence was signed on July 4, 1776

July 4th has been celebrated as Independence Day for a very long time. However, it didn't all happen on July 4, 1776. On July 2, 1776, Congress approved a resolution cutting ties with England and declaring that the United States would become independent. On July 4, 1776, Thomas Jefferson completed his draft of the Declaration of Independence. But it wasn't signed by all the delegates until August 2, 1776. A few didn't get a chance to sign it until months later.

GOTHIC ARCHES, SCOTLAND YARD AND THE UNION JACK

Gothic architecture originated with the Goths

The Goths were a warlike Germanic people who lived in Europe between the second and seventh centuries. They were considered barbarians by the Romans. Later, the term "Gothic" was used in a pejorative sense by Renaissance writers to describe the style of architecture prevalent in Europe between the 12th and 16th centuries. The Renaissance artists despised the Gothic style, and they used "Gothic" as an insult to show just how vulgar and primitive the architecture was. Today many people appreciate the elegant Gothic style expressed in buildings such as Notre Dame Cathedral in Paris and Salisbury Cathedral in England.

Scotland Yard is the headquarters for a group of special detectives

Scotland Yard refers to the London police force as a whole. The name derives from the location of London Police Headquarters in 1829, off Whitehall on a street named "Great Scotland Yard." Legend has it that the site was given to the Scottish king in 10th century Scotland to build a castle in London. In return, the Scottish king had to visit the castle once a year in a form of homage to the English king. London Police headquarters has relocated several times since 1829, but the name "Scotland Yard" has stuck.

The "Union Jack" is the English flag

The Union Jack is the popular nickname for the Union Flag, the flag of the United Kingdom of Great Britain and Northern Ireland. The English flag is white with a red cross (Saint George's cross). With its blue background and white and red crosses, the Union Jack is a combination of the English flag with both the Scottish flag (white Saint Andrew's cross on a blue background) and the former Irish flag (red Saint Andrew's cross or Saint Patrick's cross on a white background).

ROYAL HOUSES AND TOMBS

The English royal house originated in England

Most of the English dynasties came from the continent: The Anglo-Saxon rulers originated in northern Germany and Denmark; the Normans and Plantagenets in France. The Tudors did originate from the island, but were Welsh; their successors, the Stuarts, were Scottish. In 1689, William III of Orange-Nassau (1650–1702) came to the throne, and in 1715 it was the house of Brunswick-Hanover. Queen Victoria (1819–1901) eventually married Albert of Saxe-Coburg-Gotha (1819–61). In 1917, this awkward German name was changed to "Windsor." Since 1960, the royal family is known as Mountbatten-Windsor. The prince consort, Prince Philip Mountbatten (born 1921), is descended from the Danish royal house.

Richard III was a hunchback

It suited Shakespeare's dramatic purposes to make Richard III a deformed, cruel, conniving king. But the real Richard III was not crippled in any way — as can be seen in the portraits painted of him during his lifetime. And there has been much debate about whether or not he committed many of the crimes attributed to him. It was in the Tudors' interest to paint him as a wicked king, since Henry Tudor (Henry VII) killed him in battle and became King of England.

You have to be a member of royalty or a very prominent figure to be buried in Westminster Abbey

Not necessarily. There are no rules as to who may or may not be laid to rest within the hallowed walls of the ancient Abbey. The deans of the Abbey decide who shall be buried there. The site has seen the burial of kings and queens going all the way back to Edward the Confessor in the 11th century, although the present Abbey was built between 1245 and 1517. Over the centuries monks and other ordinary people associated with the Abbey have found their final resting place there, as well as kings, queens, poets, musicians and actors (for example, Laurence Olivier).

RUSSIA AND CHINA

Prince Potemkin had Potemkin villages built

Grigory Aleksandrovich Potemkin (1739–91), on the orders of Empress Catherine the Great (1729–62), colonized the area around the Black Sea. He settled farmers and townspeople there and founded many towns. In 1787, the Tsarina made a journey through the area. Meanwhile, back in Moscow, his many opponents maintained that the prince (who was also Catherine's lover) had only the time to erect blank frontages, with nothing behind them.

The Emperors of China were Chinese

The "Middle Kingdom" also saw periods of foreign rule. From 1261 to 1368, Mongol khans occupied the imperial throne and founded the Yuan dynasty. From 1644 to 1911, the country was ruled by the Manchu, the inhabitants of Manchuria, which borders China to the north. The last Emperor, Pu Yi (1906–67), descended from the Manchu Qing dynasty. Nowadays, the Manchu are a national minority in China.

In China, pigtails were the traditional hairstyle for men

In 1645, at the beginning of the Ch'ing dynasty, the Manchu promulgated a decree that every Chinese should wear a pigtail, called a "queue," to conform with the Manchu style of wearing their hair. It was bitterly resented by the conquered Chinese, but the queue was worn in China for the next 266 years. Gradually it became a source of pride. When the Ch'ing dynasty fell in 1911 and China became a republic, the wearing of pigtails was abolished by the revolutionaries and people were forced to cut off their queues.

SEATTLE AND SITTING BULL

Seattle's reply was actually spoken by him

The Suquamish chief, Seattle (1786–1866) did give a speech in January 1854 about the cession of Indian lands to the white settlers. Contrary to legend, this was not given in front of the American President, but before the Governor of Washington Territory. A journalist who attended the speech had it translated into English and published the first written version in 1887. Other written versions followed and the speech was altered every time it was printed. The best-known version, with the ecological references, first appeared in 1972. It is possible that the sentence, "Every portion of this land is holy to my people," is authentic, but it is uncertain how much of Seattle's original speech survived.

Sitting Bull was a war chief who led his warriors in the battle of Little Bighorn

Sitting Bull (1831–90) was not his name, he wasn't a war chief and he didn't fight in the famous battle where General Custer made his last stand in 1876. "Sitting Bull" was the white man's name for Tatanka Yotanka, a respected chief and medicine man who was a leader of the Sioux. When the U.S. government went back on its treaty with the Sioux, Sitting Bull opposed them, but it was Crazy Horse who led the warriors into battle.

AMERICAN CIVIL WAR: DIXIE AND SLAVES

Northerners did not keep slaves

No one doubts that there were slaves in all of the Southern colonies, but it is often forgotten that slaves were owned in the North too. Slavery was legal in many northern states in the 17th and 18th centuries. Well-attended slave auctions were held weekly, and sometimes daily, in the large ports of Boston and New York, as well as in Philadelphia and Rhode Island. Both John Hancock and Benjamin Franklin bought, sold and owned slaves. Anti-slavery Secretary of State William Henry Seward grew up in New York in a slave-owning family amid slave-owning neighbors. Even the family of Abraham Lincoln, which moved to Indiana when he was 8, owned slaves at one time. Recent archaeological finds have revealed slave quarters and cemeteries in Philadelphia and New York City.

The term "Dixie" refers to the Mason-Dixon line

There are many explanations as to why the South is referred to as "Dixie." There is no real evidence that the term comes from the Mason-Dixon line, the border between the free and slave states in the mid-19th century. It may have come from 10-dollar notes issued in New Orleans, which had the word "dix" printed on them ("ten" in French). These bills became known as "dixies" and the term caught on as a nickname for the South, popularized in songs of the time.

The cause of the American Civil War was the emancipation of slaves

The actual causes of the American Civil War were the differing economic systems in the North and the South. Whereas the South wanted free markets for its agricultural produce, the North demanded protective tariffs for domestic industries, which were just being established. In the winter of 1860–61, the Southern states left the Union, not because they were worried that the new President, Abraham Lincoln (1809–65), would forbid them from owning slaves, but because his whole policy served the interests of the North and would also establish a "pro-Northern" attitude in the new territories. The Southern states feared that in any votes they would be hopelessly outnumbered.

The Emancipation Proclamation of 1863 freed all the slaves

No, it didn't. What it did do was to proclaim the freedom of slaves in areas under Confederate control, but it did not apply to all the other states in the Union, such as all the northern states, Tennessee and parts of Louisiana and Virginia. Lincoln had the proclamation made in part to politicize the slave issue, giving the union cause more support at home and ensuring that foreign powers like France and England would not want to join with the South and be seen to be supporting slavery. In 1863 there were about four million slaves in the country. About 200,000 of them were freed as a result of the proclamation, but slavery itself was not officially outlawed until 1865, when the Thirteenth Amendment to the Constitution was passed.

Abraham Lincoln coined the phrase "Government of the people, by the people..."

In the Gettysburg Address in 1863, Lincoln used this phrase to make his point about the United States democracy: "...and that government of the people, by the people, for the people, shall not perish from the earth." However, he was not the first to use it, although he adapted it brilliantly for his purposes. A similar phrase was written by John Wycliffe in 1382 about the Bible, and in 1830 Daniel Webster wrote something very similar, as did Theodore Parker, a Boston minister, in 1850. Lincoln appreciated the phrase and used it for his own purposes.

Robert E. Lee supported slavery and the Southern cause

General Robert E. Lee was morally opposed to slavery and freed his family's slaves before the Civil War. A distinguished military commander who did not support the secession of the Southern states, he was offered the command of either the Union or the Confederate army. Because he was a Southerner, with his home and family in Virginia, he ultimately decided to lead the Confederate army.

ROUSING THE TROOPS

"Damn the torpedoes" refers to torpedoes

The famous remark made by Admiral David Farragut during the American Civil War referred to a kind of underwater mine, not what we think of today as a torpedo. During the battle of Mobile Bay on August 5, 1864, the Admiral showed his disdain for the danger embodied by these mines, beer kegs filled with gunpowder that had been placed in the bay. He allegedly said, "Damn the torpedoes — full speed ahead!" and the phrase became popular as a show of bravado in a dangerous situation. Self-propelled torpedoes were not in use until after the American Civil War.

General Sherman sent the message, "Hold the fort! I'm coming!"

When General Sherman was on his way to relieve the beleaguered soldiers at the Allatoona, Georgia, supply depot, he sent two telegrams. One said, "Hold fast!" and the other said, "Hold out!" Reporters, always on the hunt for the dramatic, condensed these messages into "Hold the fort! I am coming!" in their reports from the front. The phrase caught on and became a Union slogan.

LINCOLN AND GETTYSBURG

Lincoln spoke of forefathers in the Gettysburg Address

The famous opening of the Gettysburg Address has been misquoted so often that many people don't know the correct wording. The misquote: "Fourscore and seven years ago our *forefathers* brought forth *upon* this continent a new nation..." What Lincoln said was: "Fourscore and seven years ago our *fathers* brought forth *on* this continent a new nation..." Lincoln made the speech on November 19, 1863, to encourage and inspire his people during the American Civil War.

Lincoln wrote the Gettysburg Address on the back of an envelope

Legend has it that Abraham Lincoln wrote the Gettysburg Address on the back of an envelope on a train on the way to Gettysburg. On the contrary, he started composing it on November 8, two weeks before the day he was to give the speech, and he wrote five drafts, revising it again and again until he was happy with it.

GO WEST, O'LEARY'S COW AND THE STATUE OF LIBERTY

Horace Greeley said, "Go west, young man, go west!"

In 1851 Horace Greeley's newspaper, the *New York Tribune*, printed an article by John L. Soule that included the phrase, "Go west, young man, and grow up with the country." However, because the phrase was so closely associated with Greeley's newspaper, he was credited with the remark.

Mrs. O'Leary's cow started the Great Chicago Fire of 1871

Contrary to rumor, there was never any evidence that the O'Leary's cow started the devastating fire that destroyed 17,000 buildings and killed 250 people. The fire did begin somewhere behind the O'Leary's house, but they were asleep and the story that the cow kicked over a lantern while being milked was fabricated by a journalist looking for a good hook for his story about the fire.

The Statue of Liberty symbolizes freedom in the United States

The Statue of Liberty, or *Liberty Enlightening the World*, as the 148-foot (45 meter) statue was formerly known, is the work of the Alsace artist Frédéric-Auguste Bartholdi (1834–1904) and quite simply stands for freedom. Originally, it was intended to be erected at the Suez Canal, but when the British colonial administration there refused permission, the French state gave it to the United States. In 1924 it was declared a National Monument, and in 1984 a World Heritage Site. The colossal figure, which stands in New York Harbor, is visible from a great distance to all approaching ships. It is a symbol of hope, and not just for people who are entering the United States.

GOVERNMENT IN THEORY AND PRACTICE

A democracy is the same thing as a republic

A democracy can also be a republic, but a republic is not necessarily a democracy. By definition a republic is any form of government that does not have a hereditary ruler. A fascist country ruled by a dictator could be a republic. But a democracy is a government that is ruled by the elected representatives of the people.

Americans vote for the President

The President and the Vice-President are elected not by a direct vote of the American people, but by the members of the Electoral College. These members are elected by the people of each state and correspond to the number of senators and representatives in Congress for their respective state. The electors then vote for the President and Vice-President. The electors are expected to vote along party lines, but occasionally they don't and then the country winds up with a President that does not have the majority of popular support. Three presidents elected in this fashion were: John Adams (1824), Rutherford B. Hayes (1876) and Benjamin Harrison (1888).

The United States is governed by a "majority rule" system of democracy

Traditionally, less than half the eligible voters in the United States exercise their vote, so elected officials are not elected by the majority of the population. In addition, the technical definition of majority rule holds that the winner must have more votes than ALL the other candidates combined. The United States operates under a "plurality" rule, where the winner only has to have more votes than any other single candidate.

Communists believe everyone should receive the same salary

A common assumption is that communists believe that doctors and factory workers should all work for the same amount of money. This is not strictly true. Marx said, "From each according to his abilities, to each according to his needs." This suggests that each person should work at what they do best, and receive the salary they need. It does not define needs or abilities, but it also does not preclude differences in salaries.

U.S. MEDALS, REGIMENTS AND SHIPS

The Congressional Medal of Honor is the highest military decoration in the United States

The Medal of Honor, awarded by the American Congress, is indeed the highest military decoration in the United States, but although it is widely known as the "Congressional" Medal of Honor, its correct name is simply the "Medal of Honor." First awarded in the American Civil War, it is given "for conspicuous gallantry and intrepidity at the risk of life, above and beyond the call of duty, in actual combat against an armed enemy force."

The Rough Riders fought on horses, led by Teddy Roosevelt

The First Regiment of the U.S. Cavalry Volunteers, popularly known as the Rough Riders, certainly trained on horses, but when it came to fighting in the Spanish-American War, they had to leave nearly all their horses behind in Florida and ended up fighting in Cuba on foot. The regiment was led by Colonel Leonard Wood, and Roosevelt was second in command as Lieutenant Colonel. Together with other units, the regiment succeeded in defeating the Spanish at Santiago in July 1898.

The ship known as "Old Ironsides" was made of iron

A frigate made of wood, the *Constitution* was a warship with 44 guns that earned a reputation as nearly invincible in the War of 1812. Because it escaped serious hull damage so many times, people began to refer to it as "Old Ironsides."

AMERICAN PRESIDENTS

John F. Kennedy was the youngest American president

Kennedy was certainly the youngest president ever elected — he came to office when he was 43 years old. However, Theodore Roosevelt was the youngest President ever. When Roosevelt was 42, as Vice President, he took office as President after President William McKinley was assassinated in 1901. Roosevelt was later elected to the post in 1904 and served until 1909.

George Washington was the first President of the United States

John Hanson had that privilege. For eight years before the American Constitution was adopted, the United States existed under the Articles of Confederation. In 1781 John Hanson was elected by the Congress as the President of the United States. He didn't have the same powers later presidents had, and he only served for one year, but he was the first official President.

BEN FRANKLIN AND WAGON TRAINS

The *Saturday Evening Post* was founded by Benjamin Franklin

Although it stated on its masthead that it was founded in 1728 by Benjamin Franklin, the *Post* was founded in 1821 some 30 years after Franklin's death. Franklin owned a paper called the *Pennsylvania Gazette*, but it folded in 1815. When the *Post* was founded in 1821, they used the same printshop the *Gazette* had used. That was the only connection, but by the 1890s the *Post* was proclaiming Benjamin Franklin as its founder. A bit of a stretch, to say the least.

Wagon trains pulled into a circle at night to defend themselves

The primary reason that wagons made a circle at night was to form a corral for the horses, mules and oxen traveling with them. It also made a good defensive position in case of attack from Native Americans. But these attacks were not as numerous as rumored. During the westward migration by wagon trains, about 350,000 people died. Approximately 362 can be directly linked to attacks. Disease claimed the lives of most of these victims.

Scalping was a common Native American custom

There is no doubt that scalping was traditional for some Native North American tribes. We also know that the colonists did some scalping as well. What isn't agreed upon is who taught whom. While some historians believe that it was the colonists who "taught" scalping to the Indians, archaeological evidence now suggests that scalping was widespread in the Americas long before the Europeans arrived. Historians do agree, however, that the colonists most certainly introduced the concept of paying bounties for scalps. Not surprisingly, with money in the picture there was an increase in scalpings by white settlers. Hanna Duston, known as "The Hatchet Lady," was notorious for her scalping activities, and it seems likely that as scalping by whites became more common, so did retaliatory scalpings by Native Americans, including tribes that had not previously practiced scalping. Until the 1990s, scalps could still be seen in various U.S. museums, including the Peabody Museum of Archaeology and Ethnology.

LABOR AND LENIN

May Day labor celebrations originated in the European socialist movement

On May 1, 1886, some Chicago workers called a strike in favor of the eight-hour workday. Three days later there was a riot in Chicago's Haymarket Square, when a demonstration supporting the strike turned violent. Police and demonstrators were killed. As a result, May 1 was declared an international day of labor solidarity, with parades of union members and labor supporters taking place in many different cities around the world.

Lenin was the theorist of Bolshevism, and Stalin the despot

The system was established by Vladimir Ilyich Ulyanov (1870–1924), known as Lenin. After the fall of the Tsar, he decided to start the October Revolution against the interim government. A dreadful, five-year-long civil war followed, which claimed large numbers of civilian victims. It was not just the old elite and the Mensheviks that were eliminated, but also Ukrainian civilians. Among the farming population, the forced seizure of food supplies precipitated famine. In addition, the first two extermination camps were established. As early as 1891, Lenin had opposed humanitarian help for the famine-stricken farmers of Simbirsk, because famine furthered the desire for revolution.

Lenin said, "National health insurance is the keystone in the arch of the socialized state"

This quote has been widely used to discourage a national health insurance plan in the United States, starting in 1949 when the National Physicians' Committee came up with it to scare people away from President Harry Truman's plan for national insurance. It worked — any policy that was said to encourage Communism would not be popular, to say the least, in the Cold War atmosphere of the United States in the mid-20th century. However, Lenin never said this. Scholars have combed his works and it cannot be found. Did the doctors make it up? Whatever its provenance, the quote lives on to this day, independent of Lenin's writings.

REDS, BOLSHEVIKS AND COMMIES

Bolshevik is a Russian word for Communist

"Bolshevik" means "member of the majority." This term arose in 1903 at the second conference of the Social Democratic Party of Russia. The majority in this party consisted of the Communists under Lenin (1870–1924), and in the minority were the moderate Mensheviks ("members of the minority"). In 1912, the Bolsheviks excluded the Mensheviks from the party. The Bolshevik October Revolution overthrew not the Tsar — that had happened in February — but an interim government of the Mensheviks. The name "Bolshevik" caught on as a name for the Russian Communists, but it was seen by them as insulting and was officially abolished in 1952.

The October Revolution took place in October

According to the western calendar, the October Revolution began on November 7, 1917. According to the Julian calendar still employed at that time in Russia, it was October 25. Half a year later, in February 1918, the victorious revolutionaries introduced the Gregorian calendar (already common in Europe) to Russia, without, however, renaming their coup the "November Revolution."

Red Square is named after the Communists

"Red Square" in Russian is "*Krasnaya Ploshchad.*" "*Krasnaya,*" however, does not just mean "red" but also "beautiful." For Russians, the main square in Moscow is the "Beautiful Square." It is true, however, that the alternative interpretation of "Red Square" is appropriate for the Communists, as well as in terms of the quantity of blood that has been spilled there.

The Eastern Bloc was Communist

The states of the former Eastern Bloc saw themselves as socialist. True Socialism was considered a transitional phase on the path to true Communism. According to doctrine, in Socialism class conflict has not yet been completely overcome, which is why a dictatorship of the proletariat is required. In Communism, this dictatorship is no longer required, because by then all enmity toward the system has been eradicated.

FIRST WORLD WAR

Franz Ferdinand was killed by Serbs

The Austrian Grand Duke Franz Ferdinand (born 1863) was shot on June 28, 1914, by Gavrilo Princip (1894–1918), a Bosnian of Serbian nationality. Five others were involved in the plot: four young Serbian Bosnians and one Muslim. They had obtained the weapons for the assassination attempt from an officer in Belgrade. But neither then nor now can any link with Serbian government circles be established, although much has been speculated about the mysterious Serbian group known as the "Black Hand."

Europe slid into the First World War

This remark by the British Prime Minister David Lloyd George (1863–1945) has often been repeated. The actions that took place, however, show a completely different picture. The German government pressed the Austrians to begin a war against Serbia, even at the risk of the other great powers becoming involved. Germany blocked attempts at negotiations by the other powers, and finally declared war on Russia and France.

By sinking the *Lusitania*, Germany broke international law

International law allowed the sinking of merchant ships by submarines in war, once the crew had taken to the lifeboats. However, the British increasingly fitted their merchant ships with guns, so that it was no longer possible to make a clear distinction. The same thing happened with the British maritime blockade. It was permissible as far as war materials were concerned, but broke international law when foodstuffs for civilians were stopped. Nevertheless neither side bothered about the fine print: The Germans sank everything, and the British imposed a total blockade.

The two World Wars were the greatest catastrophes of the 20th century

Just in terms of the number of victims, the Spanish flu epidemic of 1918 to 1920, with an estimated 22 million dead, was responsible for at least twice as many deaths as the First World War. About 500 million people were infected. The influenza was first discovered in Spain, but probably arrived from North America. That influenza epidemic was the worst of its sort in modern times. The Second World War did claim more victims than the flu epidemic: worldwide, about 60 million people died during the conflict.

CHURCHILL AND BOMBS

Churchill predicted "blood, sweat and tears" in the Second World War

Winston Churchill (1874–1965) made a speech to the house of Parliament in 1940 that included this phrase about the war with Germany: "I have nothing to offer but blood, toil, tears and sweat." This was misquoted so often as "blood, sweat and tears" that many people believed that was what he actually said. Although Churchill delivered the speech himself in Parliament, an actor was hired to give it in a radio broadcast. Churchill himself was too busy to do it and the actor did a very good Churchill imitation.

Churchill came up with the term "iron curtain"

In 1946 Churchill said, "From Stettin in the Baltic to Trieste in the Atlantic, an iron curtain has descended across the Continent." But the term was in use for at least 40 years before this, and Churchill borrowed it because it was an apt description of Europe at the time. In 1914 the Queen of Belgium said about Germany, "Between them and me there is now a bloody iron curtain which has descended forever." In the old days, an iron curtain was required in theaters as a safety precaution, to prevent fire spreading from the stage to the rest of the theater. Other people used the term "iron curtain" to describe political situations, but Churchill made it famous.

The expression "weapons of mass destruction" was created to describe nuclear weapons

The first time this expression was officially recorded was in the London *Times* in 1937, referring to the aerial bombing of cities and chemical warfare. The atomic bomb had not yet been invented. Later the phrase came into widespread use to describe nuclear weapons.

The atomic bombs dropped in Japan killed more people than any other event in the Second World War

While the immediate results of the atomic bombs were devastating (75,000 people killed in Hiroshima and 35,000 in Nagasaki), and many more people died from radiation poisoning afterward, there were attacks during the Second World War that killed more people at one time. The city of Dresden, in Germany, was bombed steadily overnight and the city was completely destroyed, leaving 135,000 people dead. Another one-night attack on Tokyo in 1945 killed 85,000, after napalm was dropped on the city.

During the Second World War there was a race to develop the atom bomb

The American efforts to develop an atom bomb were driven by the fear that Germany might otherwise anticipate the Allies in doing so. After all, Otto Hahn (1879–1968) had discovered nuclear fission in 1938. However, there was never a race, because the German efforts in atomic weapons development were too tentative. By 1942 the development of new forms of conventional weapons had absolute priority. Historians nowadays assume that Germany would not have had the means to manufacture atomic weapons during the war. The Americans invested $2 billion and the work of a total of 300,000 people in the project.

THE BERLIN WALL AND THE SWISS ARMY

The closure of the border between the two Germanys happened very quickly

The border between the two German states was closed in 1951. For 10 years Berlin constituted a loophole, until building of the Wall began on August 13, 1961. Before that, 2.7 million people from East Germany had moved to the West. The border, which lasted until 1989, was secured by a death strip with mines, barbed-wire fencing and automatic firing devices.

As a neutral country, Switzerland does not have an army

Although Switzerland has upheld its constitutional policy of neutrality since 1815, the country has compulsory military service for all men between 20 and 50, as well as an active women's voluntary force. Switzerland traditionally spent more money per capita on its military than many other European countries and had a very sophisticated defence plan and mobilization strategy. In 2003 the country voted to reduce its military personnel considerably, from 524,000 to 220,000.

THE EUROPEAN UNION

Brussels is the seat of the European Union (EU)

The EU has no official seat of government. The three authorities — Executive, Legislative and Judiciary — are divided between three different cities. The EU Council and Commission meet in Brussels. The Parliament is located in Strasbourg. It is true that the parliamentary committees also meet in Brussels. The Court of Justice and the Audit Office are in Luxembourg, as is the Parliament's General Secretariat.

The EU's official language is French

The EU has 21 official languages: Czech, Danish, Dutch, English, Estonian, Finnish, French, German, Greek, Hungarian, Irish, Italian, Latvian, Lithuanian, Maltese, Polish, Portuguese, Swedish, Slovakian, Slovenian and Spanish. As working languages, English and German are used alongside French.

Every one of the territories of the EU is in Europe

The possible admission of Turkey will not be the first time that a member of the EU is not in Europe. The overseas departments of France already belong. Martinique, Guadeloupe, Réunion and French Guiana — the launching site for the European Space Agency's *Ariane* rockets — are therefore also shown on euro notes. In addition, Cyprus and some Greek islands geographically lie in Asia, and the Canary Islands in Africa.

Members of the European Parliament have no power

This is not true, but the elected members of the European Parliament actually have less authority than, for example, the members of the German Parliament, the Bundestag. Basically, the European Parliament cannot initiate anything itself, but can only refuse its agreement. So while the parliamentarians are allowed to vote on the membership of the European Commission, the individuals have been named by the various member states. In addition, their approval is sought for the budget and all laws. The initiative when it comes to laws lies with the Commission, and the first decision is taken in the Council of Ministers, consisting of the current ministers of the member states. All attempts to make Europe more democratic by giving the Parliament more powers have failed up to now, because then the individual governments would have to give up some of their own powers.

The EC is now known as the EU

In 1967, the European Coal and Steel Community, the European Atomic Energy Authority and the European Economic Community were combined into the European Community (EC). The European Union (EU) was newly set up by the Maastricht Treaty in 1992.

IDEALISM AND DEDICATION

There is an international agreement about human rights

There are two: the International Covenant on Civil and Political Rights, and the International Covenant on Economic, Social and Cultural Rights. The second agreement deals with minimum wages, the right to a healthy workplace, the right to form a trade union and the right to have access to a health system.

In the 1960s women burned bras in support of feminism

Some women threw their bras away, but there was no burning. The legend started with a 1968 article in the *New York Times* about a protest against the Miss America Beauty Contest in Atlantic City. Organizers told the paper that "they would not do anything dangerous — it's just a symbolic bra-burning." In fact, the protesters acted out a bit of street theater, throwing items of "patriarchal oppression," such as bras, girdles, makeup and high heels into a trash can.

The International Human Rights Convention forbids the death penalty

Article 6 of the International Covenant on Civil and Political Rights prescribes restrictions for those states where the death penalty exists, including rules about fair legal proceedings and restricting the death penalty to the most serious crimes and adult culprits. In addition, the United Nations' Human Rights Commission supports the abolition of the death penalty.

The "Why not?" quote originated with Robert Kennedy

In his play *Back to Methuselah*, written in 1921, George Bernard Shaw wrote, "You see things and you say, 'Why?' But I dream things that never were; and I say, 'Why not?'" Bobby Kennedy used these words as a sort of theme for his 1968 presidential campaign, and many people believed he wrote them himself. But his brother John F. Kennedy also used them in a speech in 1968, citing Shaw as their source.

The U.S. Postal Service has a well known motto about rain and snow

Many people believe that the following is the motto of the U.S. Postal Service: "Neither rain nor snow nor heat nor gloom of night stays these couriers from the swift completion of their appointed rounds." It was written by Herodotus, a Greek historian (484–425 BC), referring to the postmen of ancient Persia. The words were inscribed on the building that houses the New York City post office, and people have taken it to be the postmen's motto. But it is there for inspiration only.

PLANTS OR ANIMALS?

Living things are either plants or animals

For a long time, scientists believed that they could manage with just this simple division. But the more Nature's secrets were investigated, the harder it became to force living things that were obviously not animals into the category of plants. Since then, this scheme has been dropped. Living things are now divided into three groups, known as domains: bacteria, archaea and eukaryotes. The first two groups consist of unicellular life forms without a true cellular nucleus. However, their cellular form does show structural differences between the two domains. All living beings that have cellular nuclei and an internal or external skeleton belong to the eukaryotes.

Fungi are plants

Not any more, according to the latest classification. In this, the eukaryotes were subdivided into four groups: Animals, plants, fungi and protists. The last are unicellular (or in many cases, multicellular) simple life forms — such as algae. Fungi were separated from plants because they differ from them in many important features. For example, they do not possess any chlorophyll, nor do they strengthen their cell walls with chitin, which is otherwise found only in animals. There are even researchers who think that fungi were earlier related to animals rather than plants.

Lichens are plants

Lichens consist of two life forms, a fungus and an alga. The visible lichen body (the thallus) is the fungus. It is robust and clings to the substrate. The alga lives within the body of the lichen and carries out photosynthesis and thus is able to produce nutrients. The fungus lives on these, which it taps from the alga. To do so, the fungus is in a position to take up water. By means of this perfectly adapted partnership, lichens are able to find a habitat where no other organisms can live. However once lichens have become established, then other inhabitants do likewise.

Algae bloom

Algae cannot bloom. After all they increase by division, not by fertilization. Algal blooms are actually vast increases in the numbers of algae. Whereas in pools and streams the color of algae is a marshy green, many marine algae create a striking color in the water. *Euglena sanguinea*, for example, or *Oscillatoria rubescens*, cause a deep red "bloom."

Corals are fossils

The fiery red coral jewelry consists of the skeletons of true corals. Like all corals, these are animals. The body is generally cylindrical and fixed to the substrate with a disk-like foot. The upper opening, the tubular mouth, is surrounded by a ring of tentacles. To protect their delicate bodies, most corals surround themselves with an outer skeleton of calcium carbonate, which they excrete. Coral reefs consist of innumerable individual corals that have grown together.

Sponges consist of dead tissue

Sponges are animals. Despite its soft consistency, the material that we use as bath sponges forms only the skeleton of these extremely primitive sea creatures. In living sponges, this skeleton (which in other types of sponge may also consist of hard silica or chalk) supports the actual tissue of cells. Sponges feed on plankton, and thanks to their filtering activity, are extremely important for purifying the water.

Sea anemones are flowers

Sea anemones belong to an order of animals that includes corals, with both forming part of the class known as anthozoans. Sea lilies, plumose anemones and the various types of sea anemones all fall in the same group.

Sea cucumbers are a vegetable

These are also animals, even when they grow to up to 6.5 feet (2 meters) long, lie on the seafloor looking like brown cylinders and do not seem to be alive. They are echinoderms, related to starfish and sea urchins, and do move sometimes. But you have to be patient if you want to see this. More than 13 feet (4 meters) per hour is not likely. It gets exciting, however, if sea cucumbers are attacked. Then they squirt sticky white tubes from their insides and the attacker can get hopelessly tangled up in this spaghetti salad.

FLOWERS

Tulips come from Holland

Tulips originally came from Central Asia, and from there to Turkey. The tulip, which seems so quintessentially Dutch to us, is the national flower and the symbol of life in Turkey. In 1560 the Austrian envoy brought them from Constantinople to Vienna, where the imperial court botanist, Charles de l'Ecluse (known as Carolus Clusius, 1526–1609) developed a passion for these flowers. When he became a professor at Leiden in the Netherlands in 1593, he took tulips with him. In the 17th century, beginning with Holland, the whole of Europe became seized by "tulip mania." Tulip bulbs became the objects of speculation and were traded at extremely high prices.

Roses have thorns

Roses have spines. This is because the sharp spikes grow outside the stems and are easily broken off. Thorns, on the other hand, grow from the inside, and can only be removed by causing considerable damage to the whole plant. This is the case with cacti, for example, which therefore do not have spines, but thorns. However, the hawthorn is correctly named, because it has true thorns, and not spines.

Cloves are the dried flower heads of a sort of carnation

Cloves have nothing whatsoever to do with carnations, but are dried flower buds. They do not come from garden carnations, but from the tropical clove tree (*Syzygium aromaticum*), a plant of the myrtle family that grows primarily in the Moluccas, on Zanzibar and on Madagascar.

NUTS OR NOT?

Walnuts are nuts

Walnuts, as well as coconuts and almonds, belong to the stone fruits — as do peaches. The "nut" forms a "stone" (corresponding to a peach stone), which has a soft interior that contains cyanide and is thus poisonous. The flesh of the "fruit" of the walnut is greenish white and inedible. It breaks open and begins to rot when the nuts are ripe.

Cashews are nuts

Cashews come from a tropical fruit called the cashew apple, and they grow on trees. The cashew does not have a shell, but it grows in a pod something like a shell. The pod's covering exudes an unpleasant oil called cardol, which must be removed before the cashew can be retrieved and eaten.

The peanut is a nut

Strictly speaking, the peanut (*Arachis hypogea*) is a legume, more closely related to a pea than a nut. The "nuts" are in fact seeds.

FRUIT

A bird is named after the Australian national fruit, the kiwi

The kiwi fruit originates in China and is sometimes described as the Chinese gooseberry. However, in the 1940s it was New Zealand that first improved kiwi fruit and cultivated them commercially. Based on this, the fruit was called kiwi, after the national bird of New Zealand, which they resemble, with their brown, rounded appearance.

Apples often have maggots

The small pinkish maggot-like creatures that are found in apples are the larvae of the codling moth (*Cydia pomonella*). If the worm-eaten apple does not first fall from the tree, the fat caterpillars simply lower themselves on a thread at some point. Naturally fallen fruit often becomes food for true worms, such as earthworms.

Bananas grow on trees

The banana plant is an herb, not a tree. The fruit must be picked green and then allowed to ripen to be edible. Only when it is picked does the banana become sweet and tasty. Bananas have been cultivated to be sterile, and the plants have to be reproduced by artificial means. The most popular fruit in the United States, the banana is a quick source of potassium and carbohydrates.

Muskmelons are fruit

The classification of melons is a task in itself. If one simply takes the view that fruit is sweet, then melons are fruit. If, however, one considers their true relationship, then one has to appreciate that they are related to cucumbers and zucchini, and thus belong to the cucurbit family, which means that they are vegetables. However, if one defines fruit as the product of the fertilized blossoms of a plant, while vegetables are any other edible parts of a plant, then the whole cucurbit family becomes fruit, as do all leguminous plants and the fruits of plants of the nightshade family, such as peppers, tomatoes and eggplant. Rhubarb, which consists of the stems of a plant, remains a vegetable.

BERRIES AND CITRUS

Strawberries are berries

Strawberries are an accessory fruit: their actual fruit are the tiny green or yellow pips that are carried on the red flesh. The flesh of a strawberry is technically a vegetable.

Rowan berries are poisonous

The belief that the berries of the mountain ash or rowan are poisonous is extremely persistent. The truth is that when they are red they taste bitter and, rather like sloes (the fruit of a blackthorn), cause the mucous membranes in the mouth to pucker up. In addition, no one wants to eat many of them because they can give you a dreadful stomachache or diarrhea. However, if the berries are cooked, the astringent material is destroyed, and it is possible to make as delicious a jam as with any more common fruit. After a frost, the berries taste sweeter.

A pomelo is the same as a grapefruit

What is occasionally sold in supermarkets by the name of pomelo is really a grapefruit. True pomelos are green, not as juicy as grapefruit and may weigh as much as 4.5 pounds (2 kilograms). The grapefruit was discovered in the middle of the 18th century on Barbados, and is a naturally occurring cross between a pomelo and an orange. Crosses between grapefruit and pomelos are also occasionally offered as pomelos.

Oranges are orange

Not always. Often they're green, and if a cold snap doesn't occur before they're picked, they stay green. The bright fruit in the supermarket has often been dipped in a red dye to make them bright orange. An interesting tidbit: the color orange was named after the fruit.

Kumquats are citrus plants

They are like tiny, long mandarins and are occasionally described as dwarf oranges. Even their Chinese name *kam kwat* means "golden orange." Kumquats do not belong to the *Citrus* genus, however, but form their own genus, the rutaceous plants, the *Fortunella* or kumquat plants, of which there are many different types. But they are, of course, closely related to citrus plants.

TOMATOES AND TUBERS

Tomatoes are red

There are yellow, green, orange, mauve, pink and even almost black tomatoes. Particularly striking are tomatoes with a striped pattern. Similarly, there are violet peppers, blue corn, red, yellow and mauve potatoes and white carrots. Most of these did not arise as the whim of some mad plant breeder. On the contrary: modern plant breeding, which aims to obtain the most suitable type of plant for commercial purposes, has very sharply reduced the number of old colored types. Tomatoes must be as large as possible, uniform in size, easy to keep fresh and brilliantly red. The greatest commercial success with consumers has been achieved by tomatoes that have met these high standards. Any others are simply not purchased.

Potatoes are the fruit of potato plants

Roots or tubers are only used in colloquial language. Botanically speaking, fruit grow only above ground and are formed by the fertilized flowers of plants. Whether they are edible or not is irrelevant. Carrots, however, are the roots of the carrot plant, and potatoes are swellings that form on the spreading roots of the plants.

The Jerusalem artichoke comes from Jerusalem

No, it doesn't and it's not an artichoke. The flowering plant (*Helianthus tuberosis*) with the edible tuber belongs to the sunflower family. The Italians called it *girasole articciocco* — "sunflower artichoke." Over the years the word *girasole* was transformed into "Jerusalem."

TREES

Redwoods grow very slowly

Contrary to popular belief, the coast redwood grows quite quickly, at a rate of 170 feet (52 meters) over 50 years on a good site in California. If the growing conditions are ideal, the tree can grow as much as 1 inch (2.5 centimeters) in just one year.

In autumn, leaves turn brightly colored

On the contrary: they become bleached. In autumn, leaves lose their chlorophyll, the green pigment. As a result, the roughly 400 other pigments become visible. Anthocyanin and the carotenoids suddenly stand a chance, and cause the leaves to glow in red and yellow tones.

Redwoods are the oldest trees in the world

The North American giant sequoias (*Sequoiadendron giganteum* or *Sequoia wellingtonia*) may reach over 330 feet (100 meters) high and be several thousand years old. From the same family, the oldest known California or coast redwood (*Sequoia sempervirens*) is 2,200-plus years old, and the oldest has attained 3,500-plus years. For a long time it was believed that this would never be beaten — until the discovery in the 1950s of bristlecone pines (*Pinus longaeva*) in the Rocky Mountains. In Nevada in 1964, one "Prometheus" was felled by mistake by a young doctorate student who was searching for evidence of Ice Age glaciers and had been given permission to cut the tree. Prometheus was subsequently found to be 4,862 years old. In California's White Mountains, "Methuselah" is still alive at an age of 4,600-plus years.

Bark is all the material outside the wood

Biologists call the outermost dead layer of cells of a tree the "bark." It often falls off the tree naturally, or may be easily stripped off. Cork, for example, is obtained by stripping the outer layer of the bark from cork oaks, roughly every 10 years. Because trees increase in diameter as they grow, the outermost layer of bark breaks up from time to time and dies off, while beneath it new, fresh bark is formed.

PASTURES AND PONDS

Lean pastures appear poor

Whether an expanse of grassland is a lean pasture or a lush meadow has nothing to do with the density of the plant cover, but with the supply of nutrients. A lean pasture has a low supply of nutrients and meets only very small demands. However, the most beautiful meadow flowers have become specialized to such locations, whereas green grasses and dandelions thrive on rich soil.

More varieties of plants and animals thrive in the countryside than in towns

In general, significantly fewer animals and plants live in an agricultural landscape that has been sprayed with pesticides than do in a town. Urban conditions are very tempting for many animals. The food supply, the milder climate and the lack of natural enemies are all attractive. Research has shown, for example, that between five and ten types of birds breed in the center of towns, whereas on farmland there are no more than three. With 20 to 25 breeding varieties, birds actually do best, not only in mixed woodland, but also in parks. Swifts and kestrels are known to favor the high buildings in cities, which mimic high cliff faces. Bears, raccoons and foxes are overjoyed with the excess food found in garbage cans. Blackbirds thrive in gardens and parks because it is easier to find their prey on short, mown lawns than it is among tall meadow plants.

A garden pond is a biotope

A biotope is a location at which a specific community of plants and animals has formed that are especially suitable for the location and are in equilibrium with one another. A garden pond may be a biotope — but only if all the various cycles govern themselves and it does not need to be maintained. It doesn't qualify as a biotope if you need to cut back plants, let out water or fish out algae so that the ecological balance is not upset.

Only people and animals can suffer from a fever

By the use of infrared thermometers, American researchers have found that plants may also get a fever, either when they suffer from lack of water or when the roots are damaged and are no longer able to take up sufficient water. The disturbed water supply may cause overheating by as much as 9°F (5°C), which can be measured from the leaves.

MAMMALS AND DINOSAURS

Mammals give birth to living young

In Australia, the duck-billed platypus and the echidna first lay eggs and then suckle the young after they have hatched. The echidna is also a marsupial. It incubates the egg in a small pouch on its abdomen. How it gets there is still unknown. Like the marsupials, the egg-laying mammals (the monotremes) are a sort of "halfway stage" in the development of true mammals.

Only mammals give birth to living young

Many sharks, some other fish and various reptiles (slow worms and salamanders) give birth to living young. In contrast to mammals, however, the babies do not grow naked inside a womb nor are their needs supplied by a placenta. Instead they develop inside an egg and are fed from its supply of nutrients. But they do hatch inside the womb and are born alive. In the sand shark a long time may elapse between hatching and birth, during which the small sharks in the two wombs feed on one another, until sometimes only one is left.

Tyrannosaurus rex was the most dangerous dinosaur

Admittedly, it appears dreadful, and it is certain that it did eat meat. But researchers are by no means sure whether it did hunt and kill or whether it was more likely to have fed from carrion. Its jaws, with their 60 teeth, argue for the hunter theory, but its small stubby arms and not particularly agile body suggest that it tended to use its size to hunt smaller animals as prey. The most likely explanation is that it did both.

Tyrannosaurus rex was the largest carnivore

Even though some of these mighty dinosaurs were as tall as 33 feet (10 meters), in 1996 it was discovered that the *Tyrannosaurus* was not the largest carnivore of all times. *Gigantosaurus* was definitely bigger. It grew up to 49 feet (15 meters) tall and was slimmer, more agile and had better-developed forelimbs. The two never met. *Gigantosaurus* died out about 30 million years before the appearance of *Tyrannosaurus rex.*

The dinosaurs have died out

On the contrary: new finds indicate that all birds are descendants of the saurians. Their oldest ancestors belonged to the Theropod suborder, to which *Tyrannosaurus rex* and most other large carnivores belonged. In 2005, American research on the bone structure of a female *Tyrannosaurus* strengthened this classification. But not all reptiles that lived in the "Dinosaur Period" (235–65 million years ago) belonged to the major order of dinosauria. Even today, for example, the classification of crocodiles has not been completely clarified.

BULLS AND HORSES

Red provokes bulls

No cattle can recognize the color red. It is not the color of the bullfighter's cape (which is often red, pink or purple and always lined in gold) that annoys fighting bulls. They are bred to attack anything that moves.

Herds of horses are led by stallions

The leader of a herd of horses is always a mare. The stallion serves to produce offspring and to protect the members of the herd against attackers. The organization of the herd is the mare's job.

A thoroughbred is a horse with a pure line of breeding

Throughbreds are a breed of horse, all of which are descended from three Arabian sires bred with Royal mares in England between 1748 and 1758. Ideal for racing, these horses are sensitive and tall with good stamina and a long stride.

Horses sleep standing up

Horses can sleep standing up, but when they feel secure and they have enough room, then they happily lie down. Horse experts swear that in a herd or in a stable, not all the horses lie down at the same time. One always remains standing and keeps watch.

FOXES AND WOLVES

Foxes steal geese

No fox, unless it was very inexperienced or hungry, would choose to take a goose as prey. They are too large and too heavy for the rather dainty predator. Foxes are, on average, about 16 inches (40 centimeters) tall and weigh about 15 pounds (7 kilograms). Geese are usually not quite so heavy, but they are about 12 inches (30 centimeters) taller than a fox. In addition, they have powerful wings with which they can easily — and very effectively — give a fox a swipe. However, the fox would steal a goose's clutch of eggs if it had the chance.

Wolves howl at the Moon

By their nature, wolves stretch their necks up toward the sky in a striking manner when they howl. But this has nothing whatsoever to do with the Moon. The howling of wolves serves to demarcate their boundaries to intruders and also bring a pack back together after a hunt.

Wolves kill human beings

Wolves are extremely shy of people. There have been very few fatal predatory attacks over the last 50 years and none in North America. However, a number of people have been killed by captive wolves and wolf-dog hybrids. Research has shown that since the 16th century, most fatal wolf attacks on people have been by rabid wolves.

DEER

A stag is as old as the number of points on its antlers

For most stags this rule of thumb works only when they are young. At one year old, the stag gets its first set of antlers, which consists of two small "prickets." The next year, the animals have forked antlers, which in the majority of cases have two points, although many also have three. The set of antlers does actually get larger every year, but how fast it grows and how many new points it acquires depends on the animal's health and genetic makeup. Dominant stags, who have overcome all rivals in the area, are often so exhausted after one season that they are no longer able to maintain their status the following year, and their antlers become smaller once more.

Wolves hunt in packs

The depiction of a wolf pack as always hunting together and falling on its defenseless prey does not correspond with the facts. Only in winter, if there are too few small prey, do wolves get together in a group to attack larger prey. In addition, the proverbial voracity of wolves occurs only in exceptional circumstances. On average, a wolf eats less than 4.5  pounds (2 kilograms) a day. But one wolf can devour as much as 22 pounds (10 kilograms) at once if it has been without food for a long time.

The deer and the antelope play in the American West

Brewster Higley wasn't quite accurate in his song *Home on the Range*, which he wrote in the 1870s. It became the Kansas state song in 1947, but it has a couple of big errors. Those big hairy beasts roaming are bison, not buffalo, and there are no antelopes in North America. To give Higley credit, people in his day called the pronghorns antelope, but they don't belong to the same zoological family as the true antelope.

ELEPHANTS

Elephants have a tough, thick skin

Elephant skin is about 1 inch (2.5 centimeters) thick. It is actually extremely sensitive, and bleeds even when the gray giants are bitten by insects or horseflies. This is why they rub themselves with mud.

Elephants are scared of mice

Elephants aren't really frightened of mice. That rumor probably has its origins in a morally instructive tale that aimed to show how the largest animal could be frightened of the smallest.

Elephants drink through their trunks

They pick up water in their trunks and pour it into their mouths but they don't actually drink with their trunks. That would be like trying to suck in water through your nose.

There are elephant graveyards

Occasionally, large numbers of elephant bones are found in a single spot. This gave rise to the tale that elephants always go to particular places, known as elephant graveyards, to die. In fact, such behavior has never been observed. The elephant graveyards probably form when elephants get trapped in a swamp. Either whole herds have sunk in at once, or a marshy area with its soft plants has repeatedly attracted older elephants whose teeth were no longer in good shape.

Ivory is white

Ivory comes from the tusks of elephants and other animals such as hippopotami, whales and walrus. It is naturally discolored and must be bleached to achieve that creamy off-white color.

CAMELS, GIRAFFES AND HIPPOS

Camels store water in their humps

Camels have cells in their humps in which they store fat that may be easily broken down. That enables them to go for as long as 30 days without food. But they can also store about 26 gallons (98 liters) of water in their stomachs. That will last for just about two weeks. But the breakdown of the fat from the hump also releases water. A camel's strategy for survival also includes the fact that it begins to sweat only when the temperature reaches 106°F (41°C). A camel can lose as much as a quarter of its weight before it becomes dehydrated.

Long-necked animals have more vertebrae than short-necked ones

A giraffe has no more vertebrae in its neck than a mouse. There are seven. This applies to almost all mammals. The three-toed sloth, which has nine vertebrae, is not particularly notable for its long neck. However, it can turn its head right around toward the back. Yet sea cows, with just six vertebrae, have extremely short necks. In birds and reptiles, however, the relationship between a long neck and numerous vertebrae does hold true.

Hippopotamuses live in the Nile

They once did. But they were exterminated about 200 years ago. They are closely related to pigs, which is why they were called "river pigs" by the ancient Egyptians. Hippopotamuses generally do not swim, but they are able to walk for up to five minutes on the riverbed. When they surface, they can capsize small boats.

BIG CATS AND LITTLE CATS

Only male lions have manes

Old female lions that are no longer fertile sometimes grow a mane. But then not every male has a proper mane. Without one, they don't do too well with the lionesses, who seem to prefer lions with bushy, dark manes. The females do most of the hunting and are in charge of the prides, but the males are allowed to eat first.

Lions are only found in Africa

During the Ice Age lions still lived in the whole of southern Europe, the Near East and India, as well as in Africa. Today there are still about 300 Asiatic lions in the Gir National Park in Gujarat, India. The Asiatic lion (*Panthera leo persica*) is smaller and has a less distinctive mane than its cousin the African lion (*Panthera leo*).

The small cats are small

Small cats may be quite large. The largest is the puma, with a length of about 6.5 feet (2 meters) and weighing up to 330 pounds (150 kilograms). It therefore surpasses all the great cats, with the exception of the lion and the tiger. The smallest of the great cats, the Asian marbled cat, is not much more than 20 inches (50 centimeters) long. This traditional division of the cats is highly controversial. It is possible that in a few years a completely different classification will be used.

All cats purr

Lions, tigers, leopards and jaguars don't purr. They probably can't, although it hasn't been proved conclusively. But these four cats are the only ones that can roar.

Lions are the kings of the desert

Lions do not live in the desert, but in the savanna and semiarid plains. As far as courage goes, the "king of beasts" is not really so brave. Lazy and pragmatic, lions hunt only when they are hungry and don't attack prey unless it is definitely weaker and they're sure they can win.

Panthers are a species

Panthers are not a particular species. They can be either leopards, pumas or jaguars with black coats. Despite the dark coloring of a black leopard, it is still possible to make out its typical pattern of leopard spots under certain lighting conditions. The color is passed on via a recessive gene, so that black and spotted leopards may occur in a single litter. To date, black leopards have been found only at high altitudes and in the rain forest.

Wildcats are shy of water

Most wildcats take prolonged baths, and even hunt fish and other water creatures if they have the opportunity. Tigers, in particular, are good swimmers. Even with enormous pieces of meat from their prey held between their teeth, they cross rivers 330 feet (100 meters) wide. In contrast, most domestic cats are shy of water — but they are derived from the African wildcat, which lives in very dry savanna regions.

Siberian tigers live in Siberia

The Siberian tiger (*Panthera tigris altaica*) has died out in Siberia. Representatives of this genus now live only in the Amur region in southeastern Russia and in some areas of northeastern China. There also may be a few left in North and South Korea. An endangered species, this tiger is also known as the Amur, Korean, Manchurian, Ussuri, Korean or North China tiger. The male Siberian tiger can weigh as much as 770 pounds (350 kilograms), making it the largest feline in the world.

Cats like milk

Most pussycats are not particularly keen on it. It is also not good for them to drink milk, because they lack an enzyme that would enable them to digest it properly. That takes its toll in diarrhea. But most love cream and it doesn't have the same negative affect as milk.

MONKEYS AND GORILLAS

Monkeys can hang by their tails

Only a few monkeys are able to dangle from their tails. The spider monkeys are among the few who are able to use their tail as a kind of third arm or hand. But capuchin and howler monkeys in the South American jungle also have this ability. Other monkeys usually use their tails to help them balance.

Monkeys delouse themselves

When monkeys groom one another's coats, they are not trying to find lice in particular. The affectionate grooming serves as a form of contact bonding. It is carried out to gain affection, to establish alliances and to release tensions. Researchers have found direct links between the social structure of the group and the matter of who grooms whom and for how long. Generally, scabs and other dirt will be removed — and occasionally even a louse.

Gorillas are dangerous

Contrary to the popular image of gorillas as aggressive and violent, in their natural habitat they are gentle and shy. They can become quite nurturing toward human beings, giving them hugs and treating them as if they were baby gorillas. Gorillas are not known to attack humans.

BEARS

Polar bears eat penguins

They probably would, if they were set before them. But as polar bears live only in the northern polar regions and penguins live exclusively in the Southern Hemisphere, they never cross paths.

Polar bears like seal meat and fish

Once it has killed a seal, a polar bear eats the blubber (fat) and the skin. It might move on to the entrails and then maybe the flesh if it's really hungry, but often the meat is left untouched. They don't usually catch and eat fish in the wild, although they will in captivity.

Polar bears are the largest bears

The largest bear, and also the largest land carnivore, is the Kodiak bear, which lives in Alaska. It may reach 10 feet (3 meters) in length and weigh 1,900 pounds (850 kilograms). In addition, Kodiaks are surprisingly thin for bears and extremely fast. Polar bears, in contrast, weigh about 1,450 pounds (650 kilograms) and are also about 10 feet (3 meters) in length. Almost the same size is the Siberian Kamchatka bear. The well-known American grizzly is rather a lightweight, at around 770 pounds (350 kilograms), and is the only bear that cannot climb.

Bears hibernate

Bears sleep for a long time in the winter, but technically they do not "hibernate" in the same way as snakes, frogs, bats and ground squirrels. True hibernation involves a state of hypothermia where the animal's metabolism is lowered, involving low body temperature and very slow breathing and heart rate. A bear sleeping in the winter maintains a steady temperature and its metabolism doesn't slow down to the same extent as the true hibernators.

MARSUPIALS

Koalas are peaceful and lethargic

Only by day. Anyone who has had one of these on their arm has probably gained the impression that the cute little fellow hanging on so peacefully might be stoned. That is actually correct. The continuous consumption of eucalyptus leaves makes the nice little bears high during the day. At night, however, they become active for about four hours. Then they are fast, agile and — with their sharp claws — anything but harmless.

Marsupials are found only in Australia

There are more than 300 species of marsupials, and about two-thirds of them are confined to the relatively isolated Australia and a few neighboring islands, such as New Guinea. The rest are found in North and South America.

All marsupials have a pouch

In some of the marsupial rats, the females teats are enclosed by a simple fold in the skin. Until the young are able to cling onto their mother's fur, they swing freely from the teats.

Opossums hang by their tails

Although the opossum is the only animal in North America with a prehensile tale capable of grasping, it does not use it to hang off tree branches. Neither do baby opossums hang off their mother's tail by their tails, as is often depicted in popular culture. Opossums use their tails for balance and sometimes to grab a tree branch, but they do not hang from them. Baby opossums travel by clinging to their mother's back.

Opossums play dead when threatened

Despite the expression "playing possum," opossums do not pretend to be dead in order to escape predators. They either fight or run away, much as we would. Occasionally they have kind of paralyzing fit and lie insensible for a few moments, probably as the result of shock. This may be where the expression comes from.

Koalas are bears

They belong to the marsupials. That means that they are more closely related to a kangaroo than they are to a brown bear. Alongside the kangaroo, the wombat is also an extremely close cousin of the koala. The head, with its plush-like ears, is extremely similar in both, but the wombat appears rather like a hairy piglet. Also related to the koala and the wombat are various marsupials, such as the marsupial wolves (Tasmanian devils), dormice, opossums, rat kangaroos, echidnas, flying squirrels and many others.

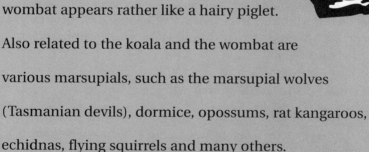

RACCOONS AND RABBITS

Hares and rabbits are related

Rabbits and hares do indeed belong to the zoological family of hares, but are so distantly related that they cannot interbreed. Most of the so-called "hares" are actually rabbits. Superficially, they are very difficult to tell apart. It is simplest when they are young. Rabbits are born naked and blind, usually in underground burrows, while hares arrive in the world fully developed, in nests above ground.

Rabbits that freeze in front of a snake are stupid

They are doing the right thing. Snakes have poor eyesight and need to see their prey move to be aware of it. Snakes cannot detect a completely paralyzed rabbit, but at the slightest movement the snake has its bearings and strikes.

Raccoons wash their food

Raccoons live on, among other things, small crabs, worms, snails and larvae, which they fish out of shallow water. Anything they have captured is first felt all over, then sniffed and finally eaten. This behavior is so pronounced that captive raccoons throw their food into water and after "catching" it again, examine it as they would in the wild. In principle, however, raccoons eat everything, which is why they feel decidedly at home wherever there is garbage to be found.

MARTENS, MOLES AND MICE

Martens like rubber

Martens eat many different things, but they will not willingly touch rubber. Nevertheless, when they bite the radiator hose in a car, there is a completely different reason. They can smell the mark of another marten, are irritated by it, and react where it is easiest for them, by chewing on the rubber hose. So one marten in a car is no problem, but the trouble arises when the vehicle is parked in the territory of another marten. The best protection, incidentally, after a hose has been bitten, is to slit the damaged hose and slip it over the new one. Martens' teeth cannot get through the doubled hose.

Moles are blind

Moles do possess an extremely weak sense of sight. However, this should not be described as a handicap, because in their dark tunnels the amount of sight available is more than sufficient. With their tiny button eyes they can differentiate between light and dark. So moles know when they come to the surface. Beneath the surface they rely upon their very sensitive snouts and their sense of smell.

Mice are the smallest mammals

The smallest mammal in the world is the Etruscan pygmy shrew. It is between 0.4 to 2.4 inches (1 to 6 centimeters) in length, so small that it can even live in the burrows of earthworms. Its tail adds another 0.8 to 1.2 inches (2 to 3 centimeters) to its length. Despite their mouse-like appearance, shrews are not mice, nor are they even rodents. Together with hedgehogs and moles, they belong to the insectivores.

ANIMALS WHO GO TO EXTREMES

Sloths are the laziest animals

Sloths are really extremely lazy. They try to survive by using the minimum amount of energy. They hardly move at all, their metabolism works in slow motion and their body temperature is 91°F (33°C) at the most. Yet koalas sleep even more than sloths, about 20 hours a day, and male lions also take a similar amount of "quiet time." However, both these animals are extremely active when awake. Some insects and reptiles have even slower metabolisms than sloths, so it hard to say which animal is the laziest.

Herds of lemmings throw themselves into the sea

The rumor about the collective suicide of lemmings is extremely stubborn but, in fact, no one has ever observed this tragedy. In the Disney documentary *White Wilderness* (1958), the event was produced artificially. Lemmings do reproduce explosively, and then major migrations take place. So, naturally, once in a while a herd may fall over a cliff. But that is not the end of the story: Lemmings can swim, although rough seas or great distances can be their undoing.

Bats can get caught in your hair

Bats navigate by means of a first-class echolocation system. They can recognize obstacles of less than 0.038 inches (1 millimeter) in size, and avoid them. These dark, flying mammals move at high speed and shoot past all obstacles, sometimes with only a hair's breadth of clearance — hence the fear that they may become entangled in a person's hair. Anyone who has had the experience of a bat that has lost its way inside a room knows how eerie these harmless creatures can seem.

Squirrels remember where they buried their nuts

Unfortunately, squirrels are afflicted with acute memory loss. They have about 20 minutes after they bury their nuts to remember where they put them, but then the hiding place is forgotten forever. However, they make up for their poor memories with their excellent smelling abilities, and they can sniff out either their own nuts or the nuts buried by another squirrel. Thus burying nuts can be seen as a kind of community effort on the part of squirrels.

There are no vampires

Vampire bats are alive and well in Mexico and many places throughout South America. Like Count Dracula, they bite their victims at night and drink their blood. But their bite is so gentle that the animal that is bitten usually doesn't wake up.

BIRDS AND AUDUBON

There is no such thing as the "third eye"

Many reptiles and birds have a form of third eye on their foreheads. It is a point where the bone of the skull is so thin that light can penetrate. It appears that animals with this eye have a form of calendar and can recognize the different seasons. When ducks had this spot covered with a hood, they no longer recognized when they should start breeding, nor when it was time to lay down winter fat reserves. Their sense of time was completely disrupted.

Birds cock their heads on one side to listen for worms

Because some birds' eyes are on either side of their heads, they tip their heads to one side to watch for the worm emerging from the ground. They're not listening — they're looking.

Feeding birds during the winter rescues them from starvation

The opposite may be the case. Their food supply is not necessarily lacking in winter, when it is cold, but in spring, during the breeding season. Then birds need insects and larvae to raise their young. If they're eating seeds from feeders they won't be as likely to search for insects, which are hard to find in tidy urban gardens.

Birds do not notice when a cuckoo's egg is foisted upon them

They would notice, if the parent cuckoo had not previously thrown one of the other eggs out of the nest before laying its own. Most birds know precisely how many eggs they have in their nests. If one is taken away, they lay another. Naturally they are not able to count, but thanks to their sensitive breast feathers they notice when their clutch suddenly feels different.

Audubon was a wildlife preservationist

John James Audubon (1785–1851) was a naturalist who made very detailed paintings of birds. However, to accomplish these paintings, he shot many birds, apparently without compunction. He needed freshly dead birds to get the color right. He often shot as many as 100 birds a day. He didn't care if the bird was rare or about to become extinct: for Audubon, painting the picture was the most important thing.

PIGEONS, PENGUINS AND PELICANS

Homing pigeons don't need to be trained to find their way home

Although homing pigeons, bred from rock pigeons, are bred to have a super-high homing instinct, they do have to be trained to return to their point of origin. It's a time-consuming process that takes patience and care. The trainer starts with a short distance of about 50 feet (15 meters) and gradually increases the distance until the pigeon can return home from a distance of many miles away. The longest flight ever recorded was over 1,600 miles (2,575 kilometers).

Homing pigeons never get lost

It is possible to confuse the orientation of a homing pigeon by transporting it in a cage that is shielded against magnetic fields. This suggests that pigeons, just like certain migratory birds, orient themselves by means of the Earth's magnetic field. They appear to be able to feel where a particular place is with reference to this magnetic field — as if they had an internal map.

Penguins are birds

That is what they look like, even though their stubby wings seem far too small. Although they are formally classified as birds (*Aves*), biologists are unable to determine a close relationship with any other form of bird. Many scientists now think that penguins may be descended directly from dinosaurs. Others assume that the ancestors of the penguins split away from other birds during the Cretaceous Period — that is, at the time when dinosaurs still existed. They see a certain relationship with the divers and albatrosses.

All penguins live at the South Pole

Of the 18 types of penguin, only two — the Emperor and Adélie penguins — live in the Antarctic. The others live in southwest Africa, New Zealand, Australia and on the west coast of South America as far north as Peru. The Galapagos penguins live nearly on the Equator. It is true that all the species inhabit coasts that are bathed by cold, and thus plankton- and fish-rich, ocean currents. The penguins' true habitat is not the land, but the water.

Pelicans feed their young with their own blood

The pelican, which allegedly feeds its young in hard times with blood from a gash in its own breast, has been a favorite Christian motif since the Middle Ages. The old legend about the pelican, the oldest version of which dates from the third century AD, runs somewhat differently. In it, the pelican killed its young because they had previously pecked it in the face. Then, out of remorse, the pelican tore its flank open, and brought its young back to life by feeding them its own flesh. What is true in all this is that some pelicans have red patches on their breasts, that they often feed their young with regurgitated, predigested fish that is reddish in color and that the greedy babies often peck their parents' faces with their considerably sharp beaks.

Pink flamingos are pink

Flamingos are gray when they're young, and their colors vary when they are adults depending on what food they eat. The way their digestive systems work is through a sieve-like filter in their bills: they drink in water and separate the good stuff from the bad. The tiny algae and creatures they end up eating turn pink during the digestive process and this color seeps into their plumage. If they are given a different kind of food to eat, they turn white.

CONDORS AND EAGLES

The largest bird of prey is the condor

For a long time anyone could show off their knowledge that the largest of the birds of prey was not an eagle but the South American condor (*Vultur gryhphus*), which weighs up to 30 pounds (14 kilograms) and has an 11-foot (3.4-meter) wingspan. However, biologists have subsequently determined that the so-called "New World vultures," which include the condor, are actually related to the storks. They do not belong with birds of prey in the family Falconiformes, which includes hawks, kites and eagles. Though there is continuing debate on the matter, condors now sit along with the other New World vultures in the order Cathartidae, which includes herons, ibises, storks, American vultures, black vultures and turkey vultures. However the ongoing debate is settled, the condor is by far the largest airworthy bird.

Bald eagles are named for their bald heads

These birds don't have bald heads. Their heads are covered with white feathers, which makes them look bald in contrast to the darker feathers on their bodies. In Old English, *balde* means white.

ORDINARY BIRDS

The Baltimore oriole is named after the city of Baltimore

The bird was widely known as the Baltimore oriole by 1669, but the city of Baltimore was not established until 1729. The black and orange bird was named after the Baltimore family, which was headed by George Calvert, who called himself "Lord Baltimore." He founded the colony of Maryland in 1632 and took black and orange as his family's colors.

White hens lay white eggs, and brown hens lay brown eggs

It is true that the color of an egg is dependent on the type of hen, but not the hen's color. Brown eggs are not healthier, nor are they an indication that they come from free-range hens, as is sometimes suggested. But ultimately there is no reliable method of telling the color of an egg from a hen's feathers. All one can really do is wait until the egg has been laid.

Ravens are uncaring parents

So long as the young are in the nest, ravens are extremely careful parents. When the young ravens have become fully fledged, however, they are unceremoniously pushed out of the nest. Many other animal parents are very rough when introducing their young to the element in which they will spend their future lives. Anyone who has seen how female otters drag their squealing young into the water and then dive with them will not find ravens so dreadful after all.

EXOTIC BIRDS

When danger threatens, ostriches bury their heads in the sand

The poor beast would suffocate, which is certainly not a better alternative. The reason ostriches often lay their heads on (not in) the ground is because they can detect vibrations. Ostriches are very fast runners: they can outrun many of their enemies and reach speeds up to 50 miles (80 kilometers) an hour. But if they need to protect their clutch of eggs, then ostriches pretend to be dead. They lie flat on top of their nests and even draw in their necks. From far away, they look like a mound of earth.

Swans sing a beautiful song before they die

There is no such thing as the famous, wonderful swan song with the approach of death. This derives from the Greek myth of Cygnus, who was mourning a friend who had died. Cygnus was turned into a swan by the gods, and shortly before his own death, began to sing a marvelous song. It was thought that the mute swan (*Cygnus olor*) made no sound throughout its entire life, but just before death broke out in a hauntingly beautiful song. However, this swan is not really mute, but makes various noises, such as croaks, hisses and raspy sounds. But none of these constitute a "song." The legend gave rise to the term "swan song" — meaning a final performance or the last great effort of an artist.

BUGS THAT FLY

Butterflies can't fly if they have the slightest damage to their wings

After minor wing damage butterflies can often still fly. Capturing them in cupped hands doesn't damage the creatures at all. Naturally, despite this, they should never be handled roughly.

Mayflies live just a single day

Depending on their type, mayflies (also known as dayflies, shadflies or fishflies) may spend the first one to four years as larvae in water. After hatching, they slough their skin again within a few hours (or sometimes even minutes) and fly off in search of mates. This search can last from a few hours to a few days. Mayflies cannot eat during this time, because both their mouthparts and intestines are atrophied. Their only task is to produce fertile eggs.

No one knows how bumblebees can fly

"According to the laws of aerodynamics, bumblebees cannot fly. It is just as well bumblebees don't know this." Thus runs an oft-repeated piece of wisdom. Until the 1990s, researchers were still fumbling in the dark for the reason why bumblebees and some other insects have the ability to fly, since their bodies are heavy and their wing beat is small. In 1996, scientists at the University of Cambridge in the United Kingdom finally made a breakthrough. The creatures do not move their wings up and down in a simple fashion, but instead follow a complicated pattern, creating vortices that provide the necessary lift for flight. In 2005, Michael Dickinson of Caltech in Pasadena, California, made a further breakthrough. His research revealed that bees wings' rotate and flip every time they flap, at a rate of 230 times a second. This extra action adds to the complexity of the vortices.

Bees and flies have some kind of internal buzzers that make them buzz

The familiar buzzing of bees and flies is caused by the rapid beating of their wings. Moths, butterflies and hummingbirds don't buzz because they beat their wings more slowly.

Ladybugs are female

The little spotted insects can be either male or female. They were named by farmers who noticed that the bugs appeared at about the same time as the Roman Catholic celebration of the Anunciation on March 25, when Catholics and some other Christians honor the Virgin Mary (the "Lady").

The age of ladybugs can be told from the number of spots

The number of spots on ladybugs has nothing whatsoever to do with their age, but with their particular species. Among others, there are ladybugs with 13, 14, 15 and 22 spots. Not all ladybugs are red with black spots; some are yellow with black spots.

BUGS THAT HURT

Mosquitoes bite

Not really. Mosquitoes have a nasty, sharp proboscis that they plunge into their victim's skin, using it to suck blood. Mosquito "bites" get itchy because their saliva, which acts as a coagulant on blood, is an irritant to the human body.

Mosquitoes can smell people with sweet blood

Mosquitoes are unable to scent blood. But they do have an astounding sensitivity to heat. They can detect differences of $0.09°F$ $(0.05°C)$. So it is no problem for them to find a tasty, warm-blooded creature on a summer evening. In addition, they are also attracted by water vapor and carbon dioxide in exhaled breath, and by certain scents — and that includes sweat as well as some ingredients in perfumes.

Ticks drop from trees

Ticks usually mate on a host animal and then the female falls to the ground to lay her eggs. The larvae often crawl to the tips of leaves of grass to wait until a new host animal passes by, and then they jump aboard. But this doesn't mean that the host animal is bitten by ticks only on the legs. The small creatures search their host's body for a particularly suitable location. They are particularly fond of hiding in hair before they bite.

Hornet stings can swiftly prove fatal

Three kill a man, seven a horse, according to the old folklore. Hornets appear menacing because they are so large. In general, however, their sting is no more dangerous than those of bees or wasps. That so few people have experienced this is because hornets are not aggressive and rarely sting. A hornet's sting can be life-threatening only if a person has an allergic reaction to the hornet's poison.

CREEPY CRAWLERS

Earwigs crawl into ears

And wherever the creatures are also known as "ear-piercers" (such as in France and Germany), it is believed that they will pinch people inside their ears, or even, in a horror-film variant, perforate the eardrum and lay their eggs inside the brain. Yet earwigs are harmless, useful bugs that feed on plant waste or small insects. Their name may derive from their ear-shaped hind wings, but it certainly doesn't come from their fondness for human ears.

Millipedes have 1,000 feet

Not quite. But they have about 200 pairs of legs, which obviously means about 400 feet. The record is about 350 pairs. They are born, however, with only a few pairs of legs — usually three. The other pairs grow when they shed their skin. The millipede family also includes the centipedes, which are small creatures with just nine pairs of legs.

Millipedes are insects

Not everything that is small and crawls around is an insect. It is reasonably well-known that spiders with their eight legs are not insects. They belong to their own class: Arachnida. It is less commonly known that ticks, mites and scorpions are also arachnids. Millipedes (order Diplopoda) and centipedes (order Chilopoda) are arthropod animals in their own subphylum, Myriapoda ("ten thousand feet"). As arthropods, they are distant relatives of lobsters, crayfish and shrimp.

Ants are always busy

Ants have the reputation as the hardest working insect. They never seem to stop. But in fact ants work only for about one-fifth of their daily lives. They have no reason to be incessantly busy. First, their food (which consists of insect larvae, honey, fruit and carrion) is very nutritious, so they do not have to arrange for large quantities to be collected. Second, within an ants' nest there is a division of labor. Some act as guards, others search for food and yet others feed the offspring and the queen. Because hundreds of thousands — or even millions — of ants live in a nest, even when just 20 percent are at work it can still amount to a busy, teeming mass.

SNAKES AND WORMS

Rattlesnakes rattle a warning before they strike

Snakes tend to shake their tails when they're frightened. When the rattlesnake's tail vibrates, its rattles start making their familiar rattling sound. Sometimes this acts as an audible warning to a potential victim. But often the snake doesn't nervously shake its tail and instead attacks without warning.

Snake charmers use music to entrance cobras

Since cobras are deaf, this would be difficult. The cobra responds to the movements of the snake charmer and his flute, and the tourists are ensnared by the music and the "dancing" snake.

Milk snakes suck milk directly from cows' udders

The *Lampropeltis triangulum*, commonly known as the milk snake, likes to hang out in barns where rats and mice are plentiful. They are not capable of "milking" cows.

If you cut an earthworm in half, both pieces continue to live

The regeneration of an earthworm is controlled by a clump of nerves that lies in its head. That means that only the front portion can form a new tail. Experts say that at least 40 segments are needed for the rest to grow again. By contrast, if the rear, headless portion is cut off, it dies. Only a worm with a different kind of nervous system, such as a flatworm, can grow a new worm from each half of its body.

Woodworm are worms

Woodworm is the name given to the larvae of several types of word-boring beetle, including the common furniture beetle and the deathwatch beetle. If you look carefully at one, you can see the tiny legs.

REPTILES AND TOADS

Crocodiles weep after feeding

There is a old story that after eating their prey, crocodiles weep "crocodile tears" of hypocritical remorse. In fact, crocodiles do have tear glands and are capable of shedding tears, but they cry at different times and not particularly after feeding.

Alligators live in the Americas, and crocodiles in other continents

Alligators and caimans are a family in the order of crocodiles. True crocodiles have several physical differences from alligators and prefer salt water, while alligators prefer fresh. Alligators live in North America and China, and caimans are found in South and Central America. But true crocodiles such as the Cuban, Orinoco, American and Morelet's crocodiles are found in the Americas, and other types of crocodiles live in Africa, Asia and Australia.

Blindworms are blind

Blindworms — perhaps better known as slowworms — can see very well. They are not snakes, as is often claimed, but legless lizards. A slowworm can shed its tail as a trick to fool predators. The tail quickly grows back again, although not to its original length.

Chameleons adapt their color to their surroundings

Chameleons do change their color, but their environment has nothing to do with it. The reasons for changing color are fear, heat or cold. Light conditions also have an influence on which color the creatures adopt. Generally the range of colors that a chameleon's skin can assume runs from green to brown, which, of course, is not bad camouflage. When chameleons are intimidated, they also appear grayer and less conspicuous than aggressive ones that want to stand out. At night, the creatures are generally quite light, and thus by no means camouflaged.

Anyone who touches a toad gets warts

Many toads produce a secretion when they feel threatened. This can cause a slight skin irritation on human skin. But a person won't get warts from it — even when the toad itself is covered in warts. Warts in humans are caused by viruses, which are transmitted from person to person.

SEA CREATURES

You can hear the sound of the sea in large seashells

That haunting sound you can hear in the spiral conch shell and some other large seashells is not a ghostly echo from the ocean. Neither is it the sound of your own blood echoing off the smooth walls of the shell. The most likely explanation is that the shell amplifies the ambient noise that is all around us every day. We block most of it out, but because of its unique spiral formation, the shell picks it up.

Only oysters produce mother-of-pearl, and it is always white

Pearl mussels and abalone also produce the beautiful iridescent material, also known as nacre. There are different shades of blue, green and gray mother-of-pearl, as well as white.

Whales blow jets of water into the air

After a dive, whales exhale the exhausted air though the blowhole on the top of their heads. During the dive, the air has become thoroughly warmed inside the whales' bodies and it condenses as soon as it comes in contact with the cooler air.

Whalebone is from the bones of a whale

Whalebone (also called baleen) is a hard substance that forms part of a whale's upper jaw. It is made up of parallel plates used for filter feeding. Its most common use was in women's corsets, used as a stiffener.

Greenpeace was the first to mobilize against whale hunting

An ecological movement whose goals were to protect nature and discourage blind faith in technology already existed at the turn of the 19th and 20th centuries. Even then the fate of whales was a matter of concern, because whaling was carried out on a massive scale with factory ships. The German philosopher Ludwig Klages (1872–1956) denounced the fact that 5,000 of the great sea mammals had been slaughtered within two years and predicted that the day was near when whales would only be found in museums.

FISH

Fish always breathe through their gills

Yes, with the exception of the subclass of the lungfish. These very old creatures, from an evolutionary point of view, are very rare and live off the coasts of South America, Africa and Australia. They must repeatedly come to the surface of the water to obtain air, otherwise they drown. Some species have additional gills, but these primarily serve to eliminate carbon dioxide.

Fish don't drown

There are many reasons why fish sometimes drown. They need oxygen to live, and if they swim into oxygen-depleted waters, they will drown. Pollution from factory waste often results in a lack of oxygen in water. Oil pollution can also cause fish to drown, as well as microscopic particles that get caught in the gills and make it impossible for the fish to breathe.

Flying fish can fly

Flying fish (*Exocoetidae*) don't actually fly: they glide. They propel themselves out of the water using their fins, which are larger than usual and resemble wings. They usually glide between 100–150 feet (30–50 meters), but sometimes they can travel much farther by using the updraft from the waves below.

The sardine is a species of fish

What we buy as sardines are actually several different kinds of small fish: herring or pilchard being the most common. The oil and spices in which the fish are packed are what give them their trademark flavor, not the fish itself.

The red herring is a type of fish

There is no fish called "red herring." Herring turns red after it is smoked and salted. It was traditionally used to throw off the scent for hunting dogs, leading them on a false trail.

Piranhas are extremely dangerous

Many types of piranha are purely vegetarian. Only three or four are dangerous to humans, most notably the red piranha. These species tend to attack bleeding and wriggling bodies. Most Amazon dwellers do not fear piranhas in running waters, but they avoid swimming in streams hit by drought. A hungry shoal of piranha that have been trapped in such a situation can be really aggressive and confirm all the horror stories of bodies being reduced to skeletons in seconds. Conversely, however, piranhas are regarded as a delicacy by humans.

Sharks often eat people

Every year about 100 shark attacks on people are recorded worldwide. About 10 percent prove to be fatal. The victims are certainly not torn to bits, but bleed to death because no help is close at hand. Usually sharks retreat after their first attack and wait to finish their kill when their victim is weakened by loss of blood. There are relatively poor chances of escaping after an attack by a common ground shark (also known as the cub, or bull shark), which, together with the white shark and the tiger shark, occur most often in attack statistics.

DOGS

A dog with a warm nose is sick

This is a common fallacy. People believe that a dog's nose should be cold and wet. But after resting, sleeping or just lying around the house doing nothing, a dog's nose is often dry and warm, and the dog is still perfectly healthy.

A barking dog is dangerous

It may be, but that's not why it's barking. Dogs in the wild never bark, and neither do wolves, their canine cousins. Barking evolved in dogs in captivity as a means of warning the "members of its pack," whether human or canine, that there is danger nearby. A growling dog is more likely to attack than a barking one.

French poodles were originally bred in France

The popular dog was bred in Germany as a hunting dog, specially trained to jump in the water to fetch ducks. Because of their noisy splashing in the water, the Germans called them "*puddel*" dogs, meaning "splash." This developed into the English "poodle." The French particularly appreciated these clever dogs, and soon they became known as French poodles. However their official name does not include "French" — they're either miniature, standard or toy poodles.

Greyhounds were named for their color

First, the elegant dogs are usually a shade of steel-blue rather than gray. Second, the word comes from an Old English word for a dog, "*grig*." They were known as grighounds, and this eventually evolved into greyhounds.

Bloodhounds were named for their sensitivity to the scent of human blood

The dogs were the first to have breeding records kept (bloodlines), and this is how they got their name.

Great Danes come from Denmark

These huge dogs are also known as German mastiffs, and they were bred in Germany. In 1876 the Great Dane became Germany's official dog. They were bred as a hunting dog from mastiffs, boarhounds, wolfhounds and greyhounds in the 17th century. They got their name when the French naturalist Georges-Louis Leclerc (Comte de Buffon, 1707–88) first saw one in Denmark and called it "*le Grand Danois.*"

The prairie dog is related to canines

Named for its funny, barking cry, the prairie dog is a burrowing rodent found on the North American plains. An adult prairie dog is between 12 to 16 inches (30 to 40 centimeters) long. They are considered a keystone species: their tunnels provide drainage for runoff and they keep certain weeds under control.

PIGS

Pigs are dirty and stupid animals

Pigs do like mud, but its because they don't have the ability to perspire, and the mud cools them off. They also like wallowing in clean water. Pigs have shown themselves to be exceptionally clever, for farm animals, and they make good pets.

Guinea pigs are a kind of pig

No, they're a rodent and they don't come from Guinea either, but that was one of their stops when they were first imported to Europe by Dutch and English traders. They originate in South America, where they were domesticated about 2000 BC, and raised for food. They are still eaten there. They do look a bit like pigs, but they are definitely not related. In the wild they travel in herds like cows and eat plants. Guinea pigs make excellent pets and come in many different breeds.

HUMANS AND THEIR BRAINS

Humans have evolved from monkeys

Humans do not originate in any of the living species of monkey. But we do have ancestors in common, and we belong to the same order: primates. The order of primates (apes) is subdivided into the wet-nosed primates and the dry-nosed primates. A suborder of the dry-nosed primates is divided into the New World monkeys and the Old World monkeys. Old World monkeys, which have no tails, form the family of anthropoid apes. This comprises the smaller gibbons and the larger apes, which are further divided into orangutans, gorillas, chimpanzees and humans.

We use only 10 percent of our brains

This theory was based on anatomical experiments in the 18th century, when it was established that it was possible to remove a large portion of the brains of animals without dire consequences. But brain scans have shown that we use far more than 10 percent — during one day a human being uses nearly every part of their brain. However, in people with brain damage, functions may be taken over to a certain extent by other portions of the brain. In babies this is possible to an astounding degree. By using sensitive instruments, it is possible to determine which parts of the brain are active, and which are inactive. This shows that although there are some particularly important centers, the rest of the brain is also involved.

Intelligent people have larger brains

The human brain is smaller than those of many other animals, but it is formed differently — with a brain stem, diencephalon, cerebrum and cerebellum. A dense network of nerves that links the parts together is crucial to the functioning of the human brain. In dementia, these links often die off. Similarly, a deficiency of nutrients during childhood can lead to insufficient development and thus to reduced intelligence. But whether the brain itself is slightly larger or smaller has no bearing whatsoever on intelligence.

Yawning increases the flow of oxygen to the brain

No, it doesn't. There are many reasons to yawn: boredom, sleepiness or because someone else just yawned and yawns are somewhat contagious. But a person does not take in more oxygen during a yawn — if anything, they take in less oxygen.

The brains of men and women are the same

The brains of men are usually about 15 percent heavier than those of women, which is what one might expect if the weight of the brain is taken relative to the weight of the body. The female brain, however, is more densely traversed by nerves and also has a more marked connection between the two halves. In the various thought processes the two halves are more equally utilized than in men.

Girls do worse at math than boys

Although for some time it was not accepted that there were any differences in the scholastic abilities of girls and boys, recently scientific evidence has highlighted fundamental variations. On average, girls do better in verbal tests, whereas boys get better results in technical disciplines. It seems the genders have very different approaches to problem solving, and this has an impact on how they perform in math.

It has been suggested that if spatial imagination and mathematical inferences are involved, boys do better, but girls are better at making calculations.

HUMANS AND THEIR BODIES

The human body is completely renewed every seven years

Although the body is always changing and new cells are born and die, each part changes at a different pace and the entire body doesn't change completely.

Blood is red

Only half the time. Blood needs oxygen to turn red — otherwise it is purplish blue. Blood leaving the heart is full of oxygen and bright red, but on the return trip is full of carbon dioxide and other wastes and is bluish. When a person is cut, the blood that flows out is red because it is exposed to oxygen in the air.

Human beings have only five senses

The five senses are sight, touch, taste, smell and hearing. But there are other ways we gather information about the world, and scientists are adding them to the list of basic senses. Balance, pain, hunger, thirst and temperature all contribute to our experience of our surroundings. There is also an awareness in our muscles of the position of our limbs, our hands and our feet (without having to look).

Contortionists are double-jointed

Nobody has "double" joints. Some people just have looser ligaments, which allow them to turn and twist their bodies in unusual ways. Contortionists work hard to make their ligaments stretch so they can perform various stunts.

Those two things on each side of your head are ears

No, they are "pinnas." The ear is an internal organ made up of the inner, middle and outer ear, and that cartilage outside is just for show. Pinnas don't really enhance sounds coming into the ear. To be able to do that they would have to be as large as your hand.

The bosom is the female breast

An old-fashioned word in many senses, "bosom" can refer to women's breasts or the chest area of a man, woman or child. In

19th-century literature both men and women speak of feelings as coming from their bosom.

Men cannot get breast cancer

Men also have mammary glands and can therefore get breast cancer. The National Breast Cancer Coalition estimates that in the United States about 1,720 men will be diagnosed with breast cancer in 2006. They predict that approximately 460 men will die from breast cancer in the same year.

BABIES AND TWINS

Women cannot become pregnant while nursing

This claim is repeatedly disproved through living examples. But despite this, it is more than an old wives' tale. For approximately half a year, during lactation, the female body produces the hormone prolactin, which not only reduces sexual desire, but which may also prevent ovulation. But the emphasis is on "may." The longer breastfeeding continues and the longer the intervals between feeding, the less prolactin is formed.

All babies are born with blue eyes

That occurs only with Caucasian babies. Dark-skinned infants usually have dark eyes. The iris of a light-skinned baby initially appears blue because not very much melanin pigment has accumulated. As the density of pigment cells increases during the first months of life, then the eyes may become gray, green or brown. All the colors are based on the same pigment. The different colors are governed by the number of pigment cells and how they refract the light.

Twins cannot have two different fathers

In 1996, a set of twins was born in England — one of the children had dark skin and the other light skin. They were conceived many days apart. Since then, several cases have been reported worldwide in which fraternal (two-egg) twins have had different fathers. The interval between conception has amounted to as much as four weeks.

A clone is an exact replicate

Cloning occurs naturally in identical twins, but although their genetic code is identical, twins have some differences. So do clones.

SKIN AND HAIR

Breathing through the skin is vital for life

James Bond is wrong: In *Goldfinger* (1964) he explained that beautiful Jill Masterson died because she was covered from head to foot in gold and her skin could no longer breathe. Because even the film crew shooting the movie believed this, doctors were on hand to supervise and actress Shirley Eaton was not as completely covered in gold paint as it appeared. We "breathe in" only about 1 percent of air through our skin — a negligible amount. However, a fever may occur when someone is gilded in this way, because the body can no longer be cooled through sweating.

After bathing, the skin shrinks

Warm water softens the skin. It does not shrink, but instead stretches, becoming a bit too large for the body that it covers. The skin takes on a pattern of folds that disappear when it dries out.

For a while after death, nails and hair continue to grow

A dead person is dead, and no "emergency reserves" allow particular parts of the body to continue to grow. The impression that the hair or nails of a corpse have grown since death arises because the skin dries out and shrinks. So nails suddenly seem to stick farther out from the fingers and toes, and stubble appears on the face.

Hair becomes gray when we get old

There is no such thing as gray hair, even though it may have the appearance of being so. In old age, growing hair contains less color pigment. The mixture of some color and white appears gray.

A person's hair can turn white overnight

This legend is lovingly cultivated by thriller writers, but in reality no one's head of hair has ever been bleached by a shock. To do so, hair would have to have nerves, and that is not the case. Only newly grown hair can bleach.

Identical (one-egg) twins are always of the same sex

The accepted rule of thumb has been that identical twins have identical hereditary characteristics, while fraternal twins resemble one another no more than ordinary siblings. However, one-egg twins are not absolutely identical — for example, they have different fingerprints. Normally, however, they are two boys or two girls. But in three cases, scientists have been able to show that a brother and a sister originated in the same egg. Sometimes a Y-chromosome gets lost during division and instead of a boy, a girl is formed with just one X-chromosome (Turner syndrome). In an extremely rare occurrence, the twins form from an egg cell that has two nuclei, and thus are not the classic one-egg twins.

SCIENTIFIC THEORY AND COUNTING

Pythagoras' theorem was discovered by Pythagoras

Euclid (ca. 365–300 BC) claimed that Pythagoras (ca. 570–500 BC) discovered the theorem that in a right-angle triangle, the square of the hypotenuse is equal to the sum of the squares of the two other sides. However, Pythagoras' theorem was clearly in use more than a thousand years earlier in Babylon and it was also used in Egyptian land measurement. But Pythagoras was certainly the first to prove it mathematically.

Charles Darwin proposed the Theory of Evolution

Charles Darwin (1809–82) didn't like to call it that. He preferred to describe his theory as "descent with modification," or "natural selection." Evolution suggests progress — an orderly development from simple to complex. Darwin insisted that the system of survival at work in nature was quite chaotic and haphazard. But the Victorians liked to think that human beings were progressing and his theory gradually became known as the Theory of Evolution.

The abacus is an ancient calculating device no longer used

The abacus is still used in many places around the world to do calculations. The simple device is made up of a wooden frame, rods and beads, and was used in various ancient cultures. The oldest abacus ever found dates from about 300 BC, used by Babylonians. Besides the basics of addition, subtraction, multiplication and division, the abacus can calculate square roots and cube roots. Very skilled practitioners can do calculations quicker than a calculator. Japan, Russia and China all have their own particular type of abacus, still in use today. The abacus is also used by the visually impaired.

Leap years occur every four years

Leap years (years with 366 instead of 356 days) are necessary to keep the calendar synchronized with the movements of the Earth, Moon and Sun. To do this, we need 97 leap years every 400 years. A leap year occurs in every year equally divisible by 4 except for centennial years, which must also be equally divisible by 400 in order to be a leap year. So 1900 was not a leap year, but 2000 was.

ATOMS AND QUARKS

The first atomic theory dates from the 19th century

In the fifth century BC, two Greek scientists and philosophers named Democritus (ca. 460–370 BC) and Leucippus (ca. 450–370 BC) developed the theory that all matter consists of similar, minute components. They called them *"atomos,"* meaning indivisible. All variations in objects and all natural processes would involve the combination and rearrangement of these atoms. Democritus wrote: "By convention there is color, by convention sweetness, by convention bitterness, but in reality there are atoms and space."

The whole universe consists of quarks

At one point atoms were considered to be the smallest components of the universe, from which all matter was constructed. But then it was discovered that atoms are themselves constructed of yet smaller particles. The smallest particle that we have discovered is a quark. That does not mean, however, that all particles consist of quarks. Only hadrons are formed from quarks. These include neutrons and protons, which occur in atomic nuclei. As well as the hadrons, however, there are the lighter leptons, such as electrons and neutrinos, which, according to our current state of knowledge, cannot be subdivided.

The word "quark" is a scientific abbreviation

The word "quark" seems rather remarkable, and many people assume that it must have a scientific origin, or that it is the abbreviation of a highly complicated term. In fact, it is completely unscientific. The word first occured in *Finnigan's Wake* (1939) by James Joyce (1882–1941): "Three quarks for Muster Mark." James Joyce loved making up words and readers often have a lot of trouble understanding exactly what his new words mean. The discoverer of quarks, Murray Gell-Mann (born 1929), felt that "quark" was an appropriate name for these mysterious particles.

LIGHT, WATER AND AIR

The speed of light and sound always remain the same

Sound travels through air at approximately 1,086 feet (331 meters) per second. This speed is valid only at a temperature of 32°F (0°C). If it is warmer, the sound travels slightly faster. The standard value for the speed of light (approximately 186,282 miles per second or 299,792 kilometers per second) is valid only in a vacuum. Light travels slower in the Earth's atmosphere, and in water it is "braked" down to about 142,915 miles per second (230,000 kilometers per second).

Water boils at 212°F (100°C)

Water boils at exactly 212°F (100°C) when the air pressure is about one bar. On mountains, where the air pressure is lower, it may boil at (say) 194°F (90°C). If it was somewhere that lay below sea level, it would need to be at more than 212°F (100°C). In a laboratory it is possible to create air pressure levels at which water can be brought to a boil at 32°F (0°C).

Adding salt to water makes it boil faster

Salted water boils at a higher temperature than water without salt, so it takes slightly longer to boil a pot of salted water. The boiling point of unsalted water is 212°F (100°C), while the boiling point of salted water is 216°F (102°C).

Stretches of water always freeze from the top downward

With very fast-running water, ground ice often forms. While the surface is continuously stirred up and thus not so easy to freeze, in the weaker flow at the bottom, ice forms on irregularities in the bed of the stream. At very low temperatures, ground ice may even form in calm lakes.

Quicksand will suck a person under the surface and drown them

Quicksand forms when fine sand becomes saturated with water to the point where it forms a kind of liquid. When a person falls into it, they will sink a bit, and then float. The best way to get out of quicksand is to relax (!) and let your body float on the surface, then roll out when you reach more solid ground.

Electric fans cool the air

Fans circulate the air and can move cooler air from one part of a room to another (say from a window). They quicken the evaporation process by drying the sweat off your body faster, but they don't actually make the air itself cooler.

Too many people in one room use up all the oxygen

When the air becomes thick in a closed room, it is not because our fellow occupants have "used" too much oxygen. The proportion of oxygen in the air (about 23 percent) is reduced by an imperceptible amount. What we are experiencing is an increased percentage of exhaled carbon dioxide from its normal concentration of just 0.04 percent. There is also a lack of negatively charged oxygen ions, which add to the "freshness" of air. These ions occur naturally at waterfalls, by open water, in the woods or in a thunderstorm.

ENGINEERING

Concrete was discovered in the 19th century

It was discovered by the Romans in the second century BC. They mixed mortar (which was already well known) with volcanic ash (*pozzolana*) to create a mixture that was much stronger than any previously known combination. Only cast concrete enabled them to erect giant structures like the Pantheon.

The Colossus of Rhodes straddled the harbor entrance

It must be confessed that no one knows what the Colossus of Rhodes really looked like. Apart from a few ancient coins that show a head with a seven-pointed crown, there are no depictions or descriptions of the legendary statue. We do know that it represented the sun god, Helios, the protector of Rhodes, and it stood about 98 feet (30 meters) high. But historians are perfectly sure of one thing: A statue with its legs straddling the harbor entrance could never have been realized technically at that time. Even today, such a feat has never been attempted.

The Leaning Tower of Pisa is going to fall down soon

The Leaning Tower of Pisa was closed between 1990 and 2001 while engineers raised it about 17 inches (44 centimeters) toward the vertical. Because the tower is partly built on firm clay and partly on fine-grained river sediments, it has been slowly sinking on one side since it was built more than 800 years ago. According to calculations by the experts, the Tower should be stable for about another 300 years.

The foundations of Venice are rotting away

The innumerable wooden piles on which the lagoon city stands are impervious to decay because they are not exposed to oxygen. But the city is slowly sinking and is also subject to flooding. The rising water level is damaging the lower levels of historical buildings. Giant sluice gates built at the entrances to the lagoon should keep floodwaters away from the city. But critics of the project fear that frequent closures will upset the ecological balance and that aggressive microorganisms will eventually destroy the wooden piles.

The longest bridge in the world spans water

The longest bridge construction in the world (and still in progress) is the Bang-Na Expressway in Bangkok, which is approximately 34 miles (54 kilometers) long. It does not bridge a gorge or area of water, but was built as a six-lane expressway, constructed as a second story over an existing expressway. The longest bridge over water is still the 23.83-mile (38.42-kilometer) Lake Ponchartrain Causeway, which links New Orleans with the northern shore of Lake Ponchartrain. Running a close second is the Donghai Bridge in China, at about 20 miles (32 kilometers) long.

ARCHITECTURE

In Greek temples, one column is an exact copy of the next one

The harmony of Greek temples rests in the fact that the relationships between all lengths, widths and heights obey a strict ratio. In older temples, an effort was made to be as precise as possible to achieve an optical balance in the building. But the Greek architects must have established that the human eye distorts exact relationships. So at some point they began designing buildings where everything appeared to be exactly balanced, but was not. In what is probably the most magnificent temple, the Parthenon in Athens, there are many compensating variations in column size.

The word "belfry" derives from the word "bell"

Although nowadays a belfry usually refers to a bell tower, the word is not connected to this function. Originally, *berfry* was a Middle English word for a siege tower, a movable tower used in battle.

Widows' walks were built so wives could look out to sea for their sailor husbands

The small railed platforms on the roofs of houses were built as an easy access to the roof to fight chimney fires. Their name came from the notion that sailors' wives would stand up there to watch for their husbands' return from sea.

AIRCRAFT AND ROCKETS

The Montgolfier brothers made the first balloon flight

Jacques Étienne (1745–99) and Joseph Michael (1740–1810) Montgolfier certainly built the first Montgolfier hot-air balloon, but they left the maiden flight in 1783 to their compatriots Jean-François Pilâtre de Rozier (1757–85) and François Laurent (1742–1809). The balloon stayed up for about four minutes.

The parachute was invented for use in airplanes

The invention of the parachute predated the invention of the airplane by about a hundred years. It was created in 1793 by a Frenchman, Louis Lenormand, as a device to save people jumping out of burning buildings. And in 1797 Jacques Garnerin jumped out of a hot-air balloon wearing a parachute and landed safely 3,000 feet (915 meters) below.

The world's first airplane was flown by Wilbur and Orville Wright

A few unmanned airplanes took flight before the famous brothers first flew a plane on December 17, 1903, but the Wright brothers are usually acknowledged as the first to successfully fly a controlled flight in a manned airplane powered by an engine. According to several newspaper reports, on August 14, 1901, a man named Gustav Albin Whitehead (born Weisskopf) flew a plane about half a mile (800 meters). But without photographs or proper documentation, his claim has been difficult to substantiate.

The Wright brothers' airplane was called the *Kitty Hawk*

The plane's original name was the *Wright Flyer*. The famous 1901 flight took place in the town of Kitty Hawk, North Carolina. Over the years their plane became known as the *Kitty Hawk*.

Lindbergh was the first pilot to fly nonstop across the Atlantic Ocean

Charles Lindbergh made the first solo nonstop flight across the Atlantic Ocean in 1927, but 66 people had flown across the Atlantic prior to this. The first transatlantic flight was made in 1919 by John Alcock (1892–1919) and Arthur Witten-Brown (1886–1949). They took a shorter route than Lindbergh, from St. John's, Newfoundland, to Clifden, Ireland, in just 16 hours, a distance of 1,980 miles (3,186 kilometers). Lindbergh flew from Long Island, New York, to Le Bourget in Paris in 33.5 hours — a total of 3,610 miles (5,810 kilometers).

Wernher von Braun invented the V2 rocket

The design of the deadly German ballistic missile was based on the extensive rocket research done by American physics professor Robert Hutchings Goddard (1882–1945). He filed patents for rockets as early as 1914. In the 1930s he made numerous experiments in New Mexico, which neither the American War Department nor the general public took seriously. Because information about Goddard's patents was freely available, he tried to warn the War Department in 1940 that the Germans could build a similar rocket. Sure enough, Wernher von Braun (1912–77) developed Goddard's prototypes into a weapon of war. Constructing the V2 rockets took the lives of 10,000 forced laborers and V2 attacks killed about 8,000 people.

INVENTORS

James Watt invented the steam engine

At the end of the 17th century, the French doctor Denis Papin (1647–1712) invented both the pressure cooker and the first steam engine, which was very small and soon passed into oblivion. In 1705, the English engineer Thomas Savery (ca. 1650–1715) built the first steam engine for pumping water from mines. This device was actually used, but had an extremely low efficiency. He later went into partnership with Thomas Newcomen (1663–1729), who had developed a different version of engine, also based on Papin's work. James Watt (1736–1819) had the merit of constructing the first truly efficient, industrially suitable engine, based on Newcomen's model.

Alexander Graham Bell invented the telephone

Yes, he did, but he wasn't the only inventor to do so. Others were working hard to invent a transmitting device, and one man in particular, Elisha Gray, perfected his invention at the same time Bell did, in 1876. However, Bell beat Gray to the patent office by about two hours, and despite years of patent litigation, Bell finally won out and was declared the inventor of the telephone.

Robert Fulton invented the steamboat

A fellow named John Fitch came up with the first steamboat in 1786, but no one was very interested and he couldn't quite get it going as a profitable venture. Other people built steamboats with varying success, but it was Robert Fulton who made it a going concern in 1807 when he started running a steamboat on the Hudson River between New York City and Albany. It caught on with the public and soon proved to be a commercial success.

Thomas Crapper invented the flush toilet

It would have been fitting if he had, but he didn't. He just sold them. Crapper (1837–1910) owned a plumbing supply company that sold a particular kind of flush toilet, which had been created by Albert Giblin in 1819. It was called the "Silent Valveless Water Waste Preventer." And the word "crap" doesn't come from his name, but derives originally the Middle English *crappe*, which referred to chaff or grain that fell on the floor of a barn, and from the Latin, *crappa*, which meant chaff.

Elisha Otis invented the elevator

Otis invented the brake system on elevators in 1952, but not elevators themselves. Human beings have been using types of hoists for centuries and elevators had been in use for freight for some time before Otis invented his brake. To persuade a doubting public that elevators were safe for humans, he orchestrated a publicity stunt. He got into an elevator and had an assistant cut the rope. The elevator's brake worked, Otis was unhurt and the elevator was soon accepted as a modern convenience.

The light bulb was first invented by Edison

The light bulb was invented in 1854 by Heinrich Goebel (1818–93), a German watchmaker who had emigrated to America. He is yet one more in the long list of unlucky inventors who did not succeed in making their discoveries public — completely in contrast to Thomas Alva Edison (1847–1931), who invented a similar bulb about 20 years later. English physicist and chemist Sir Joseph Wilson Swan (1828–1914) made his light bulb in 1860 and continued perfecting it up until 1878, when he received a British patent for it, about a year before Thomas Edison. Swan later became a partner of Edison's, doing business in England under the trademark Edi-Swan. Meanwhile, Heinrich Goebel was only able to take legal action against Edison shortly before his death. Eventually Edison pur-chased Goebel's patent from his impoverished widow.

Robert Wilhelm Bunsen invented the Bunsen burner

The handy laboratory heating device was created by Bunsen's assistant, Peter Desaga, in 1855, based on an earlier prototype developed by British chemist and physicist Michael Faraday (1791–1867). But Robert Wilhelm Bunsen (1811–99) was responsible for a much more important scientific discovery. Together with Gustav Robert Kirchhoff (1824–87), he discovered spectral analysis, which revealed that every element has a characteristic spectrum of colors similar to a fingerprint. This enabled them to track down previously undiscovered elements. Information gathered from space largely depends on the spectral analysis of the light that is captured by our instruments.

Mendeleyev invented the periodic table

The first ideas for classifying the chemical elements in a system were around as early as 1830. In 1869 two chemistry teachers independently succeeded in organizing all the elements into a complete system. One was Dimitri Ivanovitch Mendeleyev (1834–1907) from St. Petersburg and the other was Julius Lothar Meyer (1830–95) from Breslau. The system provided for still-undiscovered elements. Mendeleyev predicted the properties of gallium, germanium, rhenium and scandium.

Henry Ford invented the automobile

Nope. Two German engineers, Nikolaus Otto and Gottlieb Daimler, invented the internal combustion engine in 1876. The first motorized automobile was produced nine years later by Daimler and another German, Karl Benz.

Windmills were invented in the Netherlands

The Dutch may have improved the design of windmills by adding sails, but they were first used by the Persians between AD 500–900 to pump water. The ancient Chinese may have used them for a similar purpose, but the first record of them in China is during the 11th century, when they were used for grinding grain and separating salt from seawater, as well as pumping water. Windmills were used in the textile and manufacturing industries in Europe, and they are still used in Holland to pump water from flooded fields.

RANDOM SCIENCE

Glass is solid

Glass has more in common with a liquid than a solid: it flows at room temperature, but so slowly that you can't detect any movement. The reason we can see through glass is because of its liquid-like qualities. Its molecular structure is that of a liquid, but it has the properties of a solid, with the exception that light can pass through glass.

Diamonds are the most valuable gem

Rubies can sell for about four times the cost of diamonds, so they are more precious than diamonds. But diamonds are undoubtedly highly prized for their dazzling beauty. They are surprisingly one of the most common gems, and because of their hard consistency they are useful in industry and in science.

Diamonds are colorless

On the contrary, diamonds come in many colors. The clear ones are the most valuable, but the blue, red, orange, green and yellow ones are also in high demand. Diamonds that are darker, clouded or opaque are used in industry.

Only real diamonds cut glass

It takes a gem expert to distinguish between real and fake diamonds. The cutting test is not always definitive because some fake diamonds can cut through glass too.

Pennies are made of copper and nickels are made of nickel

Originally American dimes and quarters were made of silver, nickels were made of nickel and pennies were copper. But eventually the value of the coins became less than the value of the metal to make them. Since 1965 dimes and quarters are copper covered with nickel and since 1982 pennies are made of zinc with a thin outer layer of copper. Nickels are now 75 percent copper and 25 percent nickel.

India ink comes from India

The black ink was once used for writing and printing, but is now mostly used for drawing, and for inking comics. It did not originally come from India, but was invented by the ancient Chinese and Egyptians.

Rice paper is made from rice

Although rice is sometimes made into paper, what we call "rice paper" is not made of rice at all, but from the pith of the rice paper plant (*Tetrapanax papyrifer*).

CARS AND SHIPS

Karl Benz built the first gasoline-driven vehicle

The honors go to Siegfried Marcus (1831–98), a Jewish inventor from Mecklenburg who was living in Vienna. He built the first vehicle powered by gasoline in about 1870, when he fitted a hand-cart with a two-stroke motor. This vehicle had neither steering nor brakes, and is now known as the first "Marcus Car." All reminders of Siegfried Marcus were systematically suppressed by the Nazis from 1936 onward, but today he is well known all over the world.

Benzene was named after Karl Benz

The name benzene comes from benzol resin from which benzene was originally derived. The fluid had been known for a long time before Karl Benz began to build benzene-driven cars. Benzene had been used as a cleaning material and also in medicine for asthma and bronchitis.

Henry Ford invented conveyor-belt production

The conveyor belt was first introduced in food production. In England from about 1833 onward, ships' biscuits were prepared using conveyor belts, and about 40 years later they were used in Cincinnati slaughterhouses to carry dead animals from one cutter to the next. In the automobile industry, Ransom Eli Olds (1864–1950) initiated mass production. Starting in 1902 he arranged for cars to be pulled from one assembly station to the next on wooden pallets. By doing so, in 1904 he reached a yearly production of 5,000 cars. Ford (1863–1947) introduced the conveyor belt and the assembly line into his factory in 1913, cutting the manufacturing time for one car from 12.5 hours to 2 hours and 40 minutes.

The sinking of the *Titanic* was the greatest shipping accident of all time

It is not known exactly how many people died in the sinking of the *Titanic*, because there were no complete lists of passengers. The casualties were estimated at about 1,500. The highest death tolls at sea were caused by the sinking of refugee ships in 1945 at the end of the Second World War. On January 20, 1945, the *Wilhelm Gustloff* sank with about 9,300 passengers; on February 9, the *Steuben* with 4,000; on April 16, the *Goya* with 7,000; and on May 3 the *Cap Arcona* and two other ships carrying 7,000 freed concentration-camp prisoners. Similarly high numbers of victims occurred with the sinking of many Japanese ships in the autumn of 1944. They had mostly prisoners of war and civilians on board. The worst civilian seafaring accident was the sinking of the *Joola* off the coast of Senegal on September 26, 2002, with 1,800 deaths.

The *Titanic* was the first ship to be regarded as unsinkable

Ships had been claimed to be unsinkable much earlier. The *Great Eastern* was launched in 1858 as the largest ship ever built. It had a double hull and was divided into four sections with watertight seals between them. The *Titanic* had 16 such sections. It could probably have survived flooding of four or five of them, but the collision with the iceberg tore a hole in six. The *Titanic* was revolutionary in 1912 as far as size and furnishings were concerned, but not in any technical sense. Recent theories even suggest that faulty steel was responsible for its sinking. Scientists recovered unusually cracked sections in 1991. Extensive investigations showed that because of a high sulfur content, the steel was very brittle and consequently probably fractured extensively where a better product would only have been dented.

ATOMIC ENERGY, TEFLON AND COMPUTER CHIPS

Radioactivity is the result of the use of atomic energy

Completely natural radioactivity also occurs when unstable atomic nuclei decay and release energy. Natural radiation derives primarily from cosmic radiation and from the gas radon, which was created during the creation of the universe and is still decaying. It is widespread in air, water and rock.

Perfectly pure silicon is required for computer chips

Computer chips are made from impure silicon, but the impurities must occur with an unbelievable degree of accuracy to obtain the desired effects. The silicon is replaced with 0.0000001 percent boron or phosphorus. These tiny admixtures ensure that the conductivity of the silicon is greatly improved. Circuits are imprinted photographically and etched on the wafer-thin silicon chips. Then layers of phosphorus, boron and aluminum are deposited to create electronic circuit elements such as transistors.

No nuclear reactor in Britain has ever come close to a major disaster

In 1957, at the Windscale nuclear site (now known as Sellafield) in Britain, a reactor fire nearly became an accident of catastrophic proportion that could have been even worse than Chernobyl. A routine heating procedure went out of control and the reactor's core began to burn. None of the experts knew how to put this out. An attempt with 25 tons of liquid carbon dioxide had no effect. Finally they turned to water, even though everyone was conscious that the heat could have triggered a hydrogen explosion that would have ripped the reactor apart and irradiated a huge part of Europe. However, 2.4 million gallons (9 million liters) of water finally subdued the fire. The fire blew radioactive smoke and gases across Ireland, Britain, the Isle of Man and northern Europe. Because of the radiation released in the accident, milk from a wide area was banned.

Teflon is a byproduct of space research

As early as 1938, the American chemist Roy Plunkett (1911–94) inadvertently produced polytetrafluoroethylene by attaching fluorine atoms to a hydrocarbon chain while attempting to develop a coolant. In 1954, the French chemist Marc Grégoire (1906–96) came across this material. The idea of coating cooking ware with it is supposed to have come from his wife, Colette. Grégoire founded the Tefal firm, whose products became big sellers, especially in the United States. The suggestion that Teflon was a product of NASA first surfaced in an American publicity brochure in 1970.

DANGEROUS SUBSTANCES

Asbestos is a modern-day evil

Asbestos has always been dangerous, but people have not always been aware of its hazards. Mineral asbestos fibers, which were then known as "stone flax," were popular as early as the fifth century BC. Asbestos fibers could be bent and even woven, but their chief attraction was their resistance to fire. In the late fifth century BC, the Athenian sculptor Kallimachos was supposed to have made oil lamps with asbestos wicks. Greek doctors used cloths made from asbestos, because they could be disinfected by fire. In the late 20th century, after the fine dust from asbestos was proved to be a factor in deadly lung diseases including cancer, many countries throughout the world banned its use.

Smog first occurred with industrialization

Scientific research has shown that as early as the Middle Ages, heavy air pollution from too much dust, steam, ash and gases led to people suffering from chronic inflammation of the paranasal sinuses. This inflammation caused skeletal deformities and is thus still detectable today in human remains. The harmful material arose from the many wood, coal and peat fires, which were used not just for cooking, heating and lighting, but were also necessary in craft workshops such as smithies and brick works.

The mining of uranium is not particularly controversial

We hear a lot about the problems of atomic energy, but little about uranium mining. This is because the uranium mines are often located in remote areas, not in the high-density urban areas where nuclear energy power plants tend to be. Canada, the biggest exporter of uranium, has mines in northern Saskatchewan. During the mining process large quantities of radioactive dust are created and radon is released, which can expose workers and local inhabitants to radiation. Only about 5 percent of the material that is extracted is usable, and the remaining 95 percent sometimes remains in open waste heaps, where it continues to give off radiation.

MUSICAL ORIGINS

Yodeling is found only in the Alps

Yodeling was known in ancient China, Southeast Asia, among the African pygmies, the Inuit, in the Caucasus and in Romania before it became popular at the end of the 18th century in Austria and in the Bavarian Alpine region. The guttural cry is caused by the rapid change between the chest and head voices. Yodeling carries a long way, and helped herdsmen and hunters maintain contact over great distances.

Bagpipes were invented in Scotland

The original home of the bagpipes was most likely Asia Minor. It is possible that the Thracians invented them. They were probably brought to the British Isles by Caesar's legionaries. In the Middle Ages the instrument was known as the sack pipes. Instruments similar to the bagpipes are used in western Asia, North Africa and the Balkans. But bagpipes are known throughout Europe, from the Galician *"gaita,"* through the Breton *"biniou"* to the Swedish *"säckpipa."*

Woodwind instruments are made from wood

Woodwind instruments may also be made from metal. For example, the saxophone and the transverse flute are both woodwinds. Wooden alpenhorns are really brass instruments, which include all those in which the air flows from the mouthpiece throughout the whole instrument to the horn. If the flow of air is divided, either as it is blown, or when it is partially diverted later, then the instrument is considered to be a woodwind. Even a comb becomes a woodwind if someone blows across it. The rather remarkable division arises because the first woodwind instruments were flutes, while the first brass instruments were replicas of horns into which one simply blew.

The English horn is an English horn

Not really. The instrument known as an English horn is actually a woodwind instrument, not a horn. It is a kind of oboe that has a lower pitch than a standard oboe. The instrument came from the Near East, and first appeared in Europe in Vienna in 1760, where it was called a horn because of its shape. No one knows why it was called an "English" horn.

Johann Sebastian Bach was celebrated as a great composer during his lifetime

Although he was well known as a composer, Johann Sebastian Bach's (1685–1750) chief claim to fame was as a virtuoso organist. After his death his work was not played extensively for many years, although other musicians prized his work highly, including Beethoven, Mozart and Chopin. Felix Mendelssohn initiated the revival of his music in 1829 and today Bach is considered among the greatest European composers.

Catgut is made from cat's intestines

The tough, cord-like material used for stringed musical instruments is usually made from sheep's intestines, although sometimes other animal "guts" are used — horses, donkeys, hogs or mules. Never cats, though.

Stereo sound was invented in the 1950s

In 1881 engineer Clément Ader (1841–1946) demonstrated stereophonic sound through telephone wires at the Paris Exhibition. Two separate audio channels could be heard at the same time through separate earphones. The technique was developed further in the 1930s and 1940s, and in the 1950s the first stereo recordings were sold.

CLASSICAL COMPOSERS

Mozart's first names were Wolfgang Amadeus

The musical genius was baptized with the names Johannes Chrysotomus Wolfgangus Theophilus. Wolfgang became established as his first name. Mozart (1756–91) himself liked to use the form Amadé and usually signed himself Wolfgang Amadé. He used Amadeus, which is the Latin translation of Theophilus, very rarely. "Wolfgang Amadeus Mozart" became widespread in the 20th century.

Beethoven composed *Für Elise*

The famous piano piece *Für Elise* was actually composed for Therese von Malfatti, the daughter of a Viennese doctor, whom Beethoven was mad about in 1808. But Ludwig van Beethoven (1770–1827) had slovenly handwriting and an unknown copyist must have made a slip when deciphering the dedication at a later date. Anyone who doesn't want to commit themselves can talk of the *Bagatelle in A Minor*.

Beethoven named Opus 27 "Moonlight Sonata"

Ludwig van Beethoven (1770–1827) dedicated Opus 27 (1801) to his love interest at the time, Countess Giulietta Guicciardi, who was just 17. In 1832 the poet Ludwig Rellstab compared the music to the moonlight on Lake Lucerne, and the lovely music was known ever after as the "Moonlight Sonata."

MUSIC AND NATIONALISM

In Sparta music was considered frivolous

Music played a considerable role in Sparta, because the elite of the Spartan army were in the habit of going into battle to the sound of flutes. The best composers constantly came up with new songs for this reason, and these usually dealt with gloriously heroic death. But Sparta was not just a gloomy military dictatorship with no feeling for art. Culture flourished in the seventh and sixth centuries BC. As well as literature and the art of acting, choral lyric poetry and round dances were particularly fostered. In the fifth century, the fear of uprisings by the subjugated Messenians led to the ever-increasing isolation of Sparta, and to the orientation of everyone's life toward the armed forces.

Deutschland, Deutschland über alles was chauvinistic

The first verse of the German national anthem ("Germany, Germany above all") is nowadays regarded as chauvinistic. At the time it was composed it was not. When Heinrich Hoffmann von Fallersleben (1798–1874) wrote the text to a melody by Haydn, Germany was a federation of small states under authoritarian rule, each of which guarded its own nationality. Fallersleben wanted to overcome these boundaries with his poetry, and call for the foundation of a democratic, liberal state. For this, his professorship and his Prussian citizenship were removed, and he lived for many years in exile.

Every national anthem is different

That is not the case with one melody, the composer of which is unknown. It was first publicly played in 1745 in honor of the British King George II (1683–1760). In the Commonwealth it is the national anthem with the text *God Save the Queen/King*. It performed precisely the same function in the German Kingdom between 1871 and 1918 to the words *Heil dir im Siegerkranz*. In the United States it was used until 1913 alongside *The Star-Spangled Banner*, with the text "My country tis of thee" and in Switzerland it was the national anthem *Heil Helvetia* until 1961. That is what it remains in Liechtenstein, where it begins *Oben am jungen Rhein*.

The *sirtaki* is an old Greek dance

The *sirtaki* was invented for the film *Zorba the Greek* (1964) because Anthony Quinn (1915–2001), the leading actor, found the steps of the original Greek folk dance too difficult. However, the *sirtaki* was based on old Greek dances like the *sirtos* or the *hasapiko*. The film music for *Zorba the Greek*, and thus for the "very first *sirtaki*" was written by the famous composer and resistance fighter, Mikis Theodorakis (born 1925).

LOVE, HATE AND COLLABORATION

The Beatles and the Rolling Stones could not stand one another

The supposed enmity between the two bands was purely a publicity trick by the Stones' manager Andrew Loog Oldham (born 1944), who wanted to present his band as a wild, anarchic counterpart to the highly successful Beatles. The question "Stones or Beatles?" concerned the fans but not the musicians. The members of the two bands were friends.

The Threepenny Opera was Bertold Brecht's idea

The Threepenny Opera originates in an English ballad opera, *The Beggar's Opera*, which John Gay (1685–1732) wrote, based on an idea from his friend, Jonathan Swift (1667–1745). Brecht's collaborator, Elisabeth Hauptmann (1897–1973) translated the text and probably created additional parts of the Brecht version. It is uncertain how large her contribution was. Other female authors were also known to have collaborated with Brecht.

THE ILIAD AND THE ODYSSEY

Homer wrote *The Iliad* and *The Odyssey*

It is not even certain that Homer ever lived. Even in antiquity, his existence was a puzzle. He may have lived at some time between 800 and 600 BC. What is certain, however, is that *The Iliad* and *The Odyssey* are outstanding works of literature, and have contributed to the Greek sense of national identity. Scholars are still arguing over whether both were written by the same author. An analysis of the language appears to suggest a single author, but consideration of the content favors various authors.

Medea killed her children

In one version of the Medea saga, her children were killed by the Corinthians after Medea had killed the Corinthian king and his daughter (because Glauke had lured away Medea's husband). But the poet Euripides (ca. 480–406 BC) had his piece end with Medea herself killing her children. There are rumors that he was bribed by the Corinthians with 15 talents of silver to change the saga. There are also many versions of Medea's eventual fate. One of them recounts that she was taken to the Underworld, where she married Achilles.

The Iliad describes the conquest of Troy

The Iliad describes the "Wrath of Achilles" or, in more concrete terms, the battle between the leader of the army, Agamemnon, and the hero Achilles in the 10th year of the siege of Troy. The time covered is just 60 days. The epic ends with King Priam asking for the return of the body of his dead son, Hector. All that we think we know about the capture of Troy (even the death of Achilles) does not originate with *The Iliad* but comes from other sources.

LOVE AND LEGENDS

The *Edda* is an old Nordic epic

The *Edda* is a collection of old Nordic sagas about gods and heroes that was compiled about 1230 by the Icelandic Christian, Snorri Sturluson (1178–1241). Many of the stories were no longer known by the general public. They persisted only in idioms and allusions. Snorri wrote down the old myths so that contemporary poets would understand these references. One of his sources was later discovered, the so-called *Song Edda*, which probably dates from the ninth century.

The love triangle is central to the Arthurian saga

The famous Arthur/Guinevere/Lancelot love triangle first appeared in the tales of the French author Chrétien de Troyes (1140–90). Neither the Welsh poems about Arthur nor the works of the clerics Geoffrey of Monmouth (ca. 1100–54) and Wace (ca. 1110–71) speak of Guinevere's adultery. In his tale *Lancelot, the Knight of the Cart*, Chrétien de Troyes recounts how Lancelot frees Guinevere from her abductors and eventually commits adultery with her. Chrétien also wrote the Arthurian tales *Yvain, the Knight of the Lion; Perceval, the Story of the Grail* and *Erec and Enide*.

The legendary "Love and Peace Festival" took place at Woodstock

The concert was
supposed to take place
August 15–18, 1969, at
Woodstock in the state
of New York, but following

protests by the residents it was moved to Bethel, about 60

miles (100 kilometers) away. Despite that, more than

enough people turned up. Instead of the expected 60,000

people, about one million fans set out, of whom about

400,000 made it to the site. Even musicians became stuck

on the jammed roads and only some of them could be

flown in by helicopter.

Arthur was a legendary king

Is Arthur a figure of legend, or did he have a historical model? The tendency nowadays is toward the latter. Arthur was probably a British army leader who lived about AD 500. He does not appear on the list of British kings, although there had been an overall monarchy since the fifth century. The oldest Welsh sources describe him as "leader in battle." Some academics, however, believe that "Arthur" is just a title, not a name. One of the hot candidates for the true identity of Arthur is Owain Ddantgwyn, a powerful regional prince from the border region between England and Wales. Arthur's "Round Table" first occurs in the tales from the Middle Ages, and is also described in terms typical of that period. With time, other popular knightly epics, such as the search for the Holy Grail or *Tristan and Isolde*, were linked to the Arthurian material.

Merlin is a fictional character

Of all the characters in the Arthurian saga, one of the most unlikely of all derives from a real person: the sorcerer Merlin. His model is the Welsh bard Myrdin, who in AD 573 — and thus one or two generations after Arthur — went out of his mind at the battle of Arfderydd, and lived as a lunatic in the woods for a while.

Abelard and Héloïse left a moving exchange of letters behind them

The tragic love story between the scholar Peter Abelardus (1079–1142) and the beautiful Héloïse (ca. 1101–64), which led to the castration of Abelard, is recorded in their letters. However, their exchange of letters is worked out in such detail that historians assume that they are the work of a single writer, and suspect that Abelard wrote the whole work (*Historia calamitatum*) on his own.

Dante's lover was called Beatrice

That depends how one defines love. Dante Alighieri (1265–1321) saw the beautiful Beatrice Portinari (1266–90) at the age of 9 at his parents' party, and nine years later, fleetingly in the street. Despite this, she made such an impression on him that after her early death he unburdened himself by writing to her in the collection of poems called *La vita nuova*. Shortly afterward Dante married, but in his late work, *La Comedia*, which he began in 1307 and finished shortly before his death, he included a memorial to Beatrice, making her his guide through the realm of the dead.

Casanova could think of nothing but women

Admittedly, Giacomo Casanova (1725–89) recounts his approximately 130 love affairs at great length in his biography — including his true loves and his failures. Apart from his 12-volume memoirs, however, he also wrote about 20 other scientific and political works, including the *Isocameron*, a form of science fiction. In addition, he was a trained lawyer and studied theology, medicine, chemistry and mathematics. He worked as a theater director, an engineer, manager of a factory producing silk articles, and was a good violinist.

SHAKESPEARE

Hamlet knew Yorick well

He might have, but that's not what he said. Everyone thinks the Danish prince said, "Alas! poor Yorick. I knew him well," while looking intently at Yorick's skull. But what he really said was, "Alas poor Yorick! I knew him, Horatio" in *Hamlet* Act V, Scene 1.

Othello was not black

Shakespeare called Othello a "Moor," which at the time could have meant an Arab from North Africa or a black African of sub-Saharan descent. Some critics have suggested that Shakespeare did not want to depict a "Moor" but the Venetian mercenary leader Mauizio ("Mor") Othello (16th century). In the play, however, repeated illusions are made as to how Othello is an outsider by virtue of the color of his skin, so interpretations that ignore skin color are quite inappropriate.

SCHILLER AND GOETHE

Don Carlos fought for freedom

In Friedrich Schiller's play and in the opera by Giuseppe Verdi, Don Carlos was incarcerated by his father because he supported the oppressed people of Flanders and greater freedom in general. In addition, he had a tragic love for Elizabeth, whom his father married. However, the historical Don Carlos (1545–68) was hardly capable of political ideas. He was a victim of inbreeding, with only six different great-grandparents instead of 16 — mentally deficient with a very disturbed personality. He particularly liked tormenting his unfortunate servants. His father wanted to exclude him from the succession by means of a charge of high treason, but Carlos died before this happened.

Schiller invented William Tell

William Tell was certainly invented, even though 60 percent of the Swiss believe the legendary hero really lived. The prize for the invention, however, does at least go to a Swiss, namely the writer and politician Aegidius Tschudi (1505–72). Friedrich Schiller simply took the local story, dramatized it and decked it out with additional elements. Even the legendary shooting of the apple is found in Tschudi.

Schiller and Goethe are buried in the ducal crypt in Weimar

Johann Wolfgang von Goethe (1749–1832) is buried there. Whether Friedrich Schiller's mortal remains lie there is still uncertain. After his death, Schiller (1759–1805) was buried in a mass grave. In 1827 it was decided to move him to another grave, and a skull was chosen from the grave that resembled Schiller's death mask. In 1911, doubt was expressed, and the grave was searched again for the "true" remains of the poet. Recent investigations of the two skulls have come to the conclusion that the 1911 head is that of a woman, while the one chosen in 1827 could well be that of Schiller.

Faust was invented by Goethe

Goethe (1749–1832) was able to draw on the *Historia von D. Johann Fausten, dem weitbeschreyten Zauberer und Schwarzkünstler*, written in 1587 by an unknown writer, and on *The Tragical History of Dr. Faustus* (1590), a play by Christopher Marlowe (1564–93). Both must have been based on the story of a Württemberg doctor named Johann or Georg Faust (ca. 1480–1538), who had a reputation as an alchemist and magician.

Goethe's last words were "More light!"

Much has been read into these two words, but the complete — and rather mundane — version is found in the writings of the Weimar Chief Chancellor, Friedrich von Müller (1779–1849): "Open the second shutter so that more light may come in."

LITERARY INSPIRATION

Alexandre Dumas wrote *The Three Musketeers*

Alexandre Dumas the Elder (1802–70) is considered to be the author of about 600 thick adventure novels, most of which appeared in newspapers before they were printed as books. It was an open secret that Dumas collaborated with other authors in doing so. His closest collaborator was August Macquet (1813–88), who probably wrote much of *The Three Musketeers*.

James Fenimore Cooper invented the *Leatherstocking Tales*

Cooper's characters and stories were based on a historical model, although they were fiction. The life of the trapper Daniel Boone (1734–1820) provided Cooper (1789–1851) with the basis of the character Natty Bumppo in *Leatherstocking Tales*.

Daniel Defoe dreamed up *Robinson Crusoe*

Daniel Defoe (ca. 1660–1731) referred to the recollections of the Scottish sailor, Alexander Selkirk (1676–1723). Selkirk remained, half willingly, half abandoned, on an island in the Juan Fernandez archipelago, because the ship to which he had signed on was severely damaged (and subsequently sank). He was rescued after four years.

Johnny Appleseed was a fictional character

Johnny Appleseed was a real man (1774–1847) named John Chapman, who made it his life's mission to plant apple orchards throughout the eastern United States. He obtained his seeds free from cider mills and planted orchards in an effort to improve settlers' diets. Tall and skinny, he dressed in old clothes and spread the beliefs of Swedenborgianism, an offshoot Christian theology.

Casey Jones never existed

Casey Jones (1864–1900), made famous in the folksong *Casey Jones* by Wallace Saunders, was a real train engineer who died on the job in a train crash. A good engineer, but known for his penchant for speed and making up lost time, he apparently ignored or didn't see the flagmen waving him to stop, and crashed his train into another in Vaughn, Mississippi. Saunders, a co-worker and friend, wrote three songs about Casey Jones.

The Brothers Grimm collected and transcribed German folk tales

Jakob (1785–1863) and Wilhelm Grimm (1786–1859) certainly appreciated the old German stories, but they had their own conception of how the stories could be improved. The fairy tales they collected are considerably adapted and altered. In doing so, mothers became stepmothers, pregnancies were omitted and horrible passages were moderated.

Sinuhe the Egyptian was invented by Mika Waltari

The first Sinuhe in literary history appeared in ancient Egypt in *The Story of Sinuhe*, written in about 1800 BC. In this tale, Sinuhe was an official in the harem of Pharaoh Amenemhat I. After the latter's murder, he fled to Syria. Although he gained riches and high esteem there, he was troubled by homesickness. The work, which is written in the first person and is a song of praise for Egyptian culture, is one of the outstanding pieces of ancient Egyptian literature. *The Egyptian*, by the Finnish author Mika Waltari (1908–79), on the other hand, recounts the tale of a doctor called Sinuhe at the time of the Pharaoh Akhenaten (14th century BC).

Collected works are the same as a complete edition

Collected works are a selection of the books by a particular author that are published in a single- or multiple-volume edition. In general, they are a sort of "best of" collection. In a complete edition all the author's works must be present in unabridged form.

FRANKENSTEIN, MORALITY AND UNDERGROUND PASSAGEWAYS

For Oscar Wilde, art was more important than morality

Oscar Wilde (1854–1900) wrote many witty epigrams about art being free of morality and beauty taking priority over virtue, but if his works are looked at closely they show a high standard of morality. In the novel, Dorian Gray is punished, in his comedies the good win out in the end and in his stories eventually even beauty is sacrificed. Probably it was through Wilde's own personal tragedy that his public accepted only the frivolous, immoral image that he had himself created.

The Phantom of the Opera has nothing to do with the Paris Opera

The subterranean worlds in which the Phantom lives in the famous novel by Gaston Leroux (1878–1927) appear too fantastic to be real. But the old Paris Opera, the Palais Garnier, has labyrinthine underground foundations with endless wardrobes, workshops and storerooms. Even the lake that is mentioned in the book exists. It formed beneath the lowest story when the excavations for deep cellars encountered a water-bearing layer of ground.

Frankenstein is a monster

Frankenstein is only the creator of the monster, not the demon itself. In the introduction to the novel by Mary Shelley (1797–1851), his full name is Baron Victor von Frankenstein. He is an Ingolstadt medical student who tries to create an artificial man. But not everything goes to plan, and the monster he brings to life is soon out of his control.

FAIRY TALES

Cinderella's slippers were made of glass

In the original Cinderella stories, which go all the way back to the ninth century, her slippers were made of precious metal or some other valuable material. But when Charles Perrault translated an old French story about Cinderella, her fur slippers were incorrectly translated as glass slippers, because of some confusion about an old French word for fur. Thus the famous glass slippers became part of her story.

The Pied Piper of Hamelin is a fairy tale

Most historians are certain that there was a mass exodus of young people from Hamelin in the 13th century. But there are many theories as to what was behind this. For example, the Pied Piper may have been recruiting settlers for the eastern provinces, probably for Brandenburg. Other possibilities that have been discussed are a connection with the Children's Crusade of 1212 or with the battle of Sedemünde in 1259. The oldest known version, however, is about an elegant youth, who one Sunday in 1284, disappears with 130 kids, with no mention of rats.

El Dorado always referred to a legendary golden city

In Spanish, "*El Dorado*" means "the golden," and originally applied to a golden man. The Spanish conquerors of South America in the 17th century heard that somewhere in the interior an Indian tribe was in the habit of anointing the whole body of every new ruler with a paste of gold dust. Then he led the way to a lake, where he sacrificed many valuable golden objects to the gods, and finally washed the gold from his body. In time, this lake full of gold became a golden city, and even a golden country, which the adventurers feverishly sought.

Ali Baba was the leader of 40 thieves

Ali Baba is an honest merchant, who by accident ("Open Sesame") discovers the treasure cave of the 40 thieves. The discovery naturally places him in danger, but with the help of Morgiana, a clever slave girl, Ali Baba gradually succeeds in killing all the thieves and becomes the owner of the fabulous treasure. *Ali Baba and the 40 Thieves* was included by European publishers in the collection known as *The Book of One Thousand and One Nights*, but there is some dispute as to whether Ali Baba was part of the original Arabian Nights or not.

MYTHICAL BEASTS AND LABYRINTHS

There are no such things as unicorns

Perhaps there is no such thing as a beautiful white horse with a single horn on its skull, which can only be tamed if it lays its head on the lap of a virgin. But the horns that were displayed as proof of unicorns' existence in the Middle Ages were real. The imposing horns, which tapered to a point and were up to 10 feet (3 meters) long, did not come from a land animal, but from a sea mammal: the narwhal.

The word "nightmare" has something to do with a horse

Unless a horse is featured in your nightmare, there's no connection. The word comes from the Old English word "*mare*," which referred to a type of demon or ghost that was said to sit on a person's chest at night. The victim feels as if they're suffocating, and they experience a feeling of oppression and great weight on their chest. They often find it impossible to move. In Newfoundland this phenomena is known as "the Old Hag."

A labyrinth is the same as a maze

A labyrinth is admittedly confusing, but there is only one single tortuous way into its interior. It is not possible to wander off the path. The path through a labyrinth should stimulate meditation and help the walker to find balance in their life. In the Middle Ages pavement labyrinths were sometimes constructed in cathedrals. In a maze, however, there are numerous cul-de-sacs, so that it is difficult to find the right path.

MONA LISA AND MICHELANGELO

Only a genius can paint eyes that follow you around the room

From whatever angle one examines the *Mona Lisa*, it always seems as if she is looking directly into one's eyes. There is no magic to this, however, and neither does it need a genius such as Leonardo da Vinci to produce this effect. Basically it is a trick: one of the eyes of the sitter must lie on a line that divides the picture vertically into two halves.

Michelangelo's client was Pope Sixtus IV

Pope Sixtus IV (Francesco della Rovere, reigned 1471–84) certainly had the Sistine Chapel built, which is why it was named after him. The frescoes on the side walls were also commissioned by him. However, when it came to the roof, he had it decorated simply with stars on a dark blue, night-sky background. His nephew, Julius II (Guilano della Rovere, reigned 1503–13), however, did not like the stars, and gave Michelangelo the task of decorating the ceiling with a major set of frescoes.

The Mona Lisa is a portrait of Lisa da Giaconda

The question of who the mysteriously smiling lady is in the famous portrait by Leonardo da Vinci (1452–1519) has preoccupied art historians since time immemorial. The hot favorite for a long time was Lisa da Giaconda, the wife of a merchant. But there is some evidence that it might be Isabella of Aragon (1470–1524), the wife of the Milanese prince Gian Galeazzo Sforza (1469–94). Another theory is that it is really a man, or even a self-portrait of da Vinci himself, dressed as a woman.

The Sistine Chapel is a work by Michelangelo

The frescoes that Michelangelo Buonarroti (1475–1564) painted in the Sistine Chapel have attained such fame that it is easily forgotten that other painters were also busy there. The plans for the building originated with the sculptor and architect Baccio Pontelli (1450–92), and these were carried out by the papal master builder Giovanni de Dolci. On the side walls a series of frescoes were created by (among others) distinguished masters of the early Renaissance such as Sandro Botticelli (ca. 1452–1510), Pietro Perugino (ca. 1445–1523) and Luca Signorelli (1450–1523). However, all of this is overshadowed by Michelangelo's ceiling painting of *The Last Judgement*.

Michelangelo employed dark colors

Anyone who visited the Sistine Chapel before 1975 or who remembers old pictures of the work of art, might assume that Michelangelo reveled in earthy, brown tints. The restoration that ended in 1999 revealed that he used extremely bright colors, which have been darkened over the centuries by the soot from candles. During the restoration, overpainting was removed that had been used to hide the nudity of the figures after Michelangelo's death. Some art experts deplore the restoration because it is possible that some of the overpaintings were originally inspired by Michelangelo himself.

Michelangelo was a famous painter

Michelangelo considered himself first and foremost a sculptor. During the work on the Sistine Chapel he complained that he was not a painter and was there under false pretences. But neither his famous *David* nor *Moses* is as popular as his *Creation of Mankind*, with God reaching out his hand to touch Adam. Even more greatly overshadowed is Michelangelo's work as an architect, even though he founded the style now known as mannerism, and is, to a considerable extent, responsible for the present-day character of Saint Peter's Basilica.

PAINTINGS

Raphael's *Sistine Madonna* hangs in the Sistine Chapel

The Sistine Madonna hangs neither in the Sistine Chapel nor was it commissioned by the same pope as the Chapel itself. Raphael (1483–1520) painted the Madonna at the request of Pope Julius II, as a present for the Chapel of Saint Sistus in Piacenza. In 1754, Friedrich August II of Saxony (1696–1763) bought the painting, and as a result the Madonna may now be admired in the Old Masters Picture Gallery in Dresden.

El Greco was a Spanish painter

"El Greco" was, as the name itself implies, Greek. He was called Doménikos Theotokópoulos (1541–1614) and came from Crete. He emigrated to Toledo and under his artistic name became one of the best-paid painters in Spain. With his somber, yet impressive style he was highly typical of the spirit of the Spanish Counter-Reformation.

Rembrandt painted a picture called *Night Watch*

That was what was believed until 1911, when the old layers of varnish were removed from the dark, nocturnal painting. Underneath, brilliant colors were discovered. In reality, Rembrandt (1606–69) had not painted a night scene, but a group portrait of an Amsterdam company of militia. Those portrayed did not like the painting, however, so it ended up in a storage, where the patina developed. When the Amsterdam Rijksmuseum brought the painting by the now extremely famous artist out of its cellars in 1891, it was given the then apparently appropriate title of *The Night Watch*. The painting should really be called *The Company of Frans Cocq*.

In Roman mythology there is an "Oath of the Horatii"

After all, Jacques-Louis David (1748–1825) depicted it in his famous picture with the same name. But this oath to give one's life for the homeland had been invented by David. He painted this picture as part of an artistic project to raise public morals that Louis XVI (1754–93) initiated five years before the French Revolution. In ancient Rome, there certainly was a well-known saga about the Horatius triplets, who as representatives of the Roman army won a fight between champions against the Curatius triplets from the Alban army, but there was no talk of an oath. David himself was a Jacobin during the Revolution, and subsequently Napoleon's court painter.

Small pictures are known as miniatures

The name "miniature" does not come from "mini" but from "*minium*," the Latin name for the pigment red lead. The first initials, decorative borders and pictures in illuminated manuscripts were painted in this pigment. It makes no difference whether it was a delicate filigree or a whole page in a folio: both are miniatures. Other than painted books, however, small portraits, which became fashionable in France and the Netherlands in the 16th century, are also known as miniatures.

In antiquity, painting was not very significant

In contrast to statuary and buildings, ancient painting has hardly ever been preserved. The greatest artist was Apelles of Colophon (died ca. 300 BC). Ancient authors praise the figures, the masterly perspective and the bold depiction of shadows in his work. His fame persisted into the Renaissance period. Other famous painters were Polygnotus of Thasos (fifth century BC) who, in his monumental battle paintings must have been the first to depict perspective on a large scale, and Zeuxis (fifth to fourth century BC), whose painted grapes that were said to be so lifelike that birds attempted to peck them.

NAKED STATUES AND STONE SOLDIERS

The Greek sculptors generally depicted nude women

Until about 330 BC, the Greek artists basically depicted only naked men and clothed women. Then the famous artist Praxiteles (born ca. 390 BC) dared to exhibit his *Aphrodite of Cnidus* (a copy is in the Vatican Collection) "topless," thus causing a scandal. Although subsequently there were other statues of nude women, it was mainly later painters who showed ancient goddesses and figures from the myths in the nude.

Greek statues like *Aphrodite of Cnidus* are originals

There are very few originals of significant Greek statues. Among them are the *Barberini Faun* in the Munich Glyptothek and the *Venus de Milo* in the Louvre. All others are Roman or Etruscan copies. So it may happen that there are sometimes many examples of a statue.

The soldiers of the Terracotta Army are all individually depicted

The famous clay soldiers that guard the tomb of the Chinese emperor Shi Huang-Di (259–210 BC), were made from molds. Like modern chocolate rabbits, hollow pieces of the fronts and backs of the bodies were stuck together. Heads and hands were also shaped in molds, and then each one was individually assembled so that the attitudes of the heads and hands all appear individual. Finally, artists added details of the faces, hair and uniforms with finer clay, so that one might think that in fact 6,000 real men had served as models.

PYRAMIDS AND TEMPLES

The largest pyramid in the world is in Egypt

The largest pyramid in the world is found in Mexico, near the small town of Cholula, about 60 miles (100 kilometers) from Mexico City. It was built by the Aztecs in honor of the God Quetzalcoatl. The fact that it is so poorly known is because it has not yet been fully excavated. In addition, the Mexican building is extremely low. While the Pyramid of Cheops is 446 feet (136 meters) high, the Cholula Pyramid barely reaches 177 feet (54 meters). It has such a large area as base, however, that it is about 30 percent larger than the Pyramid of Cheops.

There are only seven Wonders of the World

Since the second century BC there has been a classic canon of the Seven Wonders of the World, and all attempts to declare a spectacular construction as the "Eighth Wonder" have changed nothing. It is true, though, that these seven Wonders were not always the same. Nowadays they are: the Pyramid of Cheops, the Hanging Gardens of Babylon, the Statue of Zeus at Olympia, the Temple of Artemis at Ephesus, the Mausoleum at Halicarnassus, the Colossus of Rhodes and the Lighthouse at Alexandria. Various ancient lists, however, mention many other Wonders vying for the top seven: the Walls of Babylon, an Altar of Artemis on Delos, a Temple of Zeus in Cyzicus, the Palace of Cyrus at Ekbatana, a Labyrinth of the Pharaoh Amenemhet III, the Coliseum, as well as the cities of Rome and Thebes.

Greek buildings and sculptures were white

During the height of classicism, when antiquity was rediscovered, lovers of art enthused over the elegant white color of temples and statues. Archaeologist Johann Joachim Winckelmann (1717–68) coined the slogan "noble simplicity and silent greatness" to describe their appeal. The theory by the Scottish painter James Stuart (1713–88) that the works of art were brightly colored was bitterly rejected. Investigations in the 19th century revealed that he was right: Greek works of art were resplendent in brilliant colors: red, blue, black, white and yellow ocher. They were also decorated with gold and bronze.

At the oracle's shrine at Delphi there was a round temple

Current photos of the shrine at Delphi show the remnants of an elegant round temple. But this building, which was constructed in the fifth or fourth century BC by Theodoros of Phocis, has nothing to do with the much older oracular site, but with the temple complex of Athena Pronaia, which lies somewhat lower than the oracle's shrine.

The Romans copied the art of the Greeks

Initially they did so. They often used Greek elements as decoration or combined solid Roman brick buildings with a Greek false façade. In doing so they created individual elements such as pilasters (projecting half-columns). In the imperial period, however, with their mastery of building arches and vaults, which were more or less unknown to the Greeks, the Romans developed their own individual aesthetic.

Galla Placida is buried in her mausoleum in Ravenna

For visitors to Ravenna the Mausoleum of Galla Placida is a must. Some of the oldest mosaics in the city can be seen on a deep blue background. But no one is buried in the small, cross-shaped space, an oratory chapel dedicated to Saint Laurence. Either Galla Placida (AD 388–450) or her husband, the Emperor Valentinian I (AD 321–375), built the chapel in the anteroom to the Church of Santa Croce.

CATHEDRALS, CHURCHES AND MOSQUES

Sant'Apollinare Nuovo is newer than Sant'Apollinare in Classe

The existence in Ravenna of two early Christian basilicas erected in honor of Saint Apollinaris is most confusing. This is compounded by the fact that Sant'Apollinare Nuovo was built first, in AD 520, while Sant'Apollinare was built in AD 549. When the relics of Saint Apollinaris no longer appeared to be safe in AD 856, they were transferred to the older church, which was renamed in honor of Saint Apollinare. In addition, Sant'Apollinare Nuovo is well-known for its breathtaking series of mosaics. In the nave, among others, there are representations of the Three Kings, the Mother of Christ enthroned between angels and Christ performing miracles.

The cathedral at Speyer dates from the 12th century

The Cathedral of Saint Mary and Stephen at Speyer is among the most significant buildings of the Romanesque period. It was constructed between 1027 and 1125. But its present-day appearance originated in the 18th century. In 1689, during the Palatinate's war of succession, the troops of the French Sun King, Louis XIV (1638–1715) burned the magnificent church to the ground. It was, however, rebuilt exactly as the original. During another restoration in 1854, various changes were made, including several to the extremely stark west façade.

The Cathedral at Cologne is the largest Gothic cathedral in the world

When comparing the sizes of churches, the winner is usually decided by the height of the nave. On that score there is one cathedral that is slightly larger than the Cologne Cathedral (built 1248–1880). Whereas the giant nave in Cologne is 141 feet (43 meters) high, the one at Saint Peter's Cathedral (built 1247–1573) in Beauvais is slightly more than 157 feet (48 meters). Even so, Beauvais doesn't really count, because the church is only a fragment. The construction was called off after numerous spectacular collapses, so that today all that is standing is the choir and transept. Because of their height they are rather disproportionate for the church as a whole.

Notre-Dame-de-la-Paix is a copy of Saint Peter's Basilica

The cathedral in the Ivory Coast is often said to be an exact copy of Saint Peter's in Rome, but slightly larger. But although the architect, Pierre Fakhoury (born 1943), obviously based it on Saint Peter's, there are many differences. The circular church building stands beneath a dome that is larger than that of Saint Peter's, supported by lower walls. It is surrounded by cross-shaped columned halls. The interior of the church, with its large, round-arched glass windows and Greek columns certainly does not resemble its great model.

Saint Peter's Basilica is the largest church in the world

The Guinness Book of Records lists Notre-Dame-de-la-Paix in Yamoussoukro in the Ivory Coast as the largest church in the world. It is true to say, however, that this record is contentious. The dome of Saint Peter's is higher, but Notre-Dame's is decorated by a 125-foot (138 meter) lantern, which brings it to a height of 518 feet (158 meters), as opposed to Saint Peter's 435 feet (132.5 meters). The interior space of Notre-Dame, at 153,924 square feet (14,300 square meters), is smaller than that of Saint Peter's, which has an area of 162,535 square feet (15,100 square meters). Notre-Dame has a larger area only if one includes the cross-shaped halls around the church.

Hagia Sophia in Istanbul is now a mosque

The "Church of the Holy Wisdom" was converted into a mosque after the fall of Constantinople to the Turks in 1453. The famous Ottoman master builder, Sinan (ca. 1491–1578) surrounded it with four high, slender minarets. In 1934 the founder of the modern Turkish state, Kemal Ataturk (1881–1938), declared that it would become the Ayasofya Museum. This way, the Byzantine gold mosaics and paintings on the walls could be revealed once more. They had previously been covered because they were inconsistent with the Islamic ban on images.

PALACES

The "Palace of the Winds" is a palace

The magnificent rose-red façade of the Hawa Mahal ("Hall of Winds") is the most famous landmark of the city of Jaipur, India. It is covered with barred windows and bay windows, each one more elaborate than the next. Many visitors are all the more surprised when they discover that behind this magnificent façade there is absolutely nothing at all — simply a set of steps. The women of the harem used to stand on the steps behind the windows to watch parades and festivities on Jaipur's main square, where they could see out without being seen themselves.

The Escorial is a palace

The Escorial, the seat of government of the Spanish king Philip II (1527–89), was conceived as a monastery and a place for the burial of Spanish kings. But then the "gloomy king" decided to integrate his living quarters and seat of government within the giant new building, which lies a good 37 miles (60 kilometers) northwest of Madrid in an isolated mountainous region. Whereas the church is magnificently furnished, the monarch's living quarters are of monastic severity and in no way like a palace.

The Crystal Palace was a particularly expensive building

In 1851, the Great Exhibition was held in the Crystal Palace in London, England. That sounds extremely grand. Actually, the Crystal Palace was a sort of giant greenhouse — similarly cheap to manufacture, and because of its modular construction, rapidly and effectively erected. The public was completely captivated by it and full of enthusiasm for this transparent exhibition building filled with light — much to the annoyance of many architects, who viewed cast iron and glass as inartistic materials.

BRIDGES, GATES AND BELLS

The Bridge of Sighs has a romantic history

"Sighs" suggests love songs and broken hearts. However, the history of the Bridge of Sighs in Venice is far more terrible. It links the Doges' Palace to the old palace prison. The bridge was the route from the palace (which was also the court) to the prison with its notorious torture-chamber, and the sight of it must have elicited many sighs from the convicts. Even worse, however, was the return journey back: that meant certain death. The sole place of execution in Venice lay between the Saint George's and Saint Mark's Columns, right by the water.

The Quadriga on the Brandenburg Gate formerly faced west

In 1807, Napoleon (1769–1821) stole the iron goddess and her quadriga (chariot) from the Brandenburg Gate in Berlin. In 1814, she was returned, and replaced — facing east. Fifty years later the rumor arose that she originally looked west, but was now turning her back on the "the traditional enemy, the French." In reality, however, the goddess was always turned toward the city center and the royal castle. She originally represented Eirene, the goddess of peace, and it was only in 1814 that she was reinterpreted as Victoria, the goddess of victory, by the insertion of an iron cross into her garland of oak leaves.

Big Ben is the clock tower of the Palace of Westminster

"Big Ben" is the name of the almost 14-tonne bell that hangs in the clocktower and strikes punctually every hour. The tower in which it hangs is officially named Saint Stephen's Tower. The bell owes its name to Sir Benjamin Hall (1802–67), the tower's architect, not Edmund Beckett Denison (1816–1905), who devised the works of the clock that is responsible for Big Ben's accuracy.

AMERICAN LANDMARKS

The Golden Gate Bridge is golden

The Golden Gate Bridge takes its name from the strait that it spans, the Golden Gate. The bridge is painted in a bright rustproof color called "International Orange." However, depending on the lighting, it gleams with various golden and reddish tints. This color was specified by the architect Irving Foster Morrow (1884–1952), who was convinced that this reddish tint toned best with the blue of the bay. Originally it was planned to be gray or metallic. The U.S. Navy even favored black with yellow stripes.

Grand Central Station is the name of the main railway station in New York City

The real name of the famous station is "Grand Central Terminal," but it's always been known as Grand Central Station. There's a subway station nearby that bears the name "Grand Central Station," but that's not where people mean when they say "meet me at Grand Central Station."

The giant Hollywood sign always read "Hollywood"

The sign was put up in 1923 to mark a new housing development called "Hollywoodland." It was meant to be a temporary sign, but in 1932 an actress committed suicide by jumping off it. In 1949 the Hollywood Chamber of Commerce took over maintenance of the sign and removed the last four letters. The letters, which were originally wood, have been replaced with steel, and the sign became a famous trademark of the Hollywood movie industry.

The most famous film prize in the world is called the "Oscar"

Its real name is the "Academy Award of Merit," and it has been awarded by the Academy of Motion Picture Arts and Sciences since 1929. "Oscar" is simply its nickname, whose source is disputed. One story has it that it was named after movie star Bette Davis' husband, Harmon Oscar Nelson. Another source suggests that an employee of the Academy spontaneously exclaimed that the statuette looked just like her uncle Oscar. When the statuette (which is not made of gold, but is only gold-plated) is awarded, the presenter does not say, "The Oscar goes to..." — but, "The winner is..."

PULITZER, OSCAR AND JAMES BOND

Pulitzer was an exemplary journalist

Joseph Pulitzer (1847–1911), after whom the famous Pulitzer Prize for outstanding journalism is named, only worked for a few years as a journalist. He was the owner and editor of various newspapers and is regarded as the creator of tabloid journalism. His papers stood out from the competition with sensational articles and comic strips, and he did not shrink from manipulations. But his newspapers also carried well-researched articles about corruption and the misuse of power. After a tumultuous career, Pulitzer provided in his will for the formation of a school of journalism, which has awarded the Pulitzer Prize since 1917.

The first two James Bond actors were Sean Connery and Roger Moore

During the 1950s there was both a television and a radio James Bond (played by actors Barry Nelson and Bob Holness, respectively). The first James Bond film, *Dr. No*, was shot in 1962 with Sean Connery (born 1930) in the role. The second actor to play Bond in the official movies was George Lazenby (born 1939) in *On Her Majesty's Secret Service*, made in 1969. Roger Moore (born 1927) first played 007 in 1973.

MOVIE MAGIC

Johnny Weissmuller produced Tarzan's famous jungle yell

The legendary yell is definitely one that has been canned by the studio. There are all sorts of stories about its composition. Johnny Weissmuller (1904–84) maintained that in his youth he had won numerous yodeling competitions, and that the Tarzan call essentially consists of his yodel. Although Weissmuller definitely produced impressive live calls himself, the most accepted explanation of the yell in his movies is that the actor's voice was augmented with a soprano's piercing rendition of a high C-note and a hyena's call played backward on a tape recorder.

John Wayne personified the typical cowboy

The Hollywood image of a cowboy as a tough guy who was an expert horseman and an ace shot was personified by actor John Wayne (Marion Michael Morrison, 1907–79). But the reality of life on the open range was far different. Men worked as cowboys if they could find no other job. Many were either vagabonds with previous convictions or men from the poorest backgrounds. About a third came from Mexico and one-sixth were black. Most were previously unable to ride, which meant that riding accidents were the primary cause of death. Shooting was, as a rule, something that they had never mastered. Hardly any cowboy wore a revolver, but some carried rifles to scare away predators.

The von Trapp family escaped the Nazis by crossing the Alps

The Sound of Music (1965) took some poetic license with the story of the musical family and their "escape" from the Nazis in Austria in 1938. They left quite openly on a train, and there was no midnight trek through the mountains. And they traveled to Italy, not Switzerland, and from there to the United States.

ANGELS, DUCKS AND LISTENING CAREFULLY

Marlene Dietrich became famous as the Blue Angel

Marlene Dietrich (1901–92) became famous in the film *The Blue Angel*. In it, however, she played the part of a revue girl named Lola-Lola. The "Blue Angel" is the name of the cabaret in which the disastrous meeting between the Professor and the seductive dancer takes place. In the original book, *Professor Unrat*, by Thomas Mann (1871–1950), the dancer's name is Rosa Frolich. The model of the cabaret must have been the Lübeck brothel called the "Golden Angel," which Mann knew well. Since 1948, the novel has also been published under the title *The Blue Angel*.

Walt Disney invented Mickey Mouse and Donald Duck

He invented neither of them. The first Donald Duck cartoon films were produced by the Disney graphic artist, Charles Alfred Taliaferro (1905–69). The actual "duck's life" universe was, however, created by Carl Barks (1901–2000). The task of creating a cheeky mouse as a new hero was given by Walt Disney (1901–1966) to his collaborator Ub Iwerks (1901–71). The "godmother" of the most famous mouse in the world was Disney's wife, Lillian, who argued that the rodent should be called Mickey and not Mortimer.

The soundtrack of *2001: A Space Odyssey* was composed for the film

Stanley Kubrick (1928–1999) used a collection of music from different composers for his soundtrack for the famous 1968 film. The title track is by Richard Straus (1864–1949): *Also Sprach Zarathustra*.

Humphrey Bogart said, "Play it again, Sam."

In *Casablanca* (1942), Bogart (1899–1957) never says this. Ingrid Bergmann (1915–82) asks the pianist to, "Play it once, Sam. For old times' sake." Later Bogart asks him to "Play it," but he never says "again."

STARS AND STARLETS

Marilyn Monroe was blonde

Marilyn Monroe (Norma Jean Baker, 1926–62) originally had natural, mid-brown hair, which she later bleached with hydrogen peroxide. In addition, she lost quite a few pounds, had operations on her nose and chin, and changed her hairline. The shape of her breasts was altered by rubber inserts inside her bra. In addition, both her voice and gestures were changed to suit Hollywood.

Elvis Presley had black hair

With Elvis Presley (1935–77) too, not everything was genuine. Hidden beneath his black, pomaded quiff was naturally sandy brown hair. He apparently wanted the dark color so that he would look like movie star Tony Curtis.

Greta Garbo wanted to be alone

The enchanting Swedish movie star Greta Garbo (1905–1990) did say she wanted to be alone in the movie *Grand Hotel* (1932). But in her real life she insisted that she never said, "I want to be alone." She said, "I want to be *let* alone."

The only real source for Santa Claus was Saint Nicholas

"Santa Claus" naturally developed out of Saint Nicholas, whose historical personage was Saint Nicholas, Bishop of Myra (today Demre in Turkey). Saint Nicholas died on December 6, 655, and was known as a great benefactor. But how did the good bishop get his reindeer? One possible source is Sari Saltuk, a wandering dervish who lived in Khorasan in Persia in the 14th century. Saltuk was generous, fond of children and very popular. After his death a host of adventurous tales grew up around him, including a story that he flew to Lapland with his winged black horse, Ankabil, and there he remains immortal. It is possible that in Lapland the winged black horse gradually changed into the more familiar reindeer.

Betty Crocker was a real person

First heard from in 1921 answering consumers' questions about products, Betty Crocker symbolized home cooking and wholesome family values for General Mills Foods. She went on to write several cookbooks and perform in radio and television shows. She even had a street named after her. However, she never actually existed. She was initially created to give a personal touch to letters to consumers, with her last name borrowed from a company director (William Crocker) and her first name chosen for its friendliness. When her picture first appeared in 1936, her features were a composite based on the faces of about 20 real women. Betty Crocker's image has changed many times over the years, updated periodically to reflect changes in American women.

Barbie is American

The famous doll first saw the light of day in Germany. She was modeled on a comic character by the name of Lilli in an illustrated paper in 1955, and was actually intended as a gag for stag nights. One year later, however, Ruth Handler (1917–2002), the co-founder of the toy firm Mattel, discovered the doll and brought it back to the United States for her daughter Barbara. A little later, she bought the rights to Lilli and introduced Barbie to the American market in 1959. The blonde's full name is Barbara Millicent Rogers.

The teddy bear was invented in America

There are numerous tales of how it happened that a plush bear came to acquire the name of the American President, Theodore Roosevelt (1858–1919). However, the stuffed bear was not invented in America, but in Germany. Margaret Steiff (1847–1909), a seamstress, invented the cuddly toy in 1880, initially in the form of a felt elephant. She quickly became a successful businesswoman, but the idea and the model for a bear came from her nephew, Richard Steiff (1877–1939). In 1902, the first "teddy" saw the light of day when it was known as "55PB" (55 centimeters, plush bear).

FUN AND FESTIVALS

Father Christmas' red coat was invented by Coca-Cola

The company is extremely happy to lay claim to this. In 1931, for an advertisement they commissioned a painting of a typical "Santa Claus." Coat and pointed hat were the typical "Coca-Cola red," with white fur trimming, bucket-top boots and a red, big fat nose. But Santa Claus had been depicted wearing a red coat since about 1885 in the United States.

The Oktoberfest begins in October

The Munich Oktoberfest begins in September and ends on the first Sunday in October. It is derived from a horse race that took place on October 17, 1810, on the occasion of the wedding of the person who later became King Ludwig I (1786–1886). The race was such a success that it was repeated the very next year, accompanied by an agricultural exhibition. Later, the festival was moved forward to take advantage of the best of late-summer weather in September.

Picnics are a British invention

Naturally, no one invented eating in the open air. However, in the 17th and 18th centuries it because fashionably romantic among the better circles in France. Marie-Antoinette (1755–93) had a particular weakness for "shepherdess idylls" in the open air. The picnic craze affected the British Isles in the middle of the 18th century.

Geishas are always female

Geishas are professional entertainers who perform traditional Japanese rituals. The first geishas were exclusively male. Female geishas ("*Onna*" geishas) first appeared in the 17th century and at first were forbidden from displaying any erotic behavior, so that they would not compete with prostitutes. However, they developed their own subtle form of eroticism.

Chinese checkers is a Chinese version of the game checkers

The game was invented in the United States and given the name "Chinese checkers" to make it seem more exotic. It is played on a six-pointed star board with six different colors of marbles. The marbles are moved around the board by as many as six players.

SPORTS AND SCIENCE

Lactic acid causes stiff muscles

An excess of lactic acid in the muscles may lead, directly after sport, to burning in the corresponding part of the body. This can be eliminated if one continues to move gently, so that the level of acid in the muscles drops. Stiff muscles, however, that occur only after a certain delay, and which may last for a long time, arise through fine tears in the muscle fibers. Stiffness occurs particularly easily in muscles that have not been properly trained. While the remedy of "doing it again" does actually help with excess lactic acid, with muscle stiffness rest is advisable, so that the fibers can heal.

Carbohydrates produce muscles

Eating carbohydrates results in a temporary surge of energy. To build up muscles, however, the body needs protein. In addition, B-vitamins, iron, zinc and folic acid are important.

Only intensive exercise strengthens the heart

The heart muscle is best strengthened by consistent exercise. Using the heart for 10 minutes every day is far better than one intensive training session every week. Even regular walking is better than an intermittent round of jogging.

Darwin preached the survival of the fittest

For one thing, it was not Charles Darwin (1809–82), but the philosopher Herbert Spencer (1820–1903) who coined the phrase "survival of the fittest." For another, what was meant by this was something completely different from what we mean by "fit" nowadays. Evolutionary biologists do not maintain that those who are most in the best shape, the strongest or the most capable ultimately succeed, but always those that are most suited to the living conditions in which they find themselves. So "fit" should be interpreted as meaning "suitable" or "appropriate."

People lose weight in fitness gyms

With regular fitness training, people build up their muscles. Certainly fat disappears in doing so, but because muscle tissue is, on average, heavier than fat deposits, it can still happen that one gains weight. However, the body's girth decreases with the alteration of fat into muscle mass.

Light blows to the back of the head increase the ability to think creatively

The opposite is the case. Scientists at the University of Helsinki did some research on athletes who occasionally receive a blow to the head, such as professional boxers or soccer players good at headers. They found that blows to the head may not only cause slight concussion but also create slight tears in the brain. Memory, concentration and rapidity of thought were measurably impaired. It is true that these deficiencies went back to normal fairly quickly. Athletes who protected their heads with helmets did not show any such symptoms in the tests — even in particularly rough sports like football.

ONE FOR, ONE AGAINST

Churchill was against sports

Whether the British Prime Minister, Winston Churchill (1874–1965), was actually the originator of the famous phrase "No sports, only whisky," is by no means beyond doubt. It is possible that he did say it. But certainly he did not mean it seriously. Churchill was a successful cricketer, golfer, swimmer and fencer. Above all, he liked to ride horses. His active war service was as a cavalryman. In addition, he was a passionate polo player, and went fox hunting into his 70s.

With his "*Mens sana in corpore sano*," Juvenal was recommending sporting activity

The Roman satirist Juvenal (ca. 60–127 AD) was making fun of the mania for fitness that was all the rage even then. In fact, he was not saying that a sound mind would be found in a sound body, but suggesting that it would be desirable if sound bodies also had sound minds. Personally, however, in view of the hordes of ancient mindless musclemen, he doubted whether there was any connection.

BASEBALL

An American invented baseball

Baseball probably evolved from an English game called "rounders," and it crossed the ocean and was adapted for American players. The first rules and diagrams illustrating how the game should be played were documented by an American engineer named Alexander J. Cartwright. He belonged to a club called the New York Knickerbockers, who played a form of early baseball in New York in 1845. Cartwright later moved to Hawaii and established a baseball league there.

The term "baseball" was coined in the 19th century

A form of baseball was played in England at least 100 years before Alexander J. Cartwright and the New York Knickerbockers made it official. The game was mentioned in a children's book called *A Little Pretty Pocket-Book* in 1744: "B is for Base-ball/the Ball once struck off/Away flies the Boy/To the next destin'd Post/and then Home with Joy." And in Jane Austen's *Northanger Abbey* (1815), baseball is mentioned in connection with one of the characters: "It was not very wonderful that Catherine, who had by nature nothing heroic about her, should prefer cricket, base ball, riding on horseback, and running about the country, at the age of fourteen, to books."

Babe Ruth ended his career with the New York Yankees

Babe Ruth (1895–1948) was traded to the Boston Braves in 1935 and he retired before the end of the season.

The Brooklyn Dodgers were named for their athletic agility

The Brooklyn Dodgers have been the Los Angeles Dodgers since 1958, but before that they were based in Brooklyn, and named after a local phenomenon. In the 1890s Brooklyn was crisscrossed with many streetcar trolley lines and people had to sort through the maze to reach Eastern Park, where the baseball team played. Brooklynites were affectionately dubbed "Trolley Dodgers" and the local team followed suit.

HOCKEY AND PING-PONG

Hockey is Canada's only true national sport

It shares that honor with lacrosse: by virtue of an act of Parliament in 1994, hockey was named Canada's national winter sport and lacrosse its national summer sport.

Ping-Pong is called Ping-Pong

The real name of the popular game is table tennis. "Ping-Pong" is a registered trademark of a company that manufactures games. Like "Kleenex" and "Velcro," Ping-Pong is one of those brand names that stuck to the product and became more common than the technical term.

Ping-Pong was invented by the Chinese

Table tennis was invented by the English upper classes in the second half of the 18th century. This game, which would happily while away a rainy weekend, was originally played in a very rustic fashion. A net was strung across a large table, balls were cut from champagne corks or rubber, and the bats were the tops of cigar boxes, frying pans or badminton bats. In 1875, the engineer James Gibb laid down the first set of rules. Sixteen years later, Gibb discovered celluloid balls in the United States, which proved ideal for the game. Their clicking noise gave rise to the name "Ping-Pong," which he promptly registered as a trademark.

FOOTBALL AND SOCCER

Cheerleading is a female sport

The first cheerleaders were exclusively male. In 1898, the University of Minnesota apparently had the first organized cheerleading team to rouse vocal support during football games. The first female cheerleaders appeared in the 1920s, and then a division of labor rapidly developed between the boys, who played football or hockey, and the girls, who pursued cheerleading as a sport.

The San Diego Chargers were named for their ability to run with the ball

The original owner of the football team, Barron Hilton, also owned the Carte Blanche credit card company. The team was named in a contest in 1959 by Gerald Courteney, a resident of Hollywood, who suggested the name because of Hilton's credit card empire.

Soccer was always the sport of the "man in the street"

In the 19th century, soccer (known as football in Europe) was popular among young English college students. In 1846, students at Oxford University laid down the first set of rules. At that time on the Continent it was mostly schoolboys and students who enjoyed kicking a ball around a field. It was only in the 1930s that the working class gradually adopted the sport as their own.

MARATHONS AND THE OLYMPICS

A marathon is the same distance as the road between Athens and Marathon

Although the length of a marathon run (26 miles, 385 yards/42.195 kilometers) is based on the distance between Athens and Marathon (21.4 miles/34.5 kilometers), it does not correspond exactly. For the first few years of the modern-day Olympics, the distance varied, depending on the route. In 1896 the distance was 24.85 miles (40 kilometers) and in 1920 it was 26.56 miles (42.75 kilometers). During the Olympic Games in London in 1908, the course was adjusted to give the royal family a good view of the race. It started in front of Windsor Castle and finished in front of the royal box in the stadium. The distance was exactly 26 miles, 385 yards (42.195 kilometers). In 1921 this distance was agreed on as the official marathon distance.

Women first started to play soccer in Europe after the Second World War

In cultures such as the Inuit and Native North Americans and in the European Middle Ages, men and women often played soccer-like games together. Frequently whole villages or tribes opposed one another. In British schools, girls first played soccer (known in Europe as football) in 1863. The first official women's soccer was recorded in 1895, and the first true international game was won by England against France in 1920. After the First World War, every English town had its own women's team, and top matches were followed by as many as 50,000 spectators. In 1921 the English Football Association banned female soccer teams from using their fields, and it didn't become official again until the 1960s.

The first marathon runner brought news of a victory

The story of the very first marathon is a legend. The way the story goes, Pheidippides, a soldier, brought news of a Greek victory over the Persians from Marathon to Athens 21.4 miles (34.5 kilometers), but then dropped dead in the marketplace. Herodotus (485–425 BC) wrote an account of the Battle of Marathon, which is probably the original source of the story. In Herodotus, a professional long-distance runner, Pheiidippides, ran from Marathon to Sparta, a distance of 155 miles (250 kilometers), in just two days. He was seeking help for the Greeks in Marathon, who were threatened by the Persians. Whether this run actually occurred is questionable, but he certainly was running for help, not to announce a victory.

Olympic medals were only ever given for sporting achievements

In antiquity, musicians and dramatists also competed for the victor's crown — although not so often at Olympia as at the other games, such as the Pythian Games, which were held at Delphi in honor of Apollo. In 1912 in Stockholm, Baron Pierre Coubertin (1863–1937) arranged for writers, architects, sculptors, painters and musicians to compete for a total of 18 gold medals. He won the title of literary Olympic champion himself. Similar contests were held six times until 1948.

CRICKET AND BOOMERANGS

Cricket is an English game

The origins of cricket are much disputed, but some evidence suggests that a version of the game originally came to Europe from Persia sometime in the ninth century AD. The name is thought to come from the Flemish, "*met de krik ketsen*" ("hit with the stick"). However, the British made it their own and then carried cricket to the countries of their former empire, where, in some cases it has become more popular than in England.

Cricket is an old-fashioned game losing its popularity

On the contrary, cricket is a thriving sport in many countries all over the world. The International Cricket Congress had 47 member countries in 1997 and by 2005 the number had more than doubled to 96. From Afghanistan to Zimbabwe, from India to New Zealand, from the West Indies to Argentina, cricket is a growing international game.

The strange scoring at tennis comes from England

People tend to blame the British for odd measurement or scoring systems. But the scoring for tennis comes from France. There, at the beginning of modern times, tennis was played for money, and the corresponding coins were worth 15, 30 and 45 sous. Probably, though verbal slovenliness, at some stage 45 became 40. Tennis is supposed to have been invented in the 13th century by French monks, who included the ceiling of the cloisters in their play.

Boomerangs always return

It is possible to throw a boomerang so that it returns — if one can. But the original hunting boomerangs did not return. The wood was curved because it was then possible to throw harder, straighter and more accurately than with a straight stick. Hunting boomerangs were up to 4.5 pounds (2 kilograms) in weight and could fly as far as 650 feet (200 meters). Returning boomerangs were used in Australia in Aboriginal contests and for driving birds into nets.

Boomerangs were used exclusively by Australian Aborigines

Many cultures around the world have used a form of boomerang, including Native North Americans and ancient Egyptians. Evidence of boomerangs has also been found in Europe, South America and India.

LANGUAGE AND NUMBERS

The Hebrew and Arabic alphabets have different origins from our own

All alphabets between western Europe and India derive from an alphabet that was introduced by the Phoenicians about 1200 BC. This was the first alphabet in which symbols did not stand for words or syllables, but for single sounds. It was a purely consonantal alphabet, as the Hebrew and Arabic alphabets still are. The Greeks were the first to add vowels, and they also altered the direction in which words and sentences were written.

Chaucer wrote *The Canterbury Tales* in Old English

Old English, a very different language than English, was spoken between AD 450 and 1100. After the Norman Conquest, the influence of the French language transformed Old English. Geoffrey Chaucer (1343–1400) wrote in Middle English, which was spoken between 1100 and 1500. Modern English has been in use from 1500 to the present. *Beowulf*, an epic poem written before 1000, was written in Old English.

Arabic numbers originated in Arabia

The system of numerical notation numbers we use now (where a number changes its value according to its position) was developed in India in about AD 500. It gradually spread to Arabia and

Persia, and from there to Europe in about 1100, replacing Roman numerals.

There is one modern Arabic language

Although a common Arabic written language, Modern Standard Arabic, is used throughout the Arab world, the spoken Arabic language varies drastically from country to country. Spoken Arabic in Morocco, for example, is quite different from spoken Arabic in Iraq.

WORDS

Everything has a name

To language philosophers, the boundaries of human speech are also those of the world. Things, conditions and feelings for which there are no words do not exist. That seems logical, but it doesn't make sense. A few years ago, for example, it was realized that no one knew a name for the thing that is used at supermarket checkouts to separate your purchases from those of the next person. Similarly, anyone who has learned some skill by themselves often does not have the name for the various tools that might be used. We store things that we do not talk about to others in our minds under "images" rather than under "words."

The expression "don't bug me" derives from insects

Ants, mosquitoes and fleas may be annoying, but bugs are unrelated to this expression. It came into popular use among African Americans, originating in West Africa, where *bagu* means "to annoy."

A dock, a pier and a wharf are all the same thing

These words are often used interchangeably, but they mean different things. A dock is the water where the boat pulls up to a wharf or pier. A wharf usually runs parallel to the shore, while a pier sticks out at a right angle from the shore.

An igloo is a domed house made of snow

"Igloo" is an Inuktitut word meaning "house." It can refer to any kind of house. The word has become associated with the traditional snow house built by Inuit in times gone by. A snow house is built from blocks of snow and is often dug partway beneath the surface of the snow for extra warmth.

A snob is someone who looks down on others

There is a much-disputed theory that the word once meant the opposite, and the word "snob" is the abbreviation of "*sine nobilitate*" (s.nob), which means "without a title to nobility." The way the story goes, upper class boys of noble birth at the prestigious Eton College in England in the 1830s referred to boys who had no title as "snobs."

American gangsters coined the term "rub out"

The colorful phrase meaning "kill" has long been associated with the American gangsters of the 1920s. However, the expression goes back to Middle English, and white trappers in North America used it in the early 1800s.

POETRY

Clement Clarke Moore wrote "'Twas the Night Before Christmas"

The name of the poem he wrote in 1822 was "A Visit from Saint Nicholas." And contrary to popular belief, the jolly old elf says "Happy Christmas" not "Merry Christmas" in the last line of the poem: "Happy Christmas to all and to all a good-night."

The sickly John Keats was forced into the study of medicine

Although John Keats (1795–1821) died of tuberculosis at the age of 25, he was not ill until the last few years of his life. Both his mother and his brother also died of tuberculosis. Keats studied medicine but dropped out before his final exams to pursue a literary career as a poet.

Lizzie Borden murdered her father and her stepmother

The jury acquitted Lizzie Borden (1860–1927) after just over an hour's deliberation. There was not enough evidence to convict her of the crime, and her guilt remains questionable. However, public opinion has always been against her. The catchy little rhyme written about her didn't help her cause: "Lizzie Borden took an axe/And gave her mother forty whacks/When she saw what she had done/She gave her father forty-one."

MARK TWAIN DIDN'T SAY IT BUT WISHED HE HAD

Naked Twain

"I would rather go to bed with Lillian Russell stark naked than with Ulysses S. Grant in full military regalia." Mark Twain (1835–1910) was often given credit for pithy sayings he didn't originate. People thought he came up with this gem, but he didn't.

Twain and smoking

"Giving up smoking is easy. I've done it hundreds of times." He didn't say this either.

Twain and lies

"There are three kinds of lies: lies, damn lies and statistics." Twain quoted this in his autobiography. He said Benjamin Disraeli came up with it.

Twain and Wagner

"Wagner's music is better than it sounds." Twain loved to quote this saying, which came from the clever and funny Edgar Wilson ("Bill") Nye (1850–96), a fellow humorist and writer.

Twain and the weather

"Everybody talks about the weather, but nobody does anything about it." Charles Dudley Warner, a journalist and friend of Twain's attributed this remark to Twain, who insisted that it was Warner who first said it. Later this same remark was ascribed to Will Rogers. Twain did have his own quote about the weather: "If you don't like the weather in New England now, just wait a few minutes."

THEY NEVER SAID IT

"Lead on, Macduff!"

What Macbeth really says to McDuff is, "Lay on, Macduff, and damned be him who first cries 'Hold! enough!'" William Shakespeare's *Macbeth*, Act 5, Scene 7.

"Methinks the lady doth protest too much"

Gertrude, Hamlet's mother, says this: "The lady doth protest too much, methinks." She's reacting to a play-within-a-play, written by Hamlet and acted out by the traveling players. *Hamlet*, Act 3, Scene 2.

"A little knowledge is a dangerous thing"

Learning, not knowledge, is dangerous, according to Alexander Pope (1688–1744), although he is often misquoted. His exact words were, "A little learning is a dangerous thing/Drink deep, or taste not the Pierian spring:/There shallow draughts intoxicate the brain,/and drinking largely sobers us again."

"Elementary, my dear Watson"

Sherlock Holmes never said it. Not in the four novels or 56 short stories written by Sir Arthur Conan Doyle. He did say "Elementary" and he did often address his friend as "my dear Watson," but the two phrases were never joined together until Sherlock Holmes started making his appearance in the movies.

"I must get out of these wet clothes and into a dry martini"

Alexander Wollcott (1887–1943), a well-known journalist never said this. It was his friend, Robert Benchley (1889–1945), a humorist and actor, who heard a press agent say it and Benchley used it in one of his movies.

"Beam me up, Scotty!"

Although this is perhaps the most famous and often-repeated line from the popular 1960s television show, *Star Trek*, Captain Kirk (played by William Shatner) never actually said this when he wanted to be teletransported back to the *Enterprise*. He got pretty close: he did say "*Enterprise*, beam us up," and he did say "Beam us up, Mr. Scott," and he even said "Scotty, beam me up," but he never actually uttered the immortal words, "Beam me up, Scotty." However, it still continues to be happily misquoted by fans of the series.

INFECTIONS AND FIRST AID

Dirt is unhealthy

Natural dirt is generally "healthy." It does indeed contain germs and bacteria, but these are normally so harmless that the body copes with them with ease. Anyone who lives in a sterile, germ-free environment cannot develop their immune system's powers of resistance.

Rusty nails can cause tetanus

Tetanus is caused by the bacterium *Clostridium tetani*, which lives in the soil, but in particular in the excrement of humans and animals. If, for example, you injure yourself on a piece of rusty wire, then the danger of tetanus only occurs if, simultaneously, earth gets into the wound, which can possibly happen outdoors. This is why it is advisable to be immunized against tetanus and have booster shots every 10 years.

Blood poisoning is indicated by a red mark, and when it reaches your heart you die

Blood poisoning, or septicemia, actually presents itself through weakness, fever and other physical disorders. The red mark that is often visible after injuries is local inflammation. This inflammation can certainly extend to the lymphatic system and eventually even lead to blood poisoning, but it doesn't "reach the heart." Nevertheless, septicemia is a serious condition. In the United States, septicemia is the 10th-leading cause of death, with over 30,000 blood poisoning fatalities each year.

Ointment helps burns

After suffering a burn, only one thing helps: cooling the tissue so that the heat that was transferred in the burn does not lead to further damage. Doctors advise that a small burned or scalded area should be held under cold water for at least 20 minutes. Only after this is it sensible to apply any ointment in an effort to soothe pain. Larger areas of burned skin or more serious burns need to be treated immediately by a physician.

Ticks should be twisted out of the skin

Ticks should be carefully pulled straight out of the skin, as quickly as possible, so that the tick has as little chance as possible to transfer the pathogens that cause Lyme disease or Rocky Mountain spotted fever that it could be carrying. Above all, when pulling a tick from the skin, you should ensure that the mouthparts are completely removed, otherwise they could result in unpleasant inflammation.

Before removing a tick, coat it in oil

Some folk remedies advise first coating the tick in oil, glue or other fluids before removing it from the skin. This is not advisable, first because it takes longer, and second because the tick may inject its stomach contents into the wound before it suffocates.

When you have a nosebleed you should hold your head back

All this will do is help prevent the blood from staining your clothes — it will not stanch the bleeding. Instead, the blood will run down into your throat. With extreme bleeding, holding your head back can even lead to choking and vomiting. When you have a nosebleed you should sit down and tilt your head slightly forward. Pinch the fleshy part of your nose with your thumb and forefinger and hold it in place for at least five minutes. Holding a tissue to your pinched nostrils will help soak up any blood.

SLEEPING AND BREATHING

Dreams last only seconds

For a long time researchers thought that any dream, even if it seemed to be very long, lasted just a few seconds. In fact, even when you nod off for a short time, it can seem as if you are experiencing a whole novel. Since then, however, it has been determined that dreams may last as long as 30 minutes. Toward morning, they are generally longer than those that occur just after going to sleep.

Many people don't dream

Everyone dreams, with the exception of rare individuals who have suffered from brain damage to the area that controls dreaming. Most people who say that they never dream still experience dreams during sleep — they just don't remember them.

Sleep before midnight is the healthiest

The greatest effect on health comes from the first two or three hours of sleep, because this sleep is deepest and thus most refreshing. Whether it occurs before or after midnight is irrelevant. Everybody has their own body rhythm, which they should try to keep to on a regular basis. Scientific investigations have produced no evidence that early birds lead more healthy lives than night owls, but regardless of your patterns, you should aim to get at least five hours of sleep per day. More may be pleasant, but is not absolutely essential for medical reasons.

Breathing from your abdomen is good

No one is capable of breathing down into their abdomen. When breathing, air enters the lobes of the lungs — and nowhere else. However, when we breathe extremely deeply the diaphragm, a muscle that separates the chest cavity from the abdomen, is stretched. This is called diaphragmatic breathing. You can try this kind of healthy, deep breathing by lying on your back while resting a small book on your abdomen, then raising the book as high as you can with each intake of breath.

EYES AND EARS

Reading in poor light damages your eyesight

No matter what your mother says, this isn't true. Reading in dim light will strain your eyes and can cause a headache, but after a rest your eyes are as good as new.

In the Middle Ages no one wore glasses

Even in antiquity it was known that shaped lenses could change images. But this knowledge was lost in Europe. It was rediscovered around 1270, when *Optics* by the Arabian mathematician Alhazen (ca. 965–1040) was translated into Latin. With this theoretical background, people soon began to shape lenses so that they would correct weaknesses in eyesight. Where and when the first eyeglasses were made is not known with certainty — the leading contender is Italy circa 1280 — but it was certainly the monasteries that played a leading role. The oldest depictions of people wearing glasses come from the middle of the 14th century and are to be found in the monastery of San Nicolo in Treviso. It is true, however, that these glasses did not have frames.

When we see spots before our eyes, they are an optical phenomenon

Frequently, small brownish gray spots appear in the field of view, and these move with every movement of the eyeball. These spots, called "floaters," are not an optical phenomenon, but tiny bits of debris in the vitreous humor, a jelly-like substance that lies behind the lens and fills the middle part of the eye. Floaters may sometimes disappear spontaneously. They are only a cause for worry if eyesight is extensively blurred or flashes of light are seen. These symptoms could indicate a detached retina.

Sugar rots teeth

Sugar is not the crux of the problem. Teeth are covered in enamel, the hardest substance found in the body. It is, however, susceptible to acids. Acids from food can attack the enamel. These are found not only in sweet foods like ice cream and candy, but also in healthy vegetable and fruit juices. Particularly dangerous, however, are sticky foods that cling to the teeth. These encourage the formation of plaque, which is a mixture of the remnants of food, bacteria and the metabolic products of bacteria. A layer of plaque can form within 24 hours. This can contain the bacteria that turn simple carbohydrates, such as those in sugar, white flour or potatoes, into acids that damage the tooth enamel. The more frequently these bacteria get fresh provisions, the more acid they produce. So it is more damaging to your teeth to repeatedly drink lemonade or apple juice than it is to eat several chocolate bars at one sitting.

Helen Keller was born unable to see or hear

Helen Keller (1880–1968) was born with normal hearing and sight, but a bad case of what doctors think was either scarlet fever or meningitis when she was 19 months old left her blind and deaf. When she grew up she became an ardent author, social activist and lecturer. Her courage and determination in overcoming the obstacles in her life have been an inspiration to many handicapped people.

TEETH

Teeth should be cleaned after eating

Generally this is fine, but cleaning your teeth is not recommended immediately after eating acidic foods, because the acids can soften the enamel, which is then damaged when the teeth are brushed. After eating acidic foods, it is advisable to first rinse out your mouth with water to remove most of the acids, and then brush away any persistent remnants of the meal about a half hour later.

Electric toothbrushes are more thorough than manual ones

That's incorrect. But children, in particular, tend to brush longer with an electric toothbrush, which is advantageous. A small brush head with good reach, and dense bristles for powerful brushing are also desirable. It is also important to clean between the teeth with interdental brushes or dental floss.

SKIN

Rosy cheeks indicate good health

Just as pale cheeks suggest illness, rosy cheeks are usually taken as a sign of good health. However, rosy cheeks in children sometimes indicates a fever, and in adults can be a sign of heart disease or heavy drinking.

Expensive moisturizers can stop wrinkles from forming

Skin becomes wrinkled from sun damage, smoking and the natural aging process. Moisturizers can help trap moisture on the surface of the skin, which makes it look younger and healthier, but no moisturizer — cheap or expensive — can stop the skin from getting wrinkles.

CELL PHONES AND SURGERY

Plastic surgery involves plastic

The name has nothing to do with plastic — it derives from *plastikos*, a Greek word meaning "to mold" or "to take form." Another common misconception about plastic surgery is that it is chiefly concerned with superficial changes to people's bodies, like nose jobs, facelifts and breast implants. However, 60 percent of plastic surgery is reconstruction surgery following serious burns, injuries or birth defects.

HEAT AND COLD

Sweat smells

In general, sweat does not smell. Otherwise people would go into a sauna with clothespins on their noses. However, sweat does contain many organic substances, and these serve as food for various bacteria. When these bacteria begin to break the sweat down, only then are nasty smelling waste products created, which can make sweat so offensive.

Deodorants freshen the body

This only appears to be true because they can feel cool against the skin. Deodorants do not prevent sweating; they hamper the multiplication of the bacteria that attack the sweat and create the troublesome smell. Deodorants are often combined with antiperspirants, which actually do reduce sweating by closing the body's pores. But that certainly does not produce freshness.

We sweat more in humid weather because it's hotter out

Humidity has no influence on the actual temperature, but a dry 80°F (27°C) day will feel cooler than a humid day at the same temperature. This is because our bodies sweat as a reaction to overheating, and on a hot, dry day, the sweat will evaporate, causing us to feel cooler. On hot, humid days, however, the ability for our sweat to evaporate decreases because the air is saturated with moisture. This lowered ability for our bodies to cool off makes the temperature seem hotter.

Cell phones are unhealthy

Specifically, there's a lot of conjecture over whether or not cell phones cause cancer. As yet there is no proof of this. That does not mean that it has already been firmly established that cell phones have no effect on health — just that there are no confirmed studies that show that they do. When cellular, or wireless, phones are being used or are in standby mode, they emit low levels of radio frequency energy (RF) in the microwave range. Although high RF levels can produce health effects by heating up tissue, exposure to low RF levels that do not heat tissue causes no known negative effects. Regardless, people who are sensitive to electrical fields do get headaches with prolonged use of these phones.

If you shave your armpit hair, you sweat less

Shaving has no effect whatsoever on the production of sweat. People who have shaved their armpits may appear to sweat more because they often end up getting wet patches on their clothing since their sweat can't be "trapped" by hair.

We get chilblains when it is very cold

Chilblains arise through a lack of blood supply, damage to the blood vessels and problems with circulation. These disorders cause an increased sensitivity of the skin in certain parts of the body to humidity and cold temperatures. Chilblains appear as bluish, flat patches beneath the skin, which are often extremely sensitive and painful, but which may also become numb. They occur less often when it is extremely cold than after a long exposure to damp, cold weather.

Colds are caused by cold weather

Colds are caused by viruses. However, if the mucous membranes in your airways are chilled, then their blood supply is reduced. In this state, they can be more easily attacked by pathogens. The mucous membranes are most susceptible in damp cold. People tend to have more colds in the winter than in the summer mainly because they spend more time indoors with others in closed spaces where there is less ventilation.

DRUGS AND DISEASE

Drugs work the same for men and women

Medical research is recognizing that this is not the case. Everybody reacts individually to drugs and, in particular, there are factors that may cause drugs to have different effects on men and women. Aspirin, for example, appears to offer men a certain amount of protection against heart attacks. It doesn't protect women from heart attacks to the same degree, but does cut their chances of having a stroke. Drugs that are fat-soluble, such as anesthetics, need to be given in different dosages to women, because most women have a higher percentage of body fat than men. The concentration of enzymes in the body can also affect the way that medicines work. This applies not just to men and women, but also appears to affect people of different ethnic origins as well.

Painkillers cure headaches

Painkillers suppress sensitivity to pain — they do not cure the cause of the pain. For this reason there is the danger of overtaxing your body, which actually requires rest to heal, because you no longer feel any pain. On the other hand, you should not simply "endure" or ignore any pain. The body seems to develop a "pain memory" for any pain that is encountered frequently, and this can persist even after the basic cause of pain has disappeared.

The plague was spread through contact with people with the disease

The bubonic plague is spread through bites from infected fleas — usually rat fleas that have fed on rodents infected with the plague bacteria *Yersina pestis*. In the 14th century, the plague killed up to one-third of Europe's population — an estimated 34 million people — and it still breaks out occasionally in parts of the world. However, keeping the rat population under control is a good preventative measure, and the disease can be treated with antibiotics.

Leprosy is highly contagious

Hansen's disease, better known as leprosy, is caused by a microbacterium, *Mycobacterium leprae*. It can occur in two different forms — tuberculoid leprosy or lepromatous leprosy. The first is milder and quickly cured, while the latter is more serious and can persist for a long time. Scientists believe that leprosy may be transmitted between people through respiratory droplets, but this has not been definitively proven. It is very hard to catch, and doctors who have deliberately exposed themselves to leprosy patients have not contracted the disease.

Polio has been eradicated

We were nearly there. In 1840, Dr. Jacob von Heine identified poliomyelitis as a contagious disease. The United States suffered its first significant outbreak of infantile paralysis in 1894, and with advances in travel, polio soon became a worldwide epidemic. The Global Polio Eradication Initiative was established in 1988 with the goal of eliminating it altogether, and within 15 years, the number of cases had dwindled to just a few hundred worldwide. But in 2003, the Nigerian government suspended immunization in its northern states and soon a new outbreak occurred. In the first few months of 2006, Nigeria had 310 cases. The nearby countries of Benin, Cameroon, Côte d'Ivoire, Ghana, Mali and Botswana also became reinfected. Polio is also firmly reestablished in Sudan, Chad and Burkina Faso, and new cases have been found in previously polio-free Yemen and Indonesia.

ALLERGIES

Hay fever comes from hay

People who suffer from hay fever are allergic to various pollens, especially ragweed. But they are not allergic to hay. And they don't get a fever.

People who live in cities are less likely to get hay fever than those who live in the country

On the contrary, research has shown that children who live on farms and who are surrounded by animals and a variety of pollens from a young age far more rarely develop hay fever or other allergies. Scientists believe that exposure to these common allergens at a young age may work in the same way that vaccinations work to prevent serious diseases.

Cat and dog hair cause allergies

Pet allergies are not caused by hair, but by dander, which is flakes of dead skin. Saliva, urine and excrement also contribute to allergic reactions. Washing a pet every week can reduce their dander by about 90 percent.

DIABETES AND HEART ATTACKS

Heart attacks are a white-collar illness

Heart attacks are an illness of the lower classes. People of lower social status have more heart attacks than managerial workers. This is thought to be because of different access to health care, and different lifestyle and behavior patterns — the lower classes often experience less healthy lives, smoke more and get less exercise. As well, on average they suffer more from stress.

You get diabetes by eating too many sweet foods

It's not that simple. There are two forms of diabetes. Those people who are unable to produce enough insulin — or produce none at all — have type 1 diabetes, while those whose bodies are insulin deficient and unable to use the insulin they produce (known as insulin resistance) have type 2 diabetes. Both types have a genetic component. Being overweight increases the risk of developing type 2 diabetes, so people who have a history of diabetes in their families are advised to manage their weight. However, just eating a lot of sugar won't cause diabetes in someone who doesn't have the genes for it, or who maintains a healthy weight.

Adult-onset diabetes only occurs in old people

Although most people with type 2 diabetes (previously called adult-onset diabetes) are over the age of 40, it has been diagnosed in children as young as 2 who have a family history of diabetes. The greater incidence of obesity and inactivity in children in recent years is blamed for the increasing number of diagnoses.

HIV AND AIDS

HIV can be transmitted through saliva

The only way HIV infection can spread from person to person is through exposure to blood, semen, vaginal fluid or breast milk. There has never been a documented case of HIV being spread through saliva.

HIV always passes from mothers to their newborn children

Before modern treatments were developed, about 25 percent of mothers with HIV infected their newborn babies. Now, with new methods of treatment and more awareness of how HIV is spread, only about 2 percent of mothers infect their babies.

AIDS can be cured

There is no cure for HIV and AIDS. Because of advances in research, medication can now control many of the symptoms of HIV. But the drugs are expensive, they have to be taken every day and the side effects can be very difficult to live with.

AIDS is a death sentence

It used to be — in the 1980s. Now people with HIV or AIDS can live long lives if they have access to good medical care and antiretroviral drugs (ARVs).

STOMACHACHES

Most stomach problems are psychosomatic

Having long disregarded the psychological components of illnesses, nowadays there is often a tendency to overestimate their significance. A specific example of this is gastritis. It was thought that inflammation of the lining of the stomach and stomach ulcers arose from suppressed anger and stress that were being bottled up by the sufferer. Certainly, this may have sometimes been the case. But this judgment did an injustice to all those whose gastritis had purely physical causes. Since then, the bacterium *Helicobacter pylori* has been discovered, which is responsible for a multitude of stomach ulcers — and it is treated with antibiotics, not psychotherapy.

Extremely acidic food can eat a hole through the stomach

This is a popular horror story with parents who want to spoil their children's excessive consumption of sour candies and other junk food, but it is not true. The human stomach contains hydrochloric acid to digest food and is not damaged by any acidic foods, although excessive consumption of some foods can cause a stomachache.

Anyone who drinks a lot of water after eating fruit gets a stomachache

There once was a certain degree of truth to this. In the past, before the age of water sanitation, drinking water contained more chemicals and particles that could cause fruit in the stomach to ferment. Nowadays, there is no need to worry about it.

THICK AND THIN

Dieting is healthy

Being overweight is a risk factor for various serious diseases. That does not by any means imply that slimming down is inevitably healthy. What is certain is that crash diets are definitely not healthy, because after them, the body eagerly stocks up on nutrients and calories, which can start the notorious "yo-yo effect." Various studies show, however, that drastic dieting may lead to as many health risks as being overweight. Diets confuse the metabolism, which may lead to a disturbance of water balance and the heart's regular rhythm, as well as problems with the liver and gallbladder. A gradual change of diet and regular exercise are far more healthy than radical measures.

Overweight people eat too much

It's not that simple. We all know people who can "eat like a pig" and always stay slender, as well as others who hardly seem to eat anything but still can't shed pounds. A variety of factors affect a person's weight, including genetics, lifestyle and metabolic rate. Basically, we gain weight when we take in more calories than we burn. So, even though we can't change our genetics, we can reduce the number of calories we take in by cutting back on high-fat and high-calorie foods, and burn more calories each day by exercising.

Diet soft drinks can help you lose weight

Perhaps, if you are simply substituting a sugary soft drink with a diet cola that is artificially sweetened — this will  save you about 100 calories per can. However, research has shown that when rats were fed artificial sweeteners, they craved more calories than those rats that were given real sugar. This has suggested the possibility that if your body thinks it's getting something that tastes like it should have a lot of calories but the calories are missing, it will crave those calories afterward. A better "diet" drink is a glass of water, with a squeeze of lemon added for flavor.

Eating late in the evening is unhealthy and makes you fat

Then the whole of the Mediterranean region would suffer, because there the time of the main meal of the day is often late in the evening. Neither is there any evidence for the idea that a full stomach leads to worse sleep, nor that calories consumed after six o'clock in the evening are particularly likely to make you fat. It is true, however, that a person's regular eating habits do play a part. Anyone who does not normally eat late in the evening will feel slightly ill after a late feast. But the same can happen to someone who is not used to having breakfast if they suddenly have a sumptuous meal in the morning.

When you go a long time with little food, your stomach shrinks

The stomach doesn't shrink. However, it can become enlarged if you eat enormous amounts of food; after digestion — and perhaps some indigestion — it will return to its previous size. But if your entire digestive system is accustomed to smaller portions, it will be overtaxed if it is suddenly required to start overworking. This means that overeating after a diet can cause a person to end up in the hospital. The size of the stomach can be reduced surgically to treat extreme obesity in a procedure commonly known as "stomach stapling."

COOKING

Adding salt to cooking vegetables keeps their colors bright

Salt has no effect on the color of vegetables. As the vegetables cook, the water's acidity and mineral content contribute to molecular changes in the vegetables, and their color often changes as a result.

Searing meat seals in the juices

Searing meat does give it a better flavor, but not because the juices are sealed in. Experiments have proven that seared meat and unseared meat both have about the same amount of juice. The improved flavor comes from the effects of a chemical process that takes place when proteins and sugars react to heat.

The cooking time for roast meat depends on its weight

Although weight is important, the shape of the roast can lengthen or shorten the cooking time. It all depends on how long it takes the heat to reach the center of the roast. For example, a short roll of meat will take the same time to cook as a long roll of meat, since the center is always the same distance from the source of heat. The best bet is to use a meat thermometer.

Alcohol evaporates during cooking

Although alcohol evaporates faster than water, it doesn't all evaporate when cooked. It depends on how you're cooking it. Two-and-a-half hours of baking will leave only 5 percent of the original alcohol, while a flambé (when alcohol is added to a hot pan to create a sudden flame) will preserve 85 percent.

You cannot deep-fry in olive oil

Because olive oil smokes faster than other oils, people think it's not good for deep-frying. But most frying is done below olive oil's smoke point of 375°F (191°C). Olive oil works just fine for deep frying, and gives a lovely flavor to the food cooked in it. Even if it smokes a little, that doesn't hurt the food. The only drawback: olive oil is more expensive than other oils used for deep-frying.

You must scald milk before using it in some recipes

Cooks used to scald milk to destroy certain enzymes that could have a bad effect on bread rising or milk thickening. But the process of pasteurization, which heats the milk, kills these enzymes. So there is no need to scald the milk, unless you are using raw milk that has not been pasteurized.

You can make a baked potato in the microwave

Microwaves don't "bake." A potato can be cooked in a microwave, but it is really being steamed, not baked, and it will not have the fluffy/crispy consistency of a real baked potato.

Water is better than milk in an omelet

Many cooks believe that adding water to eggs makes a better omelet than adding milk. But extensive tests have revealed that the opposite is true: omelets made with milk are softer, fluffier and have more flavor.

Noodles will not stick together if oil is used in the cooking water

A drop of oil in the cooking water, as used by many housewives, has no effect whatsoever. Anyone who wants to prevent the noodles from sticking together should stir in some oil after plunging the cooked noodles into cold water.

A serrated knife slices tomatoes best

A straight-edged knife will do just as good a job if it is sharp. If your straight knives aren't working on tomatoes it's probably time for them to be sharpened.

VITAMINS, MINERALS AND FIBER

Vitamins are substances that the body is unable to produce by itself

That was the original definition of vitamins. Subsequently, however, a few substances that the body can produce quite well for itself have been classed as vitamins. Vitamin D, for example, is not a true vitamin, but a hormone precursor that can be produced in the body with the help of sunlight. Vitamins B12 and K can be produced by the bacteria that are normally present in healthy intestinal flora.

People should consume as many vitamins and minerals as possible

Our bodies cannot process unlimited amounts of vitamins and minerals. Many are simply eliminated when the body is faced with an excess, while others can build up to toxic levels in the body. Vitamin overdoses can be dangerous to your health. An overdose of vitamin A may lead to headaches and nausea; vitamin C to disruption of hormone levels; vitamin D to cramps and gallstones; vitamin E to nausea, vomiting and stomach and intestinal complaints; and some of the B vitamins to itching, tingling and minor paralysis. In addition, overdoses of a vitamin or a mineral substance may restrict the absorption of other, more important, substances. Too much calcium, for example, easily leads to too little zinc. It is for this reason that artificially increased levels of vitamins are open to objection. The summaries of contents given on packaging are actually the minimum levels. But the producers include such high levels that even with vitamins that degrade, the minimum level still applies even at the end of the guaranteed shelf life.

The highest levels of vitamin C are found in lemons

This myth likely arose because lemons were eaten by British sailors to prevent scurvy. However, wild fruit such as Barbados cherries (up to 3,000 milligrams per 100 grams of fruit), rose hips (up to 2,800 milligrams) and sea buckthorn (up to 1,200 milligrams) contain the most vitamin C. Other foods that are rich in vitamin C are blackcurrants (190 milligrams), kiwi fruit (100 milligrams), green cabbage (105 milligrams) and red peppers (100 milligrams). Oranges and lemons, on the other hand contain only about 40 to 50 milligrams of vitamin C.

People in the United States and Canada don't suffer from vitamin deficiencies

Thanks to a good food supply and fortification programs that add vitamins and minerals to common foods, it is rare to see the type of deficiencies, like scurvy (vitamin C deficiency) or beriberi (thiamin deficiency), that were known in the past. However, anemia caused by iron or vitamin B12 deficiency is not an uncommon ailment. And women who are planning to become pregnant are advised to have a sufficient intake of folic acid, because a lack of this vitamin early in pregnancy can result in spina bifida in their infants.

People should eat as much fiber as possible

We obtain most of our fiber from fruits, vegetables and whole-grain products. Fiber helps to soften stool and thus improves digestion. But that does not mean that it is healthy to eat extremely large quantities. Too much fiber asks too much of intestinal flora, and may give rise to excessive and foul-smelling gas. In many cases, the intestines become irritated. Also, if an excess of fiber is combined with a lack of fluids, constipation can result. Fiber is a relatively new subject of study in dietary science. Its significance has been recognized so recently that its true nutritional value has not, as yet, been precisely determined.

AROMAS AND ADDITIVES

The smell of strawberries is made from strawberries

So-called fruit aromas are generally produced by bacteria and fungi. It would be far too expensive to make the correspondingly intense aromas from natural fruit extracts. Only if the bacteria ferment natural materials — which include wood, cheese rind or fish waste — are the resulting aromas permitted to be described as "natural."

Commercially prepared children's foods are geared to their needs

Once you get past "beginner" baby foods, like simple pureed fruits and vegetables that have no salt or sugar added, most commercial foods targeted to children are sweetened, contain artificial colors and flavors and come in bright, attractive packaging to appeal to young consumers. But none of this has the slightest thing to do with the needs of young children. Many regular "adult" foods, containing less sugar and fewer additives are far healthier.

Artificial vitamin additives and minerals make sense

Only to entice customers. Scientific tests indicate that separated and artificially added vitamins do not produce the same healthy effects as foods that are naturally vitamin-rich. As well, the additions are not always well thought out. For example, some milk products, which are already rich in calcium, have calcium added to them, which can lead to an excess of this mineral in the body.

The label shows everything that is in a food

Not all ingredients have to be declared. Substances that are used in the manufacturing process, such as the solvents used to decaffeinate coffee, and emulsifiers that make dough suitable for machine-handling, do not have to be listed. Similarly, additives in an ingredient such as a "fruit preparation" do not need to be declared if this component forms less than 25 percent of the final product. A yogurt may therefore be sold with the description "without preservatives" if preservatives are used only in the fruit-preparation stage.

"Sugar-free" means without sugar

To be labeled "sugar-free" a product must contain less than 0.5 grams of ordinary, household sugar (sucrose) per serving. However, the food can still contain other forms of sugar, including glucose, fructose, maltose and glucose syrup, and artificial sweeteners like sorbitol, aspartame and saccharin. Foods labeled sugar-free often have more carbohydrates per serving than the same product with sucrose, and are not necessarily low-calorie.

EGGS AND FATS

A low cholesterol level is healthy

Although generally a good indicator of health, a low cholesterol level may also be a sign of illness, liver damage or hyperactive thyroid.

Ketchup was purely an American invention

There are a few theories on the origins of ketchup, but none indicate that the sauce was strictly an American idea. In all likelihood, the word ketchup was introduced to the United States in the 19th century by Chinese immigrants, who referred to a particular condiment as *ke-tsiap*, which means "sauce," although it was made from eggplants, not tomatoes. F. & J. Heinz — one of the most popular tomato ketchup producers — introduced their famous red sauce in the United States in 1876.

Eating more than two eggs a week is unhealthy

This idea has arisen from worries about cholesterol. Eggs do indeed contain high levels — about 210 grams per egg — and the American Heart Association recommends a maximum of 300 grams of cholesterol per day from all food sources. However, eggs are still a very healthy food, containing vitamins A, B6, B12, riboflavin, folic acid, iron, calcium and phosphorus. As well, it is only the egg yolk that contains cholesterol. Egg whites, which have little fat and contain 15 calories per egg, are a good cholesterol-free protein source.

Brown eggs are healthier than white eggs

The color of the shell does not affect the nutritional value of the eggs. Brown eggs and white eggs are just laid by different breeds of chickens. Breeds that lay brown eggs include Rhode Island Red and New Hampshire chickens, while white leghorns lay white eggs.

Because of the danger of salmonella, eggs should be kept as cool as possible

It is true that salmonella bacteria multiplies very slowly at refrigerator temperatures. However, eggs are often sold unchilled at farmer's markets. A greater stimulus to the growth of salmonella than heat alone is a change from cold to warm temperatures. So it is better for eggs to be sold unchilled and be put in the refrigerator at home, rather than the cold chain being broken between the supermarket and home. Foods containing raw eggs should, similarly, not be exposed to such a change in temperature.

Eggs should be eaten with a plastic spoon

You can eat eggs with almost any sort of spoon. Only silver spoons should be avoided. The silver reacts with the sulfur in the yolk, causing the silver to tarnish and giving the eggs an unpleasant taste.

Margarine is healthier than butter

There is a major war of views over the butter versus margarine debate. The calorie content of both fats is approximately the same. Margarine, however, contains no cholesterol, while butter does.

But although many dieticians advise consumers to avoid taking in too much cholesterol, others are convinced that the trans-fatty acids present in margarine are equally unhealthy.

Mayonnaise spoils easily

Every summer we are warned that food made with mayonnaise will quickly go bad if not refrigerated. The truth is that store-bought mayonnaise is acidic and can actually help prevent foods from spoiling. With chicken salad or tuna sandwiches, the chicken or the tuna goes bad first. However, it is important to keep them refrigerated to avoid spoilage in hot weather, but if they do turn — don't blame the mayo.

BREAD AND FRUIT

The French invented the croissant

The croissant originated in Austria. Allegedly it was in 1683, after the siege of Vienna by the Turks. Early in the morning the bakers discovered that the Turks were attempting to place mines under the city. They raised the alarm. After the enemy was successfully put to flight, they are supposed to have created the croissant in the shape of the crescent moon. Certainly it was the daughter of the Austrian Emperor, Marie-Antoinette (1755–93), who took the pastry to France, where it was called *croissant de la lune* (lunar crescent). It is true, however, that in its new home, the croissant changed its shape slightly, and is no longer quite so sickle-shaped.

Bananas go bad in the refrigerator

While it is true that bananas will turn brown faster in the fridge, the fruit inside the skin is fine. As with other fruit, refrigeration slows down the ripening process.

Browning of apples is a sign of rot and must be prevented

When cut apples turn brown, a thin film is formed, which prevents fungi and bacteria from entering the ruptured cells. It may, perhaps, not appear particularly appetizing, but it is completely harmless. The body eliminates it, undigested. Besides, potatoes, tomatoes, cucumbers and carrots form a similar film — it is just not as easy to see. To keep apple slices from turning brown, just sprinkle them with lemon juice.

SUGAR AND SWEETS

Brown sugar is healthier than white

Brown sugar is generally just as refined as white. Its color is subsequently restored by the addition of a certain amount of molasses. The traces of minerals that are contained within the molasses are of no consequence. On the other hand, raw sugar actually still contains vitamins and minerals. It also has a strong, distinctive taste, which is not enjoyed by everyone.

Chocolate is an aphrodisiac

There is no scientific evidence that any food increases physical desire. Some, like chocolate or alcohol, may enhance sexual pleasure, but not desire. The key to a successful aphrodisiac seems to be in the mind: if people believe that it will work, it often does.

Egg cream is made of eggs and cream

The popular old-fashioned New York beverage is made with chocolate syrup, milk and soda water — no eggs and no cream. Where the name came from is lost in the mists of time, although there has been a suggestion that it was named in imitation of other soda fountain drinks that actually were made with eggs, or that it might have come from *eht*, the Yiddish word for "pure." Or it may just have been a brilliant marketing ploy — "egg cream" suggests an exotic, rich drink, as opposed to plain old chocolate soda.

A pound cake weighs one pound

Pound cake is made from an old-fashioned, simple recipe: one pound of butter, one pound of eggs and one pound of flour. Made with exactly these ingredients, this cake is rather large and weighs considerably more than a pound.

Candied lemon and orange peel is made from the peel of lemons and oranges

Candied lemon peel is made from the rind of citrons — they resemble lemons but are larger, have less pulp and a thicker rind.

Candied orange peel is made from the peel of the Seville or bitter orange. Neither are suitable for consumption raw.

Gum was invented in the United States

Chewing "gum" has been enjoyed since the Stone Age. In ancient Greece, they used the resin from the pistachio tree (the mastic tree). In central and northern Europe, people appear to have chewed birch resin. The Maya in Central America chewed *tzicli* (chicle), the thickened sap of the sapodilla tree (*Manilkara zapota*). The first commercial chewing gum was produced in the United States in 1848 from a mixture of spruce resin and beeswax. The breakthrough came in 1875, when *tzicli* began to be mixed with aromatic substances such as licorice or peppermint. For about 40 years, synthetic gums have been used.

Chewing gum takes seven years to pass through your digestive system

Parents have happily handed this down from one generation to the next to prevent their kids from swallowing gum (and then having to buy them more). The gum will pass through the digestive system in a normal amount of time and will not "stick to your insides."

LEGUMES AND MUSHROOMS

Black-eyed peas are peas

Black-eyed peas (*Vigna unguiculata unguiculata*) belong to the same family (Fabaceae) as peas (*Pisum sativum*), but they are really a kind of bean. They are a subspecies of the cowpea (*Vigna unguiculata*), which is also a bean.

You must soak beans before cooking them

Dry beans can be cooked without soaking them. They will take longer to cook than beans that have been soaked, but they will eventually become tender. What soaking does help with is the "gas" quotient of beans. If they are soaked before cooking and then the soaking water is thrown away and they are cooked with fresh water, beans lose some of their famous ability to cause flatulence.

All mushrooms with a spongy underside are edible

Collecting mushrooms for consumption is risky. Many people believe that boletes, which have spongy-looking undersides rather than gills, are always safe. However, even though most boletes are edible, there are a few exceptions. The bitter bolete (*Tylopilus felleus*) is aptly named, and can be poisonous — if someone was actually able to force down a large quantity. The devil's bolete (*Boletus satanas*) can lead to severe stomach and intestinal pains. A brown boletus, *Boletus erythropus*, on the other hand tastes wonderful, but under no circumstances should it be eaten raw.

Mushrooms should never be reheated

The flavor and quality doesn't depend on reheating. Mushrooms have a high water and protein content and spoil relatively quickly, so they should be prepared as fresh as possible. Anyone who puts the remains of food containing mushrooms immediately into the refrigerator can then reheat without worry.

FISH AND MEAT

The best caviar is black and comes from Russia

In its original state, true caviar — the eggs of sturgeon — is clear and transparent. It is only when it is preserved with salt that it darkens. The finest quality caviar comes not from Russia, but from the Iranian part of the Caspian Sea, where the water is particularly clean and deep. Generally, lighter caviar is more valuable than the darker types. Further signs of quality are a particularly soft skin and large grains.

Surimi consists of crab meat

Surimi is an imitation crab meat. Krill, or the flesh of otherwise unusable fish, is minced and gelled with sugar. This mixture is then seasoned, shaped and the surface colored with paprika extract. Originally, however, "surimi" had nothing to do with any imitation material, but simply described a method of preserving minced fish by the addition of sugar.

"Sushi" means raw fish

Raw fish is called "sashimi." Sushi is food made with vinegared rice, which is prepared by mixing hot rice with vinegar and sugar.

A variety of foods can be added to the rice, including tofu, vegetables or fish.

White meat is healthier than red meat

For a start, there is no general agreement as to what is white meat, and what is red. Many use this to distinguish between poultry and pork, beef or lamb. But a goose drumstick is much "redder" than a pale piece of veal. Analysis of the contents also provides no indication that a turkey burger is better than one made of beef. North American studies, in which "red" meat did poorly, probably did not take into account that many cuts of pork and beef are treated with nitrite salts and subsequently grilled, and that this is what is unhealthy.

Calves-liver sausage only contains calves' liver

Liver sausage does not consist solely of liver, but of a mixture of minced liver and meat. The liver content only amounts to a small percentage because otherwise the sausage would taste too strong. In calves-liver sausage the meat content must at least in part be obtained from young cattle. The liver, on the other hand, may be from any type of animal — generally cheap pigs' liver is used.

Frankfurters and wieners are the same

The confusion between these two thin boiled sausages is still unresolved. They were probably invented in Frankfurt as sausages made purely of pork meat. The Frankfurt butcher Georg Lahner (1772–1845) then introduced them to Vienna (Wien), but mixed in 30 percent beef, which was not permitted in Frankfurt, because there was a distinction between beef and pork butchers. To make the confusion even greater, it is also possible that a Berlin butcher named Wiener invented the wiener sausage. Frequently a Viennese butcher named Frankfurter is also involved in the story. Nowadays in Germany, sausages are only allowed to be called frankfurters if they are made in Frankfurt, and all others are designated wieners.

Hamburgers were originally made of ham

Yes, chicken burgers are made with minced chicken, but hamburgers were never made from ham. They are actually named after the German city of Hamburg. German emigrants took their custom of eating fried minced meat to North America in the 19th century, where their *rissoles* became known as "hamburger steaks" or "hamburger sandwiches."

Fortune cookies are Chinese

Fortune cookies first appeared in 1918 in the United States, invented by George Jung, a Chinese immigrant. He tucked messages inside a common recipe for a Chinese wafer cookie to entertain people as they waited for their food to be cooked in Chinese restaurants. The messages began as Bible verses, but soon moved on to predictions and proverbs.

your message here

CHOP SUEY AND FORTUNE COOKIES

Chop suey is a typical Chinese dish

"Chop suey" means "mixed leftovers," and was created by Chinese embassy staff in the United States. It proved so popular, however, that it was adopted by most of the Chinese restaurants in the West. Fried rice is often thought to be typically Chinese, but in fact originates in Indonesia, while *sub gum* is an Asian version of a Dutch rice dish.

The Chinese eat swallows' nests

In China and Vietnam, certain birds' nests are actually regarded as a delicacy. These nests are not those of swallows, however, which use clay and straw as building materials, but of two sorts of swiftlets that are related to the true swifts. They form their protein-rich nests from their saliva. The largest colonies of swiftlets are found in Malaysia.

Marco Polo brought noodles to Italy from China

Noodles were known in Rome and in the eastern Mediterranean area in antiquity. They probably originated in the Near East. Certainly they were also known in China for thousands of years. They were nothing new to Marco Polo (1254–1324). It is possible that he may have copied the type of spaghetti from the Mongols who ruled China at the time — if he was ever in China. Nevertheless, Mongolian "spaghetti" was made from rice flour, not the semolina flour that typifies Italian spaghetti noodles.

WHAT'S FOR LUNCH?

Fast food is unhealthy

When you hear the term "fast food," the first image that usually comes to mind is a hamburger, fries and a soft drink — a tasty treat, but not for every day. However, there are a variety of other fast foods — those that can be obtained quickly and at a reasonable price — such as pizza, sandwiches and salads, which can offer more nutrition and fewer calories. Most of the major franchises now offer a range of items and also provide nutritional information for all of the entrees, drinks and desserts on their menus. Besides, the classic burger can be make a good meal if its grilled (not fried) and topped with lettuce and tomato slices rather than cheese and mayo.

Caesar salad was named after Julius Caesar

This tasty salad was supposedly invented by Caesar Cardini, for Caesar's Place Restaurant in Tijuana, Mexico, on July 4, 1924. Traditionally the salad consists of Romaine lettuce, croutons, lemon juice, olive oil, egg yolks, Parmesan cheese, black pepper and Worcestershire sauce. It is rumored that Cardini ran out of ingredients for a regular salad and improvised by inventing the Caesar salad.

Philadelphia cream cheese comes from Philadelphia

No it doesn't and it never did. It was invented in Chester, New York, in 1872, and named "Philadelphia" because in those days the city of brotherly love had a classy reputation as a place where everything was of a higher quality, especially food. Anything named "Philadelphia" was considered a superior product. In some countries in Latin America, such as Argentina and Chile, the creamy cheese is known simply as "Philadelphia," or sometimes "Philadelphia cheese" (*queso Philadelphia*).

The Earl of Sandwich invented the sandwich

Reportedly, the 4th Earl of Sandwich, John Montagu (1718–1792), invented the sandwich so he could keep gambling with one hand and eat his supper (meat between two slices of bread) with the other. But human beings had figured out the portability and convenience of a sandwich long before the unpopular Earl made it his favorite meal. Peasants working in the fields would eat cheese between slices of bread when they stopped for lunch, Arabs stuffed pita bread with meat and Jews ate matzoh sandwiches of nuts and fruit during Passover. But after the Earl, the name "sandwich" stuck. It also stuck to the Sandwich Islands in the Pacific until they were renamed as the Hawaiian Islands. They were discovered by Captain Cook (1728–1779), who named them after the Earl, who was the acting First Lord of the Admiralty at the time.

French fries are French

Although no one can pin down exactly who invented French fries, most Europeans believe it was the Belgians. One story has U.S. servicemen in the First World War eating what the Belgians called *patates frites* and renaming them "French fries" because the Americans couldn't see a big difference between the Belgians and the French. But French fries made their way to England long before then, and Belgians claim to have been cooking and eating French fries since at least the 17th century.

Vegetarian meals are always a healthy choice

Not always, especially if they contain a lot of cheese, oil or creamy sauces, or if they're fried — these types of meals can contain a lot of fat and calories. Many meats can be healthy options, like grilled lean beef or baked chicken with the skin removed. However, it is good to include fruits and/or vegetables with every meal to meet food guide requirements.

MILK AND WATER

Pasteurization involved boiling milk at a very high temperature to kill bacteria

During the process of pasteurization, a liquid is heated to between 130°F and 158°F (54°C and 70°C) for about 30 minutes. This kills some of the dangerous bacteria in milk, but does not affect its flavor. Pasteurization was developed to prolong the storage life of beer and wine, but later it was found to have a healthy effect on milk.

Water from a bottle is better than water from the tap

There is no health difference between water that has come from a water treatment plant and runs through your taps and the bottled variety that you buy. In fact, many expensive bottled waters actually come from the city water supply in the area where they're bottled — they're just reprocessed. Those who drink bottled water because of its "superior" taste could save money by drinking from the tap. Bottled water drinkers who have taken blind taste tests frequently choose tap water over the bottled brands.

You can die from drinking distilled water

It is correct that distilled water contains none of the salts that are essential for the body. However, you can obtain these needed salts from solid food, so anyone who drinks only distilled water will not die as a result. Still, there is no good reason to drink distilled water, and anyone who does so regularly could stress their body through lack of salts.

Coffee comes from South America

The coffee bean originated in East Africa, and was ground and brewed into coffee there as early as the fourth century — by monks in Kefa (Kaffa) in Ethiopia. It was first taken to South America in the 18th century where it rapidly became one of the main agricultural products. Since then Vietnam has risen to become second to Brazil as a coffee producer. Cultivation there was massively supported from 1977 by the government. People did not want to go without one of their favorite drinks, but purchasing it from western countries required too much foreign currency.

COLA, COFFEE AND TEA

Coca-Cola has nothing to do with cocaine

Coca-Cola got its name from two specific ingredients, the caffeine-containing cola nut and the coca leaf. Cocaine is also obtained from the latter. Coca-Cola was invented in 1886 by an Atlanta pharmacist as an elixir against headaches and tiredness. But by 1903 the brown liquid had been brewed with coca leaves, from which the cocaine had previously been extracted. Apart from cola nuts, the special taste of Coca-Cola has contributions from vanilla, cinnamon, cloves and lemons, though the exact formula is kept strictly secret.

Coca-Cola can dissolve a piece of meat overnight

The meat is still there the next morning, but a process of decomposition has begun, which means that neither the cola nor the meat is particularly appetizing. In other liquids, such as juices or water, the same effect does not occur. It is true, however, that rusty bolts can be loosened after applying a Coca-Cola-soaked cloth to the bolt, thanks to the phosphoric acid contained in the cola.

Isotonic drinks compensate for the loss of minerals after exercise

To suffer from a true mineral deficiency, a person would have to perspire a great deal and for a very long time. Building workers in summer are in far more likely to suffer than "weekend warriors." But if you actually reach the limits of your capabilities, good, healthy thirst-quenchers include watermelon, or else a mixture of apple juice with mineral water.

Tea contains more caffeine than coffee

When measured in its dry form, tea does technically contain more caffeine than coffee. However, the average prepared cup of coffee contains more caffeine than an equal cup of tea.

"Tea time" in England is five o'clock

Anyone in Great Britain who expects to have the legendary "five o'clock tea" may be sorely disappointed. "Tea time" actually begins at three-thirty and is generally over by five. You would be very lucky to get a cup of tea as late as five-thirty. "High tea" combines afternoon tea with the evening meal. Particularly distinctive is southwestern England's "cream tea," which is served with scones, clotted cream and strawberry jam.

Green tea and black tea come from different plants

Only one plant produces the many different kinds of tea: *Camellia sinensis*. Different harvesting and processing methods result in green tea, black tea, white tea and oolong. The tea plant grows best at high altitudes in a tropical or subtropical climate. The major tea producers are India, China, Kenya, Sri Lanka, Taiwan, Japan, Indonesia, Nepal and Bangladesh.

DRINKING AND SMOKING

White wine is made from green grapes and red wine from red grapes

The color of the grape has nothing to do with the color of the wine. The color of the juice from grapes without their skins is nearly always clear. During the wine-making process, the skins of the grape are removed during fermentation to make white wine, but left on to create red wine.

Alcohol-free beer contains no alcohol

Alcohol-free beer is heated under a vacuum, which removes the alcohol produced during fermentation. A small residue of alcohol is tolerated. According to U.S. and Canadian food standards, a beverage with less than 0.5 percent of alcohol may be described as alcohol-free.

A food or beverage only contains alcohol if it says so on the label

There are minute traces of alcohol in more foods than you would think. It is not just "alcohol-free" beer that contains about 0.2 to 0.4 percent alcohol. Alcohol also occurs in ripe fruit. As well, food that has undergone a fermentation stage during its preparation also contains alcohol. In the production of sauerkraut, for example, there is a lactic acid fermentation rather than an alcoholic one. Despite this, about 0.5 percent alcohol may be produced.

Vodka is made from potatoes

The traditional raw material for vodka is rye. But potatoes, wheat, corn or molasses may also be distilled. After all, with vodka it is not a question of retaining any of the taste of the original substances, because as much as possible is removed by filtration. A good vodka is distinguished by a neutral taste. But the original source does still have an influence on the consistency. Vodka from rye is the most popular, generally regarded as being particularly rounded, smooth and mellow. Potato vodka tastes more distinctive than grain vodka. Molasses, which retains a sweetish taste, is in many respects the cheapest source.

After a heavy meal, a glass of liqueur aids digestion

The alcohol dilutes the hydrochloric acid in the stomach that breaks down fats. So it is a hindrance to digestion rather than a help. Conversely, fat interferes with the breakdown of alcohol, which then remains longer in the body.

Alcohol is unhealthy — with red wine being the only exception

Studies have shown that it is not just red wine that has healthy effects. Moderate drinkers live longest — even longer than teetotalers — and the alcohol consumed can be red wine, white wine, beer or even the harder liquors. Moderate, in this context, means 12 ounces of beer, 5 ounces of wine or 1.5 ounces of 80-proof distilled spirits per day for women, and twice that for men. However, some people, including pregnant women, anyone with liver disease or those who are taking prescription medication, should abstain from drinking alcohol.

Alcohol warms the body

Alcohol dilates the blood vessels at the body's surface. (The stereotypical red "drinker's nose" is a result of dilation of the blood vessels.) This creates a subjective feeling of heat. Warmed alcohol, such as mulled wine, is particularly rapidly absorbed by the body and its effects are correspondingly stronger. However, a body with good circulation gives off more heat and cools more quickly; also, sensitivity to cold is reduced. This is why a drunk person can easily freeze to death outside in winter.

Pot is harmless

The condemnation of cannabis products is currently questionable. They are less addictive than alcohol and nicotine, and the symptoms of many diseases, such as AIDS and cancer, seem to be alleviated by them. But they are not harmless. The drug restricts speech, the ability to think, memory and reaction time. It is just as dangerous to drive when stoned as it is when drunk. Repeated consumption makes people passive and lacking in motivation. School, work, relationships and one's own health may become unimportant.

Cigarettes have a calming influence

In smokers, smoking does actually cause them to relax. This is not, however, because nicotine has a relaxing effect, but because in nicotine addicts, turning to a cigarette quells withdrawal effects. Smokers thus combat a stress that nonsmokers never have in the first place.

QUALITY, STANDARDS AND REPUTATIONS

Everyone should try to have at least one hot meal a day

It doesn't make the slightest difference whether you eat hot or cold food. The body is not dependent on the warmth of heated meals. What is important is that you eat a balanced diet, and many foods that are part of a balanced diet need to be cooked before they are eaten.

English cooking has always had a bad reputation

"The English invented table-talk so that people would forget their food" was a malicious remark made by the French author Pierre Daninos (1913–2005). In fact, in the 19th century English cooking had a fine reputation. Part of the negative view of English cooking arose thanks to the two World Wars, when many food ingredients were unavailable, leading to a more limited menu. Today, English fare can hold its own in the world, and chefs like Jamie Oliver are turning around England's reputation for cuisine.

Hotels can have a maximum of five stars

There is no overall international classification system for hotels, only the systems used by national associations, most of which award up to five stars, but which are by no means comparable in the criteria that they use. So there is nothing saying you can't award more than five stars. The Burj Al-Arab hotel in Dubai, United Arab Emirates, for example, has been described as a seven-star hotel, because of its luxurious accommodations, unique architecture and outstanding location on an artificial island.

TOOLS AND MATERIALS

Lead pencils contain lead

In antiquity and in the Middle Ages, people did actually work with lead pencils and round disks of lead alloy. However, the material was very hard, which made it easy to damage the paper, and it was also extremely unhealthy (a fact that was not known at the time). In England in the 17th century, graphite was found to be a good substitute. However, people believed graphite was lead ore, which is why pencils are still known as lead pencils even though they contain no trace of the metal. Nowadays, the "lead" in pencils consists of a mixture of ground graphite and clay, in different grades of hardness.

Stainless steel is the sharpest type of steel

Stainless steel is a particularly pure steel. It is generally corrosion-resistant and rarely forms rust. However, it has a different structure and is softer than normal steel, so it is not suitable for ultrasharp blades. Good knives and professional shears — the type that gardeners use, for example — are therefore not made from stainless steel, but rather from heat-treated or carbon steel. Stainless steel knives and blades should therefore be regularly sharpened.

Matches were invented before lighters

The first lighter was constructed by Johann Wolfgang Döbereiner (1780–1849) in 1816. Hydrogen was produced by a reaction between hydrochloric acid and zinc, and this was ignited by a catalytic reaction with platinum. Matches with a head of phosphorus, which ignited when rubbed, were introduced later — in 1832. However, these first matches ignited all too readily, frequently requiring only the gentlest, accidental rubbing to flare up. In 1848, Döbereiner's pupil, Rudolf Christian Böttger (1806–81), introduced safety matches with less easily ignited sulfur heads.

Tinder is dry wood

Nowadays, we tend to think of tinder as fine shavings of dry wood that burn well, but tinder can be any easily flammable material used to start a rudimentary fire. Originally, however, before the invention of matches and lighters, people used a fungus to kindle a glow, specifically a bracket fungus that grows on broad-leaved trees. This fungus could be ignited by sparks, rather than an existing flame. "Ötzi the Iceman," a well-preserved mummy of a man who lived circa 3300 BC, had some of this sort of tinder as one of his possessions, along with flint and pyrite to create sparks.

TELECOMMUNICATIONS AND HOUSEHOLD ITEMS

The United States has the highest number of cell phone users

As of 2003, high-density Hong Kong won the prize for the most cell phone users. Statistics showed that 1,079 of every 1,000 people in Hong Kong subscribed to a cell phone service that year — which meant that some people had more than one cell phone. Italy was next on the list, with 1,018 cell phones per 1,000 people, then Sweden with 980. United States had "only" 546 cell phones for every 1,000 people. The countries with the fewest cell phones were Cuba, Eritrea, Ethiopia, Myanmar (Burma) and Nepal.

The fax machine is a 20th-century invention

The fax machine was developed by Scottish watchmaker Alexander Bain (1811–77) around 1843. Instead of the beam of light that is used today, a pendulum connected to an electrical supply was used to "read" line by line with each back-and-forth movement. As well, the document that the pendulum was to scan had to be made of electrically conducting material. An Italian named Giovanni Caselli (1815–91) developed the machine further, and his Pantelegraph, produced in 1861, even predated the invention of the telephone.

The standard "QWERTY" keyboard was designed for maximum efficiency

Not exactly. When the typewriter was patented by Christopher Sholes in 1868, he set it up with the keys in alphabetical order. But he found that they frequently jammed because the most-used keys were too close together. So his brother-in-law, who happened to be a mathematician, designed a new layout in which the most frequently used keys were as far apart as possible to prevent sticking. With the advent of computers, however, this measure is unnecessary. Since Sholes's time, other keyboard arrangements have been created, including the Dvorak Simplified Keyboard, which has the most commonly used letters (A-O-E-U-I-D-H-T-N-S) on the home row. However, the QWERTY keyboard remains the most popular.

A divan is a piece of furniture

Well then, what did Johann Wolfgang van Goethe (1749–1832) mean when he called his collection of poems *West-Östlicher*

Divan (*Poems of the East and West*)? In Persian, a "divan" was originally an archive or an office. Over time, this became a room where a ruler conducted business. Depending on the way this office was used, it could be more of a reception hall, a court of justice or a small cabinet room, to which only a very restricted number of advisers were admitted. In the Ottoman Empire, the term came to be applied not just to the conference room in which the state council met, but also to the council itself. In the Orient, however, comfortable, easy furniture was always part of the decor of such a room, which is why, from about the beginning of the 19th century, the word "divan" came to be applied in Europe to an upholstered bench seat. Goethe, who was exceptionally well-read, saw his *Divan* in the original sense as an "archive" of Western and Eastern wisdom.

CLOTHES AND ACCESSORIES

Corsets were made from fish bone

Actually, they were made from whalebone. However, this is deceiving because whalebone is not the bone of a whale, but rather baleen from its baleen plates. These comblike plates are found in a whale's jaws and are used to filter organisms from the water. Baleen is made of keratin — the same material that is found in animal horns and nails — and has a stiff, but flexible quality. Baleen, or whalebone, thus had the ideal properties to stiffen corsets, and was also used for parasol ribs.

Panama hats are made in Panama

The brimmed hats are made in Ecuador. Made from the woven leaves of the panama-hat palm (*jipijapa* or *toquilla*), the hats gained widespread popularity during the construction of the Panama Canal, where they shielded many a tender head from the burning sun.

The handkerchief was invented for the purpose of blowing your nose into it

Handkerchiefs came into fashion in the 15th century in Italy, and were used to wave around in an elegant and dignified manner. They were correspondingly expensive, and decorated with lace and embroidery. The custom of using them for nose blowing first arose in the middle of the 18th century. Today most people use disposable tissues for this messy job.

Buttons were invented as fasteners for clothing

Buttons were originally nothing more than ornamentation sewn onto clothing. The first may be traced back to 2000 BC, and even in antiquity, otherwise plain togas and tunics were ornamented with sewn-on buttons. It was only about AD 1300 that the idea arose of using the buttons as fasteners. The immediate result was a rise in particularly close-fitting fashions. During the Renaissance, a veritable "button mania" broke out. Many pieces of clothing were inundated with hundreds and even thousands of buttons, and they all needed to be buttoned up.

The ten-gallon hat holds 10 gallons of liquid

If you were so inclined as to pour liquid into a ten-gallon hat, you could probably fit in about three-quarters of a gallon (2.8 liters). The hat was named after the Mexican *sombrero galon*, a braided Mexican hat popular in the 1800s. *Galon* referred to the braid on the hat, but in the translation into English it became "gallon."

Levi Strauss invented jeans

Only partially. Genuine "jeans" are distinguished by a sturdy cotton cloth, indigo-blue color and rivets. The haberdasher and cloth merchant Levi Strauss (1829–1902) cut his first trousers for gold diggers in San Francisco from brown tarpaulin. The idea of reinforcing the stitching with rivets was that of the tailor Jacob Davis (1834–1908), an immigrant from Latvia. Because he did not have the money to apply for a patent, he turned to Levi Strauss. At about the same time, Strauss started to make his trousers from blue denim. In 1873 the blue, riveted trousers were patented. Strauss and Davis held the patent together.

The miniskirt and bikini first appeared in the 20th century

They are age-old. As a bog body and many bronze figurines show, women in ancient Europe wore extremely short "miniskirts," which sometimes consisted of just a double row of vertical cords wrapped around the hips. As well, among the items left for posterity from ancient Rome is a leather bikini, which, as mosaics show, was worn as such, and not hidden under clothing as lingerie is.

Ties are pieces of civilian clothing

Today's neckties are descendants of the cravat, which has a military history. In the 16th century, Croatian mercenaries under the employ of King Louis XIII of France (1601–43) wore neck bands as a part of their uniforms. Parisian gentry found these neck bands so appealing that they turned them into a fashion item. In doing so, the cloth became smaller and was either given long, hanging ends or was tied into a bow, which later became the bow tie. The name "cravat" derives from the French *cravate* — this may be a corruption of *hvrat*, which was what the Croats themselves called the neckwear.

Only silkworms manufacture silk

True silk is produced by the silkworm (*Bombyx mori*), which is the larva of the mulberry moth. However, thread from spiders may also be turned into silk, which is even finer and lighter than "caterpillar silk." Although spider silk is currently manufactured on the Solomon Islands, the effort involved is incomparably greater than that used to make silk from captive-bred silkworms.

The most expensive sheep's wool is cashmere

Pure cashmere does not come from sheep, but from Kashmir goats, a breed that originated in China and Mongolia. Their fine, white undercoat cannot be removed as a single fleece as with sheep, but must be carefully combed out from the coat, a process known as de-hairing. This is why cashmere products are so pricey.

Pearls are white

Typically, pearls are white, but they can be found tinted with other colors, including yellow, blue and purple. Around the Polynesian islands in the Pacific there are also black pearls, which are rare and thus very expensive. They are formed by the black-lipped oyster, *Pinctada margaritifera*.

HEALTH, SAFETY AND HYGIENE

One hundred strokes with a hairbrush daily is good for the hair

Intensive brushing stimulates the sebaceous glands in the scalp. If a person has oily hair, then a lot of brushing should be avoided. Dry hair, however, will become more glossy, supple and robust with brushing. With long, thick hair, the hundred strokes with a hairbrush may be necessary to reach all the hair, right down to the ends. Whatever the case, you should only use a gentle brush with natural bristles to prevent damage to the hair.

Condoms were invented in Paris

Although condoms were sometimes known as "French letters," they have been in use in many different cultures since antiquity. Generally they were made from sheep's intestines or other animal membranes. It was only in the second half of the 19th century that condoms made from vulcanized rubber were introduced. In his biography, Casanova (1725–98) wrote of *vêtement anglais* (English garment), one of the names given to condoms at the time.

Costume jewelry is inexpensive

The origins of what we think of as costume jewelry date back to the 1920s and 1930s, although cheap jewelry made of glass "jewels" and inexpensive metal was also available before then. In the '20s and '30s, costume jewelry became trendy as an inexpensive way to coordinate jewelry with current clothing fashions. However, as time went on, large U.S. costume jewelry companies like Coro and Trifari produced items of different qualities for different sectors of the marketplace, including sterling silver and vermeil jewelry, as well as pieces with high-quality rhinestones and even semiprecious stones. Some costume jewelry makers, like Miriam Haskell, Coco Chanel and Theodor Fahrner, produced designs that are very collectable today and sell for hundreds or even thousands of dollars at auctions.

The Pill comes from the United States

The contraceptive pill was developed at Syntex, a small laboratory in Mexico City in 1951. Working there at that time was the American chemist Carl Djerassi (born 1923), originally from Vienna. He had the idea of artificially synthesizing progesterone (which during a woman's pregnancy prevents a further conception) as a method of contraception. At the same time, a Wisconsin laboratory was involved in the analysis of the artificial hormone, but the patent for the first chemical contraceptive was granted to Djerassi's Mexican employer.

Plastic is more hygienic than wood

Specifically, it is thought to be better to use a plastic cutting board rather than a wood one. However, in scientific tests in which wood was exposed to troublesome bacteria such as salmonella or E. coli, it was established that practically all the bacteria died quite rapidly. But on a plastic surface bacteria not only survived longer, but sometimes even multiplied. In any case, it is always a good idea to disinfect cutting boards with a diluted bleach solution and to use a separate cutting board for raw meat.

Toilets are particularly unhygienic

Toilets, being repeatedly flushed with water, have far fewer germs than would be believed. On the other hand, scientists who have searched for household germs have made the astonishing discovery that an incredible number of bacteria are present on and in computer keyboards. Perhaps the worst household offender, however, is the kitchen sponge or washcloth — bacteria just love to fester there.

Spiders get into the bathtub from the drain

Nope. A spider in the bath has likely just slipped in from the edge and been unable to get out again. Incidentally, it is actually quite difficult to wash a spider down the drain. Even in the swirling water of a drain pipe, this eight-legged creature is able to make its body sufficiently buoyant, allowing it to reach the surface of the water very quickly. This is why spiders that are thought to be dead suddenly crawl out of the drain.

In Australia, bathwater runs down the drain the other way

Supposedly, the Earth's rotation (through the Coriolis effect) causes the water in a bath in the Southern Hemisphere to drain clockwise, and in the Northern Hemisphere counterclockwise (and many people believe the direct opposite). But the tiny hole from a bath drain is far too small to be affected by the Coriolis effect. The direction that the small whirlpool adopts is ultimately dependent on purely local factors, such as movement in the water, surface tension or even air currents in the room. Moreover, even at the Equator the water flows out as a small whirlpool, and not as a straight flow down. Low-pressure areas in the atmosphere, however, do actually rotate clockwise in the Southern Hemisphere and counterclockwise in the Northern Hemisphere, thanks to the Coriolis effect.

Walking is more strenuous than standing

This seems logical. After all, one involves movement, and the other doing nothing. But then why does standing for a long time make you feel tired? Standing is more strenuous than walking because both legs are constantly carrying weight. By contrast, when walking every step takes the burden off one of the legs.

People are not "walking disaster areas"

Evaluations of insurance claims suggest that there are actually "accident prone" individuals. Many people do really seem to attract bad luck. Psychologists, however, maintain that it is not bad luck, but early childhood experience that has led to inattentiveness. And it seems to occur most often in people who were brought up in a very authoritarian manner. Later they rebel against any authority and restriction, and in doing so, they tend to completely ignore common sense and caution.

VEHICLES

Car speedometers always read 10 percent too high

This misconception could lead to you getting a speeding ticket if you thought you were driving slower than you actually were. However, these days speedometers are calibrated extremely accurately at the factory, using the stock tires and gears that come with the car. In the United States, federal standards allow a maximum 5 percent error on speedometer readings. If you make aftermarket changes, such as different tire or wheel sizes or different gear systems, you could have inaccurate readings on your speedometer. And because the speedometer and odometer are connected systems, if your speedometer is inaccurate, so is your odometer reading.

People flash their headlights to intimidate other drivers

Drivers flash their headlights as a way to communicate with other drivers for a variety of reasons — to inform an oncoming car that their headlights aren't on or if one is burnt out; to warn oncoming traffic about a police speedtrap they passed; or to indicate to the driver ahead that they would like to pass. A single short flash is usually an indicator of communication. On the other hand, repeated flashing combined with tailgating is considered intimidating, aggressive driving — and this is a punishable offence.

You should never flash your headlights at a car whose headlights are out or you could be killed by a gang

This urban legend, known as "Lights Out," has never been substantiated. It reached its height thanks to e-mail alerts that were forwarded by endless Internet users in the 1990s. It was also featured in the horror movie *Urban Legend*. According to the legend, new gang members will drive around in cars at night with their headlights off. When a driver flashes their headlights at the gang members' car, they will race them down and kill the car's occupants as part of their initiation into the gang. The legend does appear to be related to a single incident. In 1992, a driver hand-signaled a car to let them know their lights were off; the teenage occupants of the car mistook the hand signal as a rude gesture and shot and killed one of the other car's occupants. However, the teens were not in a gang, and there was no "initiation" rite.

The rickshaw is a traditional form of transportation in Asia

Invented by American Baptist minister Jonathan Scobie in 1869, the rickshaw soon caught on as a cheap and cheerful way to get around Yokohama, Japan. From there it spread to other Asian countries. Scobie's wife was an invalid, and he created the hand-drawn passenger cart so she could be pulled around the city. The original name for the cart in Japan was *jinriksha*, which means "human-powered vehicle," whereas the shortened version simply means "powered vehicle."

RIGHTS AND LEGAL ISSUES

The United States led the world in giving women the right to vote

In 1776, New Jersey women who owned over $250 were given the right to vote. However, this was done accidentally, as the word "people" instead of "men" was used in the documentation — and this right was rescinded in 1807. The Pitcairn Islands, a British colony in the southern Pacific Ocean, first gave women the vote in 1838. New Zealand introduced universal suffrage in 1893 — the first country to do so. Other countries followed, as did some individual states in the United States. However, it wasn't until 1920 that the 19th amendment to the Constitution gave all U.S. women the right to vote.

Murder is planned and manslaughter is committed in the heat of the moment

Murder can also occur in the moment. Although a premeditated murder is what is commonly thought of as murder, if a person is killed "in the heat of the moment" during a felony crime — including kidnapping or burglary — it is also classified as murder in the first degree. Manslaughter is the unlawful killing of a person without malice. Only voluntary manslaughter is considered as a "heat of the moment" killing. A death is labeled involuntary manslaughter if it occurs during a non-felony crime or when someone is acting in a "reckless or wanton" manner, for example, by running down and killing a pedestrian when driving recklessly.

A verbal agreement may be made with confidence

A verbal agreement is just as binding as a written one — at least in theory. However, according to U.S. law: "To be legally binding as a contract, a promise must be exchanged for adequate consideration." So, if there is a dispute, the defendant will need to establish that there was a verbal contract and also what was actually agreed upon. This is easier if one end of the deal has already been put in place. So, if a purchased article has been handed over, a house occupied, work begun or a check cashed, then the other party will have difficulty in proving there was no contract. It is more difficult when the matter is still undecided. If a landlord, employer, purchaser or seller backs out, it is generally not possible to establish that there has been a binding contract, unless some or all compensation has been made already. In practice, anyone who can produce a signed piece of paper or proof of adequate compensation made is far better off.

A retrial is the same as an appeal

In an appeal only the legal procedure and applicable laws will be examined to determine if there were errors of procedure. In a retrial, on the other hand, the whole case will be reiterated. The facts that led to the conviction in the first case will be examined again, and the witnesses recalled.

"Assault" and "battery" are the same thing

Assault includes the threat of force and does not necessarily involve physical contact; battery involves using force against someone. So a mugger who holds you up at gunpoint but doesn't touch you can be charged with assault, but as soon as he slugs you, it's assault and battery.

All the silly, outdated U.S. laws you read about on the Internet are made up

Although it is hard to find reputable sources online, it is true that there are still many outdated state and city laws on the books. In Massachusetts, there are laws that prohibit "embellishing" the national anthem, spitting on a steamboat or going to a bar for the purpose of seeking sex. In Fairbanks, Alaska, you are prohibited from giving alcoholic beverages to a moose. And in Missouri, a person under the age of 21 can be charged with illegal possession of alcohol if they take out the trash and it contains any empty alcoholic beverage containers. Many states, however, are actively changing these out-of-date laws. In 2005, the New York City Council Small Business Committee amended the law that required a business owner to obtain a license to wash the street or sidewalk in front of their store.

Outdated laws are just for amusement — no one is ever charged

Tell that to the "cussing canoeist." In 1999, a 25-year-old man who fell out of his canoe and into the Rifle River in Michigan was convicted for violating an 1897 law that prohibits cursing in the presence of women or children. His sentence? Four days work in a child-care program plus a $75 fine. However, in 2002 the law was struck down by the Michigan Court of Appeals and the conviction was thrown out.

MERCHANDISE AND STORE POLICIES

Products on sale can never be returned

Faulty goods may always be returned. However, merchants are not legally required to offer refunds, exchanges or credits on any items — on sale or otherwise — that are not faulty. So if a person suffers from "buyer's remorse" after hastily buying an item and bringing it home, they have to hope that the merchant will be willing to oblige in taking the item back. Many companies do offer compensation, even on sale items, but it is always worthwhile to know the company's exchange/return policy before purchasing an item — including any time limitations. Practically speaking, a sign or notice that sale items cannot be returned only advises clients that there is no readiness to oblige in this case, but no one has to resign themselves to putting up with a piece of equipment that does not work, nor with a shirt that loses its color after the first wash.

If the wrong price is advertised, that's the price you pay

When a mistake is made in advertising, such as a television set advertised at $10.00 instead of $100.00, you can't get the TV for 10 bucks. As long as it can be proved that it was a typographical error, the business has no obligation to sell the item at the lower price. When an item is ticketed incorrectly, some stores have a policy to honor the lower ticketed price, but they don't have to.

COINS AND BILLS

Dollar bills are made of paper

Actually, all American greenbacks, from $1 and up, are produced from a blend of 25 percent linen and 75 percent cotton, at a cost of 5.7 cents each. The new color notes contain a variety of red and blue synthetic fibers distributed evenly throughout the paper. Prior to World War I, the fibers were made of silk. Canada uses 100 percent cotton for its "paper" currency, and some of it is even recycled from blue jeans!

The words "In God We Trust" appears on all U.S. currency

It does now, but if you enjoy collecting currency, you likely know that these words first appeared on U.S. money in 1957. It has appeared on all U.S. currency since 1963.

Thanks to new technology, it is easy to make counterfeit bills

With improved reprographic technology, such as color printers and sophisticated scanners, governments have had to take steps over the last two decades to include security features to prevent counterfeiting. Canada and the United States use various measures, including shiny patches that appear to change color, micro- and raised printing, serial numbers, planchettes (small green discs that can actually be removed from the bill to leave a round inkless space underneath), and features that glow under ultraviolet light. Treasuries also change designs every 5 to 10 years to stay ahead of the counterfeiters. Some countries, including Canada, are considering use of a polymer material for their bills, while Australia, Haiti and Costa Rica have already converted to plastic money.

All bills last about a year or two

It all depends on the denomination of the bill. The United States Federal Reserve estimates the average life span of a $1 bill at 21 months, $5 and $10 bills at two years, a $20 bill at 22 months, a $50 bill at 4-1/2 years and a $100 bill at five years. On average, it takes about 4,000 double folds (forward and backward) before an American banknote will tear.

An American flag is flying over the Parliament buildings on Canadian paper money

On $5, $10 and $50 bills from the "Birds" series, a Canadian Red Ensign flag (which was a former flag of Canada) is flying over the Parliament buildings. In the upper left corner of the flag is a Union Jack, which contrasts with the rest of the flag, similar to the way the canton of 50 stars on the American flag contrasts with the alternating stripes on the remainder of the flag. Because the Canadian Red Ensign flag is not depicted in full color on these bills and it makes up such a small part of the image, to the naked eye it resembles the flag of the United States.

It is not against the law to burn money

Happy millionaires who light their cigars with $100 bills could be charged with a crime. This is according to Title 18, Section 333 of the United States Code, which states: "whoever mutilates, cuts, disfigures, perforates, unites or cements together, or does any other thing to any bank bill, draft, note, or other evidence of debt issued by any national banking association, Federal Reserve Bank, or Federal Reserve System, with intent to render such item(s) unfit to be reissued, shall be fined not more than $100 or imprisoned not more than six months, or both."

The cashless transaction is a modern achievement

It is older than money itself. The oldest letters of credit that have been found date from 2500 BC and consist of clay. In the high cultures of the Near East, the temples functioned as banks and administered the traders' accounts. Instead of operating with unwieldy goods of exchange, trade was carried out with credit notes. Coins, on the other hand, were invented in Lydia (now part of Turkey) around 650 BC.

GOLD AND STAMPS

The largest gold reserves in the world are at Fort Knox

The United States stores a major portion of its own gold holdings at Fort Knox. Currently this amounts to 147.3 million ounces, or about 4,520 tons. The largest amount of gold, about $90 billion worth, representing roughly one-quarter of the world's official reserves and weighing in at 7,715 tons, is stored in the vaults of the Federal Reserve Bank of New York. It was there that, during the Second World War, European countries stored their gold reserves. Many other smaller countries also used the secure vaults at the bank, so that around 1970 almost a third of the world's total gold holdings were stored there — about 12,125 tons. Since then, the European nations have, to a large extent, withdrawn their gold, so that currently there is no more than about 8,800 tons stored there, or about one-quarter of the world's gold.

The British "Penny Black" is the rarest stamp in the world

The "Penny Black" was the world's first official adhesive postage stamp. It was issued for use in 1840. However, because there are many examples of the "Penny Black" still in existence in the world, a used stamp can be bought for $200 and an unused stamp for about $3,000. The rarest stamp is the "Treskilling Yellow."

The "Mauritius Blue Penny" is the most valuable stamp in the world

Since 1996, the most valuable postage stamp is the Swedish "Treskilling Yellow," or "3 skilling banco error of color." At an auction in Geneva, Switzerland, it went for US$2.5 million. The "Treskilling Yellow" is also the rarest stamp in the world, as there is one single known specimen. It was issued in 1855 as part of the first series of postage stamps in Sweden, but was inadvertently printed not in the intended shade of green, but in a yellowish orange tint, which was intended solely for the 8-skilling stamp. A "Mauritius Blue Penny," of which there are a total of 12 known specimens, was last sold in 1993 for about US$1.7 million.

WORK AND DEATH

In the past, work was not regarded as shameful

Well-known philosophers such as Plato (427–347 BC) and Aristotle (384–322 BC) even went so far as to deny that craftsmen and day-laborers were perfectly human, because they had no time at all for spiritual and cultural creativity. In the Middle Ages as well, work was seen as a necessary evil for the lower classes. It was only in the 18th century, with the rise of the bourgeoisie, that people began to connect work with achievement, meaning of life and self-realization.

Police officers perform one of the most dangerous jobs in society

It would seem that garbage collectors are injured far more often than police officers, and taxi drivers are more likely to be shot on the job than cops.

After death your body can be sold

It is illegal to sell a body or body parts — it is punishable by fines and imprisonment. However, you can donate organs, including your liver, lungs and heart, as well as your eyes, body tissues and bones. You can also arrange to have your entire body donated to science.

By donating your body to science, your family won't have to pay funeral costs

Although most medical schools will accept bodies that are donated to them, they are not required to do so. Donated bodies can be rejected by medical schools for a variety of reasons, including contagious disease, severe trauma, if the body has been embalmed or if there is a space limitation at the school. If rejected, the family will be required to pay for funeral costs. As well, even if a body is accepted, many medical schools require the deceased's estate to pay for the travel expenses.

Plantation wood is better than wood from old-growth forests

Frequently, vast stretches of old-growth, or primeval, forests are burned to the ground to create plantations. In order to grow big-leaf mahogany, for example, which is so desirable for flooring and furniture, forests in Central and South America are being cleared on a large scale with overharvesting, selective cutting and illegal trading threatening the viability of the forests as well as the economies of these countries. In addition, the property rights of plantations are often unresolved. In the case of some tropical woods, natural forests are claimed to be plantation wood. But for plantation wood to be truly sustainable it must carry the FSC stamp, which is given only under specific circumstances that promote environmentally appropriate, socially beneficial and economically viable management of the forest.

WOOD, PAPER AND THE ENVIRONMENT

A "two-by-four" is 2 inches by 4 inches

Nope, and it never was. Its measurements are 1-1/2 to 1-5/8 inches by 3-1/2 to 3-5/8 inches. The inconsistency stems from the way logs are measured when they are cut. The wood is first cut to roughly 2 by 4 inches and is then planed down to 1-1/2 to 1-5/8 by 3-1/2 to 3-5/8 inches.

Boycotting tropical woods will save the rain forests

A boycott achieves nothing, primarily because, worldwide, there is an increasing market for tropical wood. As Brazil is actually the world's largest consumer of tropical wood, the behavior of North American buyers could be considered unimportant. Rain forests may be preserved effectively either by law, or by being managed in a careful, sustainable, environmentally friendly manner. North American consumers can have an impact, then, by purchasing tropical wood products that have been certified by the FSC (Forest Stewardship Council), an organization that guarantees that lumber has been obtained by methods that have not damaged either the environment or indigenous peoples. Buying tropical woods with this seal is not only harmless, but a genuine contribution to the protection of forests, and it is available at your local building supply center. If it isn't, ask for it. Demanding a certain product is more effective than simply not buying one.

There are no old-growth forests left in the United States

On the contrary, there are several old-growth forests in the United States, including the redwood and giant sequoia forests in California and North Carolina's bald cypress forests. There is even a small section of ancient pitch pines in the Hudson River Valley that lies about 50 miles (80 kilometers) away from New York City. In Europe, there is still primeval forest in northern Scandinavia, Germany and the Bialowieza National Park on the Poland-Russia border.

Air pollution is increasing year by year

According to the U.S. Environmental Protection Agency, between 1970 and 2001, there was a 25 percent decrease in the six principal air pollutants (nitrogen dioxide, ozone, sulfur dioxide, particulate matter, carbon dioxide and lead). This is encouraging, considering that over the same time period the U.S. population increased by 39 percent, energy consumption increased by 42 percent and vehicle miles traveled increased by 149 percent.

NUMBERS, FLAGS AND MORSE CODE

Numerals are Arabic

True, we acquired the numbers 0 to 9 in the 14th century from the Arabs. They replaced Roman numerals, which became very long and complicated for large numbers, and were badly suited to calculation. However, in Arabic countries, our "Arabic" numerals are known as "Indian" because the Arabs imported them from India in the 10th century. They replaced the Indian word *sunya* (empty) for zero with the word *sifr*, which was again altered in Europe to the Italian *nulla* (null), while *sifr* became "cipher."

The sentence "The only statistics I believe are those I falsified myself" originates with Winston Churchill

It originates with Joseph Goebbels (1897–1945). In his numerous instructions to the German Press to defame his wartime opponent, he attributed it to the British Prime Minister, Winston Churchill (1874–1964). In reality, Churchill took statistics very seriously.

Only Switzerland has a square flag

Both Switzerland and the Vatican City have square flags. Otherwise all countries have rectangular flags, except Nepal, which has a two-tiered pennant. Paraguay is the only country with a flag that does not appear the same from both sides — in the middle of the white stripe on one side is the national coat of arms, and in the middle of the other side is the seal of the Treasury. The sole country to have a flag of just a single color is Libya. The Libyan flag is completely green, which is the traditional color of Islam, the state religion.

Recycled paper is gray

It was, once upon a time. Today there is white recycled paper of the highest quality. Consumer-group tests and the American National Standards Institute have determined that it is suitable for printers and photocopiers. In fact, recycled paper often exceeds virgin paper for opacity — it is harder to see through. Businesses and governments set standards for the recycled paper products they purchase. Since 2001, for example, the U.S. government has required that papers and publications be printed on paper that is 100 percent recycled with a minimum of 50 percent post-consumer content. It should also, whenever possible, be labeled PCF (Process Chlorine-Free).

SOS stands for "Save Our Souls"

No. Neither does the distress signal stand for "Send Out Sailors" or "Save Our Ship," although it was first used as the *Titanic* sank in 1912. The signal SOS has no deeper meaning whatsoever. The combination of letters was chosen as the international distress signal in 1909 at the International Conference for Wireless Telegraphy, simply because it is easily remembered and so simple to broadcast. The signal consists of three short, three long, and three more short tones. Translated into Morse code it becomes "SOS." There is, however, no pause between the individual "letters."

LIFE, SCHOOL AND LANGUAGE

"We learn for life, not for school"

This saying is attributed to Seneca (4 BC – AD 65). However, he said exactly the opposite: *Non vitae, sed scholae, discimus!* (We do not learn for life, but for school). The reversal is not completely arbitrary, however, as Seneca's saying was meant to be critical of the way things were, not the ideal of how things should be.

The most widely spoken language in the world is Chinese

After all, there are 1.3 billion Chinese people, but only 440 million people whose mother tongue is English. But there is no such thing as *the* Chinese language. The official language of China is Mandarin, which is spoken by "only" 850 million people. However, relatively few non-Chinese speak one of the Chinese languages, but about 1.5 billion people speak English as a second language. So English is, despite everything, the most widely spoken language in the world. If we consider only a person's mother tongue, however, then more people grow up speaking Mandarin than any other language in the world.

MARRIAGE AND CHILDREN

The nuclear family barely exists anymore

In the United States, the traditional nuclear family of a mother and father with children still makes up the majority of family types, comprising about 53 percent of U.S. families. And if you stretch the definition of "mother" or "father" to indicate a step-parent, then 73 percent of American families are nuclear families.

Having children increases marital bliss

According to a variety of studies, the birth of a child often does exactly the opposite. Specifically, following the birth of a first child, there is increased stress in the marriage that may drive the husband and wife apart. Children also do not help to cement a troubled marriage — the arrival of a child will not prevent the marriage from ending in divorce. However, overall, North American couples with children have a slightly lower divorce rate than couples with no children.

In the 18th century, you could be married by the smith at Gretna Green in Scotland

At the end of the 18th century, ad hoc weddings were carried out at the legendary smithy in Gretna Green, and this caused many lovers, whose families objected to a proposed marriage, to flee to the Scottish border. But it was not the smith who carried out the weddings, but an alcoholic priest named Thomas Brown.

Catholic countries have the highest birth rates

The average world birth rate is about 20 births per 1,000 population. Although the Catholic religion's stance on birth control is a factor in birth rate, a country's economic level is another important indicator. The traditionally Catholic countries of Spain and Italy currently have some of the lowest birth rates in Europe, hovering at about 10 births per 1,000 population, although Paraguay, which has a prominent Roman Catholic population, has a rate of 29 births per 1,000. The highest birth rate in the world is in Niger, Africa, a predominantly Muslim country, with 51.3 births per 1,000 population.

The great blackout in New York City led to a baby boom

This rumor was started by the New York Times. The story held that significantly more babies than usual were born in two local hospitals exactly nine months after the great power outage in New York (November 9, 1965). The headline treatment of this story gave rise to the rumor that most people had used the blackout to devote their attention to their partners since they couldn't watch television. If they did so, then they must have taken proper precautions, because examination of the complete birth statistics for New York revealed no extraordinarily high numbers for August 1966.

PARTNERSHIP AND GOOD BEHAVIOR

Grand gestures hold a relationship together

It would appear instead that it is the small things that cement a relationship: the daily rituals; the private jargon that only the partner, and no outsider, can interpret correctly; and the common habits. Couples that share many small things together seem to get over conflicts better than those who have very different habits.

Saying "sorry" once is enough

The renowned American marriage researcher John Gottman, who has observed thousands of couples in arguments and discussions, has determined that saying sorry once is actually not enough. After every hurtful remark there needs to be about four positive words or gestures of apology before the other person is prepared to forgive.

With any problem, it helps to "talk it over"

Most therapy for couples or families encourages talk as a method of resolving problems. But talking alone is not inevitably positive. It all depends on how the conversation is carried out. If the partners speak solely to deliver their point of view for the umpteenth time — in the belief that the other has simply not understood — then the argument can easily escalate and make the problem even worse. For a discussion to work, the partners in the conversation need to show a proper interest in the other's point of view and indicate possible solutions.

When making small talk, you should avoid discussing money and politics

When it comes to small talk, it is permissible to talk about anything that is agreeable to your conversational partner and that would not offend any third party who accidentally overhears the discussion. If you can conduct a cultured conversation about money or politics, then you are certainly allowed to do so. In addition, small talk is not a synonym for a superficial conversation, as is often assumed. Small talk is a conversation that does not depend on its content or theme, but on the chance to get better acquainted with someone in an informal way.

O CAPTAIN, MY CAPTAIN!

The captain must go down with the ship

This has never been true. The captain has the responsibility to make sure that the crew and passengers are safely stowed in lifeboats. He or she is often the last to leave a sinking ship because of the responsibility for keeping the ship's cargo out of the hands of pirates, but there is no rule that the captain must sacrifice his or her own life and sink with the ship.

The captain of a ship has the power to perform the marriage ceremony

Somehow this has become an accepted belief, but in reality it is illegal for the captain of a ship to marry people unless he or she has a license to do so on land.

INVENTED BY WHOM?

Bloomers were invented by Amelia Bloomer

Amelia Bloomer (1818–94) and Elizabeth Miller (1822–1911) were both reformers who championed women's rights. It was Miller who in the 1850s started wearing bloomers — long trousers for women that were worn under skirts and gathered at the ankle. But it was Bloomer's name that was eventually associated with the garment. In the 20th century, bloomers became a term that referred to a kind of underwear with baggy legs that girls wore under gym skirts or school uniforms.

Zippers were invented by Zipper

No one named Zipper had anything to do with this type of fastener. In 1851, Elias Howe filed a U.S. patent for a fastener similar to the zipper, but it wasn't terribly practical. Then in the early 1890s, a similar device was marketed by Whitcomb L. Judsen. However, both of these "zippers" used hooks and eyes, not the interlocking teeth we are familiar with today. That was the invention of Gideon Sundback, who patented his "separable fastener" in 1917. It wasn't very popular, however, until the B.F. Goodrich Company ordered over 100,000 of the fasteners for use in their rubber galoshes. The company coined the name "zipper" based on the sound that the fastener made when being used.

Venetian blinds were invented in Venice

These slatted blinds gained wide popularity in Venice in the 1600s, but they originated in Japan, where they were originally made with strips of bamboo.

The Turks invented the Turkish bath

A Turkish bath is a kind of steam bath. Although the Turks perfected the rituals of this kind of public bathing in their traditional *hamam* baths, the Spartans in Ancient Greece were doing it centuries before it became a custom in Turkey. The bather moves through a series of hot rooms, followed by a cold plunge, a wash and sometimes a massage, and then spends some time in a cooling-down room. In Victorian times, Turkish baths became very popular in Britain.

Molotov invented the Molotov cocktail

The Molotov cocktail is a Finnish invention. During the Winter War of 1939–40, the Finns hurled gasoline-filled bottles, plugged with burning rags, at the tanks of the Red Army. They called the simple bombs Molotov cocktails, because they were directed at the then Soviet Foreign Minister, Vyacheslav Mikhailovich Molotov (1890–1986) and his troops.

THE TITANS

The Titans were the greatest of the Greek gods

In Greek mythology, the Titans were the first, but not necessarily the greatest gods. They were defeated by the Olympian gods under the leadership of Zeus. The Titans were known for their great strength, their wild natures and their lack of civilization. They were not invincible, however, and Zeus was able to conquer them. In various myths, individual Titans (such as Prometheus) tend to play a tragic role.

THE OLYMPIANS

The Greek gods lived on Olympus

The most ancient Greek gods were the 12 Titans, and they did not live on Mount Olympus. The more famous Titans were Cronos, Uranus, Gaia, Prometheus and Atlas. The 12 Olympian gods were Zeus; his wife Hera; his brothers Hades and Poseidon; his sister Hestia; Ares and Hephaestus, the sons of Zeus and Hera; as well as Zeus' children Athena, Artemis, Apollo, Hermes and Aphrodite. This familiar group was documented in the literary works of Homer (ca. eighth century BC) and Hesiod (ca. 753–680 BC). There were many other Greek gods that did not dwell on Mount Olympus, such as Dionysus, the Pleiades, Pan and Heracles.

Zeus was the mightiest Greek god

Zeus, like all the other gods, could fall victim to the goddesses who represented major passions. The dangerous female gods included Alecto (irreconcilable resentment), Tisiphone (blood vengeance), Megaera (envy), Nemesis (rightful fury), Hybris (arrogance) and Ate (dangerous passion).

Zeus was the greatest skirt-chaser of all the Greek gods

If you counted all the names of his known lovers from all the Greek myths, then Zeus had "relations" with 31 women. His brother, Poseidon, on the other hand, had a total of 34 playmates, although he didn't get as much publicity as his famous brother. Yet Poseidon produced some very interesting offspring, such as Charybdis, the sea-monster and whirlpool; the Cyclops Polyphemus; and Pegasus, the winged horse.

Religion and Philosophy

Atlas carries the globe on his shoulders

There are portrayals of Atlas that show him in this fashion, but they do not correspond exactly to the Greek sagas. According to these, the Titan Atlas has to carry the heavens on his shoulders as punishment for his part in the fight against Zeus. In another story, Perseus, to whom Atlas had refused hospitality, turned him into the Atlas Mountains (located in present-day Morocco) by showing him the severed head of the Gorgon, Medusa, whose gaze turned everything to stone.

Apollo was the Greek sun god

Apollo was the god of poetry, music and prophecy. The sun god was Apollo's son Helios, who drove a golden chariot across the sky. Helios had the epithet Phoebus, which was later merged with that of his father, Phoebus Apollo. During the Baroque period, Apollo was seen as the sun god. The "Sun King," Louis XIV (1638–1715), for example, was happy to be depicted as Apollo.

Aphrodite was born from sea foam

This is one of the various accounts about her origin and comes from the poet Hesiod. He recounts how Cronos flung the severed genitals of Uranus into the sea, where the semen mixed with sea foam and gave rise to the Goddess of Love. According to other accounts, Aphrodite is quite simply the result of a liaison between Zeus and Dione, a daughter of the sea god Oceanos. But most artists are happy to depict Aphrodite rising from the sea.

According to the Greeks there were gods and demigods

Not exactly. There were Greek gods and then there were Greek heroes. According to Homer, these heroes were normal mortal men who required divine assistance in their adventures. Hesiod calls them a separate race who lived before modern-day humans. The heroes gained a quasi-divine status, and although they were sometimes called demigods, they did not have any divine abilities.

THE ROMANS

Romans and Greeks had the same gods

There is a general tendency to equate the two: Zeus is Jupiter, Hera is Juno, Athena is Minerva, and so on. In doing so, however, one does the Roman religion an injustice. Even if the Romans gradually brought their own gods into line with the Greek gods, and even though in the end they subscribed to the Greek myths, they always knew how to differentiate between the literary and political sides of the religion. For example, the figure of Jupiter in the formal Roman culture had very little in common with the Zeus who was always chasing after women. And in everyday life, the original Roman divinities such as Lar, the Penates, Janus and Bona Dea played a much greater part than the Greek imports.

The Vestals were not allowed to marry

They certainly could — but only after they had completed their service as priestesses. That lasted 30 years, so only very few actually married. The Vestals were the priestesses of Vesta, the goddess of fire and purity, guardian of the hearth and patron goddess of bakers. The Vestal Virgins were the only priestesses in Rome. They had to come from noble families and were chosen between the ages of 6 and 10. Their task was to ensure that the sacred fire of Vesta burned perpetually. They enjoyed the very highest respect and took part in official rituals, but certainly had no say over the actual exercise of power. Because a Vestal could not be killed, they were buried alive if they broke their vow of chastity.

The Campus Martius was in Rome

The Campus Martius (Field of Mars), the 600-acre (243-hectare) ground on which the army assembled, originally lay outside the walls of the city of Rome. The Romans dedicated it to the God of War, whom they wanted to appease, but at the same time they wanted to keep his influence outside the walls of the city. Foreign dignitaries who could not enter the city of Rome would be received on Campus Martius, and competitions were held all year round to honor Mars. Between public assemblies, festivals and parades it was also used as grazing for horses and sheep. Later, the Circus Flaminius was built there for chariot racing. It was only in the first century AD that the Campus Martius became a location for new buildings. Eventually Campus Martius would come to include much of central Rome's most impressive architecture.

OEDIPUS AND THE GREEK PHILOSOPHERS

Oedipus was punished for marrying his mother

Oedipus was punished for the sins of his father. He was powerless to change his destiny. His father, Laius, was cursed after kidnapping and raping a boy. The boy's father cursed Laius, saying his son would kill him and marry Jocasta, his wife. Although Laius, Jocasta and Oedipus all did everything they could to avoid this fate, it caught up with them eventually. As king of Thebes, Oedipus was an intelligent and just ruler. When he learned that he had unknowingly killed his father and married his mother, he blinded himself and became a beggar.

Xanthippe was a quarrelsome old hag

Xanthippe, the wife of Socrates (ca. 470–399 BC) has entered history as the prototype of the nagging married woman. She is supposed to have overwhelmed her husband with words, and once supposedly emptied a chamber pot over his head. On the other hand, she had to feed three sons, and her husband refused to take any money from his many students (some of whom were the sons of the richest citizens in the city). Socrates was about 50 when he married and, apparently Xanthippe was a much younger woman. Socrates never had anything favorable to say about the marriage. Xanthippe is the subject of a humorous, rhyming quatrain known as a clerihew:

Whenever Xanthippe
Wasn't feeling too chippy
She would say to Socrates:
"Why can't you have been Hippocrates?"

Hedonism is the philosophy of pure pleasure

Hedonism — living in accordance with the principles of pleasure — was introduced as an idea by the Greek philosopher Epicurus (ca. 341–270 BC). But he did not advocate overindulgence in pure sensation, because it could lead to pain. He wanted to avoid pain and pursue pleasure. Epicurus held that the basis for a life full of pleasure was modesty. Anyone who leads a healthy, simple life can gain more pleasure from a banquet, for example, than someone who is used to eating rich food every day.

HOLY INDIA

There are no Buddhist legends

A religion without a god, one might think, could not have any legends about gods. But there is a Buddhist mythology that is just as colorful as those of other religions. Many legends surround the Enlightened One, Buddha Gautama, in which he attains a godlike status. Some even recount encounters between him and old Indian gods, such as Indra or Brahma. Other legends are woven around the lives of the bodhisattvas. These are beings who were capable of attaining full enlightenment, but who do not take this step out of compassion for other people, and are thus repeatedly reborn to do good in the world.

Buddha is a god

Buddha ("The Enlightened One") is one of the titles of the Nepalese prince Siddhartha Gautama (ca. 563–483 BC). He taught that by conquering their desires, human beings can find inner peace (nirvana) and obtain release from the cycle of rebirth. There are no gods in Buddhism; neither are there priests. Theoretically anyone can obtain full enlightenment and thus become a Buddha.

Rama and Krishna are Indian gods

Rama and Krishna not gods, but avatars. Both are considered to be human incarnations of the god Vishnu. An avatar is a human being who is the incarnation of some aspect of an immortal being, but still remains a human. Rama, considered to be the ideal man and ruler in the first versions of the Ramayana epic (second century BC), is still a mortal man. Only later does he become the manifestation of Vishnu. And Krishna was also a human being, represented at times as an uncouth rascal with supernatural powers.

Suttee was based on religion

Suttee, the notorious custom of a widow burning herself alive on her husband's funeral pyre, is named after Sati, the wife of the god Shiva. Shiva immolated himself with shame because his unruly wife had interrupted a sacrifice to the highest gods. The basis of the custom comes from the Ramayana epic, in which Sita, the wife of Rama, burns herself to death for (not with!) her husband. Suttee, however, first became a custom in the eighth century AD, when the Hindus wanted to differentiate themselves from Muslims. Though not prescribed in Hindu scripture and never a duty, it spread widely as a result of social pressure. The British banned it in India in 1892.

Yoga is a form of Indian gymnastics

Yoga (Sanskrit for "union") is a system of physical and spiritual exercises that will help one to enlightenment and thus to eventual spiritual release. The union is between body, mind and spirit. Yoga is one of the six classical systems of Indian philosophy, which start with the assumption that the visible world is just an illusion, and that truth may be attained only when one separates oneself from material things. Yoga was first developed around 500 BC.

GODS AROUND THE WORLD

Chinese religion has no gods

There is an extremely colorful Chinese heaven with gods, dragons and other fabulous creatures, but it is part of popular belief, not a religion. Ever since the sixth century BC, Chinese thought has been governed by the philosophy of the Master, K'ung-fu-tzu (Confucius, 551–479 BC). During the Han Dynasty (202 BC–AD 220), Confucianism became the official doctrine, and it remained so until the end of imperial rule. Most Chinese philosophers ignored popular beliefs and their gods. In the People's Republic of China, Chinese mythology is officially regarded as superstition.

The supreme god of Native North Americans is called Manitou

Gitche Manitou (Great Spirit) is a deity only among the Algonquian peoples. Gitche Manitou is not so much a personal god, but rather an abstract, spiritual force that inhabits everything. Many other Native American mythologies have a high deity who is responsible for creating the world. The Lakota Sioux also recognized a similar supreme, spiritual authority figure, whom they called Wakan Tanka (Great Spirit). Among the Iroquois, Orenda (also meaning Great Spirit) played a similar role.

Ayers Rock is the most sacred place to the Australian Aborigines

The Australian Aborigines venerate many different sacred sites, and Ayers Rock, now officially named Uluru, is the location of many sites that have great meaning for the local Aborigines. But there are others in the area, and elsewhere in Australia, some of which are unknown outside the aboriginal communities. Kata Tjuta (the Olgas) is another unusual rock formation about 15 miles (25 kilometers) from Uluru. This series of oddly shaped small hills is also the location of ancient, sacred sites. The Anangu, who now live near Uluru, try to discourage tourists from taking pictures and climbing near the sacred sites at both Uluru and Kata Tjuta.

Sun gods are always male

Female sun gods are found in many different cultural traditions. Among the Germanic tribes, Mani, the Moon, was male, and Sol, the Sun, was female. This is reflected in the language: *die Sonne* (the Sun, feminine) and *der Mond* (the Moon, masculine). Japanese tradition holds that the imperial family is descended from Amaterasu, the sun goddess. The Hittites in ancient Turkey had Arinna, a female sun goddess who represented fertility. In New Guinea, the Moon was regarded as male, because men hunted at night. The Sun, on the other hand, was female, because it was mainly the women who worked beneath its light. Many Native American traditions have a female sun god and a male moon god, a sister and a brother who became forbidden lovers. When they discovered they were related, they tried to avoid being in the sky together, and the Moon flees in shame when the Sun appears.

Fallen warriors were taken to Valhalla

Only when they were worthy warriors who had died heroic deaths. In Norse mythology, the Father of the Gods, Odin, assembled all the noblemen who had fallen in single combat in his palace of Valhalla. Noblemen who had not fallen in a direct duel, but who had nevertheless died in battle, were taken by the God of War, Tyr. Fallen farmers had to make do with Thor's castle — which was said to be the loudest and most cheerful place.

The Celts had gods that resembled men

Initially, they did not. As early as the third century BC, the Celts made fun of the Romans, because the latter viewed their gods as persons and erected statues to them. For the Celts, however, gods were specifically linked to particular places and were worshipped there. For example, many European rivers are named for Celtic gods: the Marne (Matrona), the Seine (Sequanna), the Saône (Souvonna) and the Severn (Sabrina). It was only later that personified gods such as Lugh, Toutatis, Belena or Epona appeared among the Celts. But there was no family of gods, just as there was no supreme god.

Zarathustra founded the first monotheistic religion

During Egypt's 18th Dynasty, pharaoh Amenhotep IV (reigned ca.1350–1334 BC) introduced a new religion, and renamed himself Akhenaten, meaning "servant of Aten." Of all the gods, only Aten was to be worshipped. It is uncertain, however, whether Akhenaten believed Aten to be the only god. At the end of the seventh century BC, Zoroaster (or Zarathustra) (ca. 628–551 BC) claimed that the Persian god Ahura Mazda was the sole creator of the world. At about the same time, the Jews asserted that god, Yahweh, was the only god.

ISLAM

Islam does not allow for a separation of religion and state

For a very brief period (AD 632–61), religious and political power was united in the Muslim state in Mecca. Since then, the king or sultan has remained separate from the religious leaders in many Islamic countries, including the Ottoman Empire and Saudi Arabia.

Islam is a religion of the desert

Muhammad was born in Mecca and is thought to have originally worked as a merchant. Islam developed as an urban religion, in part as a reaction against the tribal society of the nomads of the desert.

Muslims pray to Muhammad

The Prophet Muhammad (ca. 570–632) is greatly venerated by Muslims, but prayers are not addressed to him. He is not considered a god or the Son of God, but simply a prophet. Followers of Islam therefore disapprove of being called "Muhammadans," i.e., followers of Muhammad. "Muslim," on the other hand, means "those who follow Islam." The word Islam is translated as "acceptance of the will of God."

What the Bible is to Christians, the Qur'an is to Muslims

For most Muslims, the Qur'an is the literal revelation from God, or Allah. Muslims think of the Qur'an as presenting the same message that God had previously sent down in the Torah, through Moses, and in the Gospel, through Jesus. Many Muslims disapprove of translations, because these inevitably falsify the original text. There are Muslims who will only touch a copy of the Qur'an after special cleansing rites. Christians believe that the Bible is the word of God sent forth in the words of human beings under divine inspiration. The Bible has been translated into many different languages, and is open to a greater variety of interpretation than is the Qur'an.

The Dome of the Rock is a mosque

The Dome of the Rock on Jerusalem's Temple Mount is, for Muslims, the third-holiest shrine after Mecca and Medina. The building with the splendid golden dome was erected over a rock, from which the Prophet Muhammad was supposed to have ascended to Heaven. But it is not a mosque. For this reason, Sultan Al-Walid (reigned AD 705–715) built a huge mosque nearby, called the Al-Aqsa Mosque. But Muslims consider the whole area of the Noble Sanctuary (Temple Mount) to be part of the mosque. Thousands of worshippers overflow to fill the courtyards outside the Al-Aqsa mosque every Friday for prayers.

JUDAISM

The Star of David is an old symbol of Judaism

The six-pointed star that later became known as the Star of David was a decorative motif in the Middle East and Africa that had long been associated with good luck. In the Middle Ages, Jews, as well as Christians and Muslims, began to use the Star (a hexagram) and the five-pointed pentagram as talismans against evil. It was particularly popular among the Jewish population in Prague from the 14th century onward, and can be seen on Jewish tombs dating from that time. Mystics created a link between the Star and King David's shield. It first became a general Jewish symbol in the 18th century, when Jews were seeking a symbol that could represent their religion in the same way as the cross symbolized Christianity.

The Jewish Torah corresponds to the Old Testament

The Torah includes only the first five of the books of the Old Testament: Genesis, Exodus, Leviticus, Numbers and Deuteronomy, which are also known as the five books of Moses. The whole Jewish Bible is known as the Tanach. It consists of the Torah, the books of the prophets (Nevi'im) and additional works (Ketuvim). The books of the prophets are Joshua, Samuel, Judges, Kings, Isaiah, Jeremiah, Ezekiel, and the *Trei Asar* "Twelve." The Ketuvim include the Psalms, Proverbs, Job, Song of Songs, Ruth, Lamentations, Ecclesiastes, Ezra, Nehemiah and Chronicles.

ADAM AND EVE

Adam and Eve were created on the sixth day

In the Bible there are two creation accounts. In the first, God makes the world in seven days, and on the sixth day he creates land, animals and people. This version says God created man and woman in his image, but they do not have names. The second creation account begins with Adam being created from earth, but God doesn't create woman until some time later, as a companion for Adam. She isn't named until after the expulsion from Eden, when she is called Eve.

Lilith was Adam's first wife

In Jewish mythology, Lilith was Adam's first wife, who was banished when she refused to obey her husband. The two different creation accounts in the Bible are interpreted to suggest that Adam must first have had a wife of equal standing, and that only later was Eve created from his rib. Lilith is thus an icon for feminist theology. Jewish theologians such as Pinchas Lapide (1922–97), however, considered that "rib" is an incorrect translation. The correct interpretation would be that Eve was created from Adam's side, which would mean that she was considered his equal. A subordinate creature would have been created from his feet. Lilith, however, is actually an importation from Mesopotamia. There she was one of the powerful female demons. In Hebrew, her name means "nocturnal ghost."

Adam and Eve were banished from Eden because they succumbed to temptation

It was not giving in to temptation that got them kicked out of Eden; it was the fact that they were disobedient. Technically speaking, you could say that temptation led them to disobedience. But the message of the story is that if only humans would obey God, they could live in harmony and peace.

Eve tempted Adam with an apple

Nothing in the Bible says anything about an apple. The fruit in question came from the "tree of knowledge." In addition, it is not really possible to talk of "temptation." The passage simply says "… she took some and ate it. She also gave her husband some and he ate it." The fateful piece of fruit might have become an apple later, because *malum* in Latin means both "bad" and "apple." Or it may have changed to an apple because apples were associated with the Greek goddess of love, Aphrodite. In the Bible, however, there is no mention of apples.

Eden is a word for Paradise

Genesis 2:15 states: "Then the Lord God took the man and put him in the Garden of Eden to tend and guard and keep it." "Eden" is an old Sumerian word for desert or steppe. When Paradise is mentioned in the Old Testament it is as "the garden *in* Eden," meaning a garden in the desert. It was Martin Luther (1483–1546) who first turned this into "the Garden *of* Eden" in his translation of the Bible from Greek to German. Later translations, including the King James Version, the precursor of all Modern English bibles, relied on Luther's *Die Heilige Schrift*. The debate continues as to exactly where this garden was located.

OLD TESTAMENT

David killed Goliath

In the New English Bible, the 17th chapter of the First Book of Samuel recounts how David killed the giant Goliath. The Second Book of Samuel (21:19) states "... Elhanan son of Jair of Bethlehem killed Goliath of Gath, whose spear had a shaft like a weaver's beam." A different translation, the King James Version, has Elhanan killing Goliath's brother. There has been some debate as to which is the more accurate, with some biblical scholars arguing that Elhanan killed Goliath but David was given the credit to build up his reputation. There is no definitive proof either way.

Moses had horns

Many representations, including the famous statue by Michelangelo, show Moses with horns. This oddity has arisen from a translation error in the fourth century AD by Saint Jerome (AD 347–402). In Exodus, it states that after Moses had received the tablets with the Ten Commandments for the second time, he had rays of light (*karan ohr*) coming from his head. In Hebrew, *karan* can mean either "ray" or "horn."

The Sixth Commandment says: "Thou shalt not kill"

Yet another translation error. The Commandment reads: "Thou shalt not kill outside the law." So only murder is prohibited, not the death penalty.

The Bible instructs parents: "Spare the rod, spoil the child"

Somebody did some paraphrasing here. The closest the Bible comes to saying something like this is in Proverbs: "He that spareth his rod hateth his son: but he that loveth him chasteneth him betimes." (Proverbs 13:24, King James Version) The meaning is a little different; translated into modern English it says "if you don't discipline your son, you don't love him, but if you love him you will discipline him." The spoiling is inferred.

JERUSALEM AND THE TOWER OF BABEL

Jerusalem was founded by the Jews

Jerusalem was the capital of the Jebusites, a Canaanite tribe. It was captured by King David (reigned ca. 1004–970 BC), who enlarged it and made it his own capital. Previously, the Hebrew nomads had no capital at all. Jerusalem is probably one of the oldest cities in the world, and even at the time of its conquest by David was 2,000 years old.

The tower of Babel is purely legend

During the exile of the Jews in Babylon (586–538 BC), a high tower was actually completed there. It was a ziggurat, a stepped pyramid in honor of the Babylonian city god, Marduk, built to a height of 330 feet (100 meters). It is possible that Jewish forced laborers participated in building the tower. It is quite certain that in the multicultural trading metropolis that was Babylon, they encountered a bewildering mixture of languages.

ANGELS AND PROPHETS

Cherubim were angels

Originally, in the Old Testament, cherubim were creatures resembling the winged, human-headed bulls that were guardian figures in front of Babylonian and Assyrian palaces. They definitely had wings, but they weren't angels. They evolved into angels later. For example, Psalm 80: "Thou that art throned on the cherubim," and the Second Book of Samuel (22:11): "He rode on a cherub, he flew through the air." Angels, on the other hand, did not have wings. Many angels in the Old Testament appeared without being recognized as such. It was only in the fourth century AD that they were depicted with wings.

Prophets were clairvoyant

Many biblical prophets prophesied disasters. But these did not always occur. The citizens of Nineveh, for example, changed their ways, and the destruction prophesied by Jonah was avoided. Other prophets such as Aaron made no prophecies at all. Prophets were not known for foreseeing the future, but rather as people who would pronounce and interpret God's will. They were preachers and admonishers, but not clairvoyant. It was only in the translation into Greek (*prophemi* = predict) that the Jewish prophet became an oracular priest of the Greek type. The numerous allusions by the Evangelists in the New Testament to the fact that things occurred "and thus fulfilled the words of the prophet" clearly show how the authors were influenced by Greek thought.

Isaiah foretold the birth by a virgin

The Book of the Prophet Isaiah 7:14 reads: "Therefore the Lord himself shall give you a sign: A young woman is with child, and she will bear a son, and will call him Immanuel." In the Hebrew text the word *alma* means "young woman." It was Martin Luther (1483–1546) who first changed this to a virgin, which in Hebrew would have been rendered as *betula*.

NEW TESTAMENT

The founder of the Christian religion was called Jesus

He was called Joshua or Jeshua, which means "he who will save." Jesus is the Greek version of these names. The title "Christ" was first bestowed upon him by his followers after his death. It is also Greek and means "the Anointed," translated from the Hebrew term *masiah* (messiah).

Jesus said he was the Son of God

According to the Gospels, he never did. Jesus referred to God as his father, but he referred to himself as "the Son of Man."

The New Testament was written in Hebrew

The Old Testament was mostly written in Hebrew, but the original language of the New Testament was Greek, which was the common tongue in the eastern Mediterranean at the time. Jesus and his followers probably did not speak Hebrew, but Aramaic.

There are only four Evangelists

The four best known Evangelists were Mark, Luke, Matthew and John. But there were also apocryphal (secret) Evangelists who were not accepted into the canon of the Bible because they were viewed as more-or-less questionable. These include, for example, the Protogospel of Jacob, the Gospel according to Thomas, the Gospel of Pseudo-Matthew, and many more. They are, however, the source of many elements in popular thought, such as the ox and the ass, accounts of the childhood of Jesus, Mary's eternal virginity and the depiction of Joseph as an old man.

CHRISTMAS AND THE STAR

Jesus was born in year zero

No one at all was born in the year zero. There never was such a year, because zero was not used in the Roman counting system. In the sixth century AD, the monk Dionysius Exiguus (ca. AD 470–544) was asked by Pope John I to determine the dates of Easter for the years 527 to 626. Using the years of Rome's founding as a starting point, Dionysius's carried out computations that showed that Jesus had been born in the year 753 in the Roman calendar (since the foundation of the city). He established this as the year AD 1: "Anno Domini," meaning the first year of Our Lord. It was only in relatively modern times, when people began to use negative dates (i.e., BC: Before Christ) that AD was equated with "after Christ." A year zero was never introduced, however, so that 1 AD followed immediately after 1 BC. On this basis, the third millennium also began on January 1, 2001, as the 20th century did on January 1, 1901.

Jesus was born in the year 7 BC

To calculate the date of Jesus' birth, many have used the Star of Bethlehem as a starting point. Even the author of the laws of planetary motion, Johannes Kepler (1571–1630) assumed that the Star of Bethlehem was a conjunction of Jupiter and Saturn in the year 7 BC, which means that both planets appeared so close together that they shone like a single, particularly bright star. In ancient astrology, Jupiter represented the supreme ruler, and Saturn the Kingdom of Judah, which made it the perfect event to mark the birth of the Son of God. However, there were other conjunctions of planets around this time that could have resulted in what looked like a very bright star. For example, in the year 2 BC, Venus and Jupiter came unusually close. His birth date has never been conclusively established.

Jesus was born when Herod was King of Israel and Quirinius was Governor of Syria

Luke the Evangelist appears to give very precise details, saying that Jesus was born during Herod's reign and at the time of the census conducted by Syria's governor, Quirinius. Unfortunately, he was mistaken in at least one of his facts. By most accounts Herod died in 4 BC, though some say as late as 1 BC, while the date at which Quirinius took office and the tax census occurred is a full 10 years later, in AD 6.

Jesus was born in Bethlehem

Unfortunately that doesn't make sense. Church historians now assume that Jesus came into the world perfectly normally in the house of his parents. In their view, the stories about Bethlehem arose later because of the Jewish prophecy that this town would be the birthplace of the Messiah. Even if there had been a tax census and Joseph had property in Bethlehem, there would not have been the slightest reason for him to have had to take his pregnant wife with him.

Jesus Christ was born on December 25

The exact day of Jesus' birth is unknown. December 25 was chosen in about AD 354 to celebrate his birth. It was chosen to take advantage of existing celebrations: the observance of the Winter Solstice on December 21, and a traditional Roman feast day on December 25.

"Xmas" is a modern, commercial abbreviation for Christmas

"X" has been used as an abbreviation of the word "Christ" for hundreds of years. It is the first letter of his name, *Christos*, in Greek, written as Χριστος. Xmas has been used as a shorter form of Christmas since about 1755.

Three Wise Men visited the baby Jesus in the stable in Bethlehem

Although tradition would have it that three wise men, or kings, from the east came on camels to pay homage to the Christ-child, the factual evidence of their visit is not conclusive. The Bible says that "wise men from the east" came, but it doesn't specify how many, how they got there or when they visited Jesus. Most likely they were magi, learned men who studied astrology, perhaps connected to the Zoroastrian religion, which was based in Persia. But they probably walked rather than rode camels, and they may have arrived up to a year after Jesus' birth, in which case he would no longer be living in the stable, but in a house.

There is just one account of Jesus' birth

Two may be found in the Bible. One is in the Gospel according to Luke. It is the well-known Christmas story: Mary and Joseph make their way to Bethlehem, where they find no place at the inn, and the Christ-child is born in the stable. Matthew, on the other hand, recounts how Mary and Joseph live in Bethlehem with their small son. Attracted by a star, the Magi come from the east and honor the child, but also bring his birth to the notice of King Herod, and the family are forced to flee to Egypt. The Evangelists Mark and John say nothing about the matter.

Herod was a Jewish king

Herod the Great (73–4 BC) was the son of an Idumaean father and a Nabatean mother. The Idumaeans, also known as the Edomites, lived in southern Judea. The Nabateans were an Arabic tribe, whose capital was Petra in Jordan. Herod's family was probably forcibly converted, and was thus not regarded by the Israelites as true Jews. He was king by Rome's approval. In securing his rule he was certainly not squeamish, but the legendary "Massacre of the Innocents" undoubtedly did not take place. He rendered outstanding service, primarily through his building projects, but also through his sound administration.

PHARISEES AND PONTIUS PILATE

The Pharisees were hypocrites

According to the Evangelists, the Pharisees were religious hypocrites and the fiercest opponents of Jesus. Religious experts, however, are certain that this cannot have been the case. The Pharisees certainly took the laws extremely seriously, but there was no prohibition on healing or saving lives on the Sabbath, for example. In addition, they did not demand that their religious opinions be shared by everyone. In much that Jesus said and did, he was very close to the Pharisees, particularly to the famous Rabbi Hillel, known as Hillel the Elder (active ca. 30 BC – AD 10), who must have lived at about the same time. Many Biblical scholars believe that the Evangelists glossed over the role of the powerful Romans, and thus made the Jews appear worse than they actually were.

Pilate did not want to condemn Jesus

This is a matter of conjecture. Pontius Pilate was Prefect of Judaea from AD 26–36. Authors such as Philo of Alexandria (ca. 20 BC– AD 50) and Flavius Josephus (ca. AD 37–100) confirm that he discharged his office in a cruel, hard manner. Philo recounts constant executions, corruption and a strong enmity toward the Jews. Among other things, Pilate seized the treasures of the Temple for building projects and had the protesting crowds beaten to the ground with clubs. In AD 36 he was recalled because of corruption and a massacre of Samaritans. With a reputation like this, it seems quite likely that he would willingly order the execution of Jesus as a means of calming the situation, which was quite a standard response for Roman governors.

Jesus had to carry the cross to Golgotha

Both the flogging scourging and the "Way of the Cross" were customary in a Roman crucifixion. However, the convicted men did not carry the whole cross, but only the crossbar, to which they were already fastened. Generally they were tied to it. Nailing was extremely rare.

PAUL AND PETER

The Pauline letters were written by Saint Paul

The New Testament contains 14 letters that are supposedly written by the Apostle Paul (ca. AD 5–65). Bible researchers are not completely in agreement as to which were actually written by him. Some may have been written by his disciples. The letters in question are the Letter to Hebrews, the two Letters to Timothy, the one to Titus, as well as the Letters to the Ephesians, the Colossians and the second Letter to the Thessalonians.

The Bible states that "Money is the root of all evil"

Saint Paul says: "For the love of money is the root of all evil: which while some coveted after, they have erred from the faith, and pierced themselves through with many sorrows." (I Timothy 6:10, King James Version). It is clearly the *love* of money, not money itself, that causes all the problems.

Jesus was crucified on a cross

Well, yes, but not the Latin cross that has since become the symbol of Christianity. Romans used a T-shaped cross for crucifixions, and it is most likely that Jesus was crucified on one of those. The traditional Christian cross may have developed as a result of the first two letters of Jesus' name in Greek: XP, which formed a cross when written together. Jesus was often referred to by the first two letters of his name. Most early Christians were illiterate, but they came to recognize this short form of his name, and eventually it evolved into the Latin cross associated with Christianity.

The first Christians lived on the Mediterranean

Shortly after the death of Jesus, Paul began intensive missionary work over the whole of the area around the eastern Mediterranean, creating individual congregations. The first country to declare its faith in Christ and to make the new beliefs its official religion, was Armenia in the year AD 301. It was converted to Christianity by the Apostles Thaddeus and Bartholomew. The Armenian Church is called Apostolic in their honor.

Saint Peter was executed in Rome

Documentary evidence of this is a single sentence in the first Letter of Peter, which, however, was not written by Peter: "Greetings from her who dwells in Babylon ... and from my son Mark." In this, "Babylon" is supposed to be employed as a cover name for Rome. The first to report that Peter and Paul were executed in Rome was Irenäus of Lyon (ca. AD 135–200). In the second century, the first bishop of Rome was recorded as Saint Linus (died AD 79). It was only in the third century that it was asserted that Peter was the first bishop of the Roman congregation.

The first Christians held secret services in the Roman catacombs

Services in the catacombs were certainly illegal because Christianity was forbidden, but did not need to be held in secret because according to Roman law, burial places were inviolable. And the catacombs themselves were not secret, but completely legal burial places. But because the space was restricted, large masses were probably not celebrated there, but only memorial services for people who had died.

INQUISITION

No one had a chance when faced with the Inquisition

The Inquisition (12th–15th centuries) was actually a process of ecclesiastical law that dealt with heretics, set up by Pope Gregory IX (reigned 1227–41). Its primary aim was the conversion of heretics, not their destruction. After three detailed cautions, if a person persisted in his views, he was considered a heretic. But even that did not lead inevitably to being burned at the stake. There were Inquisitors who did not pass a single death sentence. But equally, there were those who believed that heretics should be mercilessly exterminated, and that 1,000 wrong verdicts were preferable to missing just a single one.

Bernard Gui was a particularly terrible Inquisitor

This is according to author Umberto Eco (born 1932). The sinister figure from his historical novel, *The Name of the Rose*, did really exist. Bernard Gui (ca. 1260–1331) was a committed Inquisitor, but he had the reputation of being very conscientious in finding out whether the accused really held heretical views. Of the 930 charges of heresy he handled, 42 people were burned at the stake, approximately 300 were imprisoned for life, about 130 acquitted and the remainder sentenced to undertake pilgrimages, acts of penance or to have their houses destroyed.

POPES AND ANTIPOPES

There was a Pope John XX

There was no such pope. John XX was simply forgotten. There was John XIX (Romanus of Tusculum), who reigned 1024–32. Petrus Juliani (reigned 1276–77) adopted the name of John 250 years later, but he called himself John XXI. Neither was there a John XVI. Johannes Philagathos (reigned 997–998) who bore this name, was never officially recognized. One would also seek in vain for Popes Martin II and III, because for a long time, two Popes named Marinus were erroneously listed as Martin. There was no officially recognized Felix II either, with the numbers jumping from Felix I to Felix III. There was a Felix II (reigned 356–358), but he was considered an "antipope."

The Pope is infallible

Popes have claimed repeatedly that they and the Church are infallible. According to the dogma of 1870, however, only pronouncements "ex cathedra" (from the bishop's throne) are infallible. The two dogmas that have been pronounced "ex cathedra" since then are among the most controversial: the Immaculate Conception and the physical admission of Mary into Heaven. Apart from that, the Church has even condemned one Pope as a heretic. Honorius (reigned AD 625–638) was admittedly a very worthy man, but he believed that two natures, one human and one divine, were present in Jesus, and because of this he was anathematized (excommunicated) in AD 680, 40 years after his death.

Popes cannot have legitimate children

Any widower with children is allowed to take up a priestly career. Nowadays it is unlikely that he would ever become Pope, but over the course of history, this has happened. Felix III (reigned 483–92), Clement IV (Guy Foulques, reigned 1265–68) and Pius IV (Giovanni Angelo Medici, reigned 1559–65) all had several children. Felix V (Amadeus VIII of Savoy, reigned 1440–49) was not actually a Pope, but a deeply religious man who, after the death of his wife and his oldest son, withdrew into a monastery. Through his second son, he was the ancestor of the later kings of Italy.

No Roman Catholic priest has been married

Although marriage is forbidden for priests in the Catholic church, it is possible for someone who has previously been married to become a Roman Catholic priest.

There are no female Catholic priests

In the Czech underground church, women were ordained from 1970 onward, because men stood no chance of being allowed to provide pastoral care for Catholic prisoners in women's jails. How many women in all have been ordained is unknown, although we do know about the "Danube Seven," a group of women who were ordained on the Danube River in 2002. Since then, similar ordination ceremonies have occurred in the United States, Canada, Spain and Switzerland. The Catholic church continues to excommunicate the ordained women.

SAINT PATRICK AND ATHEISTS

Saint Patrick was Irish

Only in spirit. Saint Patrick (ca. AD 386–493) was born Maewyn Succat into a wealthy family living in the Roman province of Britannia (now Scotland), some time in the late fourth century. As a young boy of 16 he was kidnapped by pirates and taken to Ireland, where he was sold as a slave. At 22 he escaped to Gaul, where he sought the guidance of Saint Germanus, Bishop of Auxerre (died ca. AD 449). For the next 15 years Succat studied for the priesthood and in AD 432 he received a calling to return to Ireland. Before leaving, Pope Celestine (reigned AD 422–32) consecrated Maewyn Succat, baptizing him Patricius. He would spend the next 30 years in Ireland, where he converted many of the Irish to Christianity.

The American South has always been deeply religious

Not so. It was not until 1850 that the southern states became more fundamentalist in their approach to Christianity. Prior to that and as far back as the 1600s and 1700s, the northern states had a higher proportion of fundamentalist Christians, largely because of that region's promise of freedom from persecution. By the mid-1800s, however, churchgoers in the south outnumbered those in the north twofold.

Atheists are not interested in God

Atheists do not accept the existence of a God nor of supernatural forces. To arrive at this certainty, however, one must first have extensively considered the question of these forces. The writer Heinrich Böll (1917–85) even once maliciously remarked that in his view, atheists talked about God too much.

PHILOSOPHY

Logic has something to do with common sense

Scientific logic is completely unrelated to the content of a statement. Logic seeks laws, which when correctly applied, inevitably lead to true statements. That can also apply to variables. For example: for every A, B applies. C is an A. Therefore C also applies to B. Insects have six legs. Beetles are insects. Therefore, beetles have six legs.

Machiavelli was an evil man

Niccolo Machiavelli (1469–1527) wrote a book in 1515 called *The Prince*. Based on Machiavelli's lifelong study of politics and government, the book describes how a ruler must be cruel to retain power. The term "Machiavellian" came into use as a description of someone who was calculating and deceitful like the character in *The Prince*. But Machiavelli himself was a philosopher, a musician, a playwright and a poet, and was not guilty of any of the cruelty he discussed in his famous book.

"Desiderata" was written in 1692

The famous words of wisdom, featured in a widely circulated poster in the 1960s, were written by Max Ehrmann in 1927. His copyright did not appear on the poster, and it was falsely attributed to an anonymous writer in the 17th century, and purported to have been "discovered" in Old Saint Paul's, a church in Baltimore.

Rousseau demanded a return to nature

The Swiss philosopher Jean-Jacques Rousseau (1712–78) did not suggest that humans return to a natural state and live like animals. He did support the idea that people were fundamentally good, but civilization was often a path to misfortune and injustice. As a way forward, he proposed a voluntary, democratic social contract between individual people and an education that did not destroy the natural tendency for good in children.

Kant preached a sense of duty and was humorless

The philosopher Immanuel Kant (1724–1804) did lay great stress on duty. He emphasized that valid ethical rules must be applied under all circumstances. Compliance must not depend on the actual situation, nor be interpreted in the light of the possible outcome, nor a person's personal sympathies. This stringent application of ethical rules gained Kant the reputation for being dry and humorless. But Kant was an amusing conversationalist, a legendary host and a witty, imaginative lecturer. In addition, he always championed people's freedom to shape their world for themselves.

Nietzsche was anti-Semitic and a nationalist

Both German and Italian Fascism referred to Friedrich Nietzsche (1844–1900). Theories of the *Übermensch* (Superman) and of a *Herrenmoral* (morality of masters) were particularly well suited to Fascist propaganda. But Nietzsche was, above all, a radical individualist, to whom only individual genius counted, not a group, a race or a nation. He spoke out against anti-Semitism. His sister, Elisabeth Förster (1846–1935), however, used her brother's estate and his writings to promote Fascist propaganda.

Nietzsche wrote *Will to Power*

Purported to be Nietzsche's magnum opus, the 20-volume *Will to Power* was posthumously published by his anti-Semitic sister, Elisabeth Förster. He wrote parts of it, but his sister cut and pasted the manuscript and essentially rewrote it, using it to promote her own beliefs. Scholars researching it decades later found Nietzsche's original pages and it became clear that Förster had subverted her brother's words and intent to such an extent that he can no longer legitimately be named as the author of the book.

GEOGRAPHY LESSONS

England is a country

England, Scotland and Wales are political divisions within the country of the United Kingdom.

Americans are people who live in the United States

"Americans" refers to all people who live on the continents of North and South America, from the Arctic to the southernmost island in the archipelago of Tierra del Fuego. However, it has become a worldwide custom to refer to inhabitants of the United States as "Americans."

The Pennsylvania Dutch are Dutch

This group of settlers came to the Pennsylvania area in the 1600s from Germany. They called themselves *Deutsch*, which was mangled into "Dutch." Some Pennsylvania Dutch (the Amish and some Mennonites) have retained their traditional language and customs, living much the way their far-off ancestors did. But many have assimilated into modern American culture.

Illinois lies east of the Mississippi River

Most of Illinois does lie east of the great river. However, in the 19th century, after a big flood, the river cut itself a new channel near Kaskaskia, Illinois. Now this small part of Illinois lies west of the river.

The Black Hills of South Dakota are hills

Technically, they're not hills but mountains. Many of them are higher than 6,000 feet (1,830 meters) above sea level, and the highest, Harney Peak, rises to 7,242 feet (2,207 meters).

The United Nations is located in the United States

The United Nations headquarters occupies an 18-acre (7-hectare) piece of land on the East River in New York that is officially international territory. It was given to the world organization by John D. Rockefeller Jr. (1874–1960) in 1946. The complex was designed by a consortium of architects from 11 countries, including the United States, the Soviet Union and China.

The Klondike is in Alaska

The site of the Gold Rush of the late 1890s was the Klondike River near Dawson City in Yukon Territory, Canada. The discovery of gold in the river in 1896 heralded a frenzied gold rush, with a total of about 100,000 people making the difficult journey from the United States and elsewhere in Canada to the Yukon.

The Panama Canal cuts across the Isthmus of Panama from east to west

Because of the twisty nature of the Isthmus, the canal actually runs north-south and then east. The Pacific end of the canal (in the Gulf of Panama) is 20 miles (32 kilometers) east of the canal's entrance in the Caribbean. When traversing the canal, ships are said to be traveling south if they're going to the Pacific, and traveling north if they're heading to the Atlantic. The canal took 34 years to build and was finally completed in 1914. It provides a vital time-saving link between the Atlantic and Pacific oceans, shaving 8,000 miles (12,875 kilometers) off the journey.

WHAT'S IN A NAME?

Chicago is called the "Windy City" because of its weather

It certainly is windy many days of the year in Chicago, but in fact it was christened the "Windy City" by the editor of the *New York Sun*, Charles Dana, during the World Exposition held there in 1893. Weary of the long-windedness of politicians' incessant boasting about the city and its Expo, he referred to it as the Windy City.

Pennsylvania is named after William Penn, who founded the state

When William Penn (1644–1718) founded Pennsylvania in 1681, he called it *Sylvania*, which was Latin for "woods." But King Charles II, who had given the land to Penn, asked that it be named "Pennsylvania" in honor of Penn's father, Admiral Sir William Penn (1621–70).

Hell Gate on the East River in New York was named after hell

The Dutch who originally settled in Manhattan called the East River *Die Helle Gat*, which means "beautiful passage" in Dutch. This phrase became "Hell Gate" in English and soon was associated with the dangerous passage between the East River and Long Island Sound.

The Canary Islands were named for canaries

The seven Canary Islands lie off the northwest coast of Africa and belong to Spain. The largest of the Canary Islands was named *Insularia Canaria* by ancient Romans. This means "island of the dogs" in Latin. Apparently the island was inhabited by packs of large, wild dogs when the Romans landed there.

Devil's Island owes its name to its very hot climate

Devil's Island, off the coast of French Guiana, was not named for its climate. The water around it is extremely turbulent, and this gave rise to its name. Long used as a penal colony, the name is very apt for the nature of the prison there: disease-infected and surrounded by jungle, it housed both political prisoners and criminals. Many of them died from malnutrition and bad treatment. The prison was used from 1852 to 1946.

Iran is the modern name for Persia

The country was called *Iran* (Land of the Aryans) from the third century AD onward, although it had been called *Pārsa* before that. The Greeks called it *Persis*, and the Latin form is *Persia*. It was widely known as Persia for many centuries, but in 1935 the Shah of Iran made a proclamation that the country would once again be known as Iran. But "Persia" and "Persian" are still sometimes used.

THE EARTH AND ITS POLES

The Earth is a sphere

In fact, the Earth does not resemble a perfectly round ball, but rather an apple or gourd. It is slightly flattened at the poles, more at the South Pole than at the North Pole, and bulges out at the Equator. Sea level there is about 13 miles (21 kilometers) farther from the center of the Earth than at the poles. The reason for this deformation is the Earth's rotation, and the proximity of the Moon and the effects of its gravitational pull. To be scientifically correct, the Earth is a "flattened rotational ellipsoid" or an "oblate spheroid."

There is one North Pole and one South Pole

There are two North Poles and two South Poles. The *geographic* poles are fixed by the Earth's rotation and are located at the ends of the Earth's rotational axis, where all lines of latitude converge at 0° longitude. The other two poles are the *magnetic* North and South Poles. There is, of course, no giant magnet inside the Earth. However, the Earth does have a magnetic field, as if a giant bar magnet were located inside the Earth. The exact reason for the magnetism is still not fully understood.

Robert Peary was the first to reach the North Pole

Although nearly everyone knows of the thrilling competition between Robert Falcon Scott (1868–1912) and Roald Amundsen (1872–1928) to reach the South Pole, the first explorers to reach the North Pole is not so clear cut. Robert Edward Peary (1856–1920) was supposed to have arrived there on April 6, 1909, with his assistants Matthew Henson (1886–1955) and four Inuit. But he probably never reached it. The data given by his measurements were more accurate than was technically possible at the time, and Peary reported covering distances each day that were unbelievable. Even more dubious were the details given by both Frederick Cook (1865–1940), who was supposed to have made it to the North Pole a year before Peary, and Richard Evelyn Byrd (1888–1957), who supposedly flew over it on May 9, 1926. The first men to reach the Pole were probably Roald Amundsen, Umberto Nobile (1885–1978) and their crew, who flew there with the airship *Norge* on May 12, 1926. Nonetheless, Peary, Henson, Cook and Byrd were significant polar explorers.

THE COLD PLACES

The Arctic is an island

There is no land beneath the ice in the Arctic. If the ice cover were to melt, there would only be a giant ocean around the North Pole. The Antarctic, by contrast, is a true continent.

The Arctic lies outside any national boundaries

The territory of the Arctic is divided between seven countries. It belongs to the United States, Canada, Russia, Norway, Sweden, Finland and Denmark. The Antarctic, on the other hand, is international territory. The Antarctic Treaty was signed by 43 countries and runs until 2041.

There are no flowers in the Antarctic

A type of dianthus and some flowering grasses grow in Graham Land, a northern peninsula, and on a few islands. Sweet vernal grass and chickweed have also been imported by humans and have survived. Most of the approximately 600 different types of plant in the Antarctic are algae, lichens and mosses. About 98 percent of the total of more than 5,405,430 square miles (14 million square kilometers) of surface is ice, comprising 90 percent of the world's ice and nearly 70 percent of its fresh water.

Compass needles always point north

There are in fact two "north" poles. Compass needles point to the magnetic North Pole, which at this time lies slightly less than 1,250 miles (2,000 kilometers) from the geographic North Pole, which is located on the polar ice cap among the Queen Elizabeth Islands in Canada. The magnetic South Pole is located about 1,550 miles (2,500 kilometers) from the geographic South Pole, which is located in the sea 1,000 miles (1,600 kilometers) off the Antarctic coast, in the direction of Australia. This disparity is because the Earth's magnetic field shifts over time. Eventually, over the course of millions of years, it will completely reverse its polarity. Tests of the paleomagnetism of Earth's rock layers has revealed that the magnetic field has reversed completely several times over the planet's lifetime. The last reversal occurred about 750,000 years ago. Although scientists do not expect the next one for some time, the last thousand years has seen a significant shift in the magnetic North Pole between northern Canada and Siberia.

Inuit traditionally live in igloos

Inuit usually live in huts and tents. They only build igloos on their hunting trips, when they have to spend the night on the ice.

Scandinavia is a term for the northern European countries

Neither Iceland nor Finland belong to Scandinavia. Originally the term was applied only to the Scandinavian peninsula, which includes Norway and Sweden. Culturally, however, Denmark is also included in Scandinavia. Finland, on the other hand, was under Swedish sovereignty from 1154 to 1809, and as such was included in the term "Scandinavian." In 1809 Finland was annexed to Russia as an autonomous Grand Duchy. But even today, many Finns are not at all happy if they are described as Scandinavians. Finland, Iceland, the three Scandinavian countries and the autonomous regions of Greenland and the Åland Islands together call themselves the Northern Lands.

THE HOT PLACES

The Sahara is the greatest sand desert

The Sahara, which extends over approximately 3.5 million square miles (9 million square kilometers), is indeed the largest desert in the world, but most of it consists of rock, and only a very tiny fraction is sand. The largest sand desert in the world is the Great Arabian Desert, or Rub-al-Khali, in the southeast of the Arabian Peninsula. It covers 250,000 square miles (650,000 square kilometers). Some of its dunes stretch for several miles and reach heights of 3,300 feet (1,000 meters). The Rub-al-Khali is one of the least accessible regions of the world.

In any desert there are traces of life

For most deserts this is true. However, scientists have discovered an area in the interior of Iran in which, up to now, no traces of animal or plant life has been discovered. This is the Dasht-e Lut Desert in central Iran, which is about 62,000 square miles (160,000 square kilometers) in size. One of the driest and hottest areas on Earth, it has never been inhabited by human beings.

Deserts are hot and absolutely dry

At nighttime, the temperatures of deserts may drop below 32°F (0°C), and on an average day temperatures can plummet 50°F–70°F (28°C–42°C) from the daytime high to the nighttime low. Generally, deserts are dry, but despite this, hundreds of people have drowned in them. When it rains, the dry river beds are subject to dramatic flash floods. Otherwise, you would have to dig deep to find water in a desert. Millions of tons of fossil water are stored beneath the Sahara, at a depth of about 33,000 feet (10,000 meters).

The water in the Dead Sea contains more salt than anywhere else in the world

The Dead Sea, situated between Israel and Jordan, has a salt content of more than 30 percent. But Lake Asal in central Djibouti, Africa, contains even more salt. It lies 500 feet (150 meters) below sea level, the lowest point of the African continent, and contains almost 35 percent salt. Two things contribute to its extreme saltiness: the lake is fed by water from the Indian Ocean, and it experiences extremely high evaporation.

Arabs are peoples of the desert

Most Arabs in Saudi Arabia are either farm workers or city dwellers. Only a quarter of the Arabian peninsula is true desert, and the nomads that live there are a minority in the country as a whole.

EXPLORERS

Ferdinand Magellan was the first to sail around the world

The Portuguese explorer Magellan (1480–1521) undertook two great voyages. In 1505 he sailed by the eastern route to the Moluccas (the Spice Islands) in Indonesia. In 1519, he wanted to reach the Moluccas by the western route, but he was killed in the Philippines. If both his voyages are taken together, he did sail around the world. But the first true round-the-world sailors were the 18 members of Magellan's crew who survived. Led by the former helmsman Juan Sebastian Elcano (ca. 1476–1526), they finally reached Spain in September 1522.

The southern tip of Africa is the Cape of Good Hope

The southernmost point of Africa is Cape Agulhas (Needle Cape), which is about 90 miles (150 kilometers) east of the Cape of Good Hope, and lies about 40 miles (65 kilometers) farther south. Bartholomew Diaz (1450–1500), who was the first to describe both capes in 1488, spoke about *Caba tormentosa* (stormy cape), but it is not clear which cape he meant, nor which he measured. The more distinctive feature for sailors is the Cape of Good Hope, which was so named by the Portuguese King John II (1455–95), who hoped that they had discovered the sea route to the Indies.

Australia was discovered by James Cook

If we neglect the Aborigines, who must also have discovered Australia at some stage when they migrated there, then it was probably Spanish or Portuguese sailors who discovered Australia in the 16th century. The earliest record of a European reaching Australia was the Dutchman Willem Janszoon (ca. 1570–1630) in the year 1606. In the following decades, other Dutch sailors traveled to Australia, but the colonization of the fifth continent began in earnest with James Cook (1728–79), who took possession of the country for the British Crown in 1770.

MOUNTAINS

Edmund Hillary was the first person to climb Mount Everest

First of all, the New Zealander Edmund Hillary (born 1919) was not alone when he climbed Mount Everest on May 29, 1953. He was accompanied by the Sherpa Tenzing Norgay (1914–86). In addition, it is possible that George Mallory (1886–1924) and Andrew "Sandy" Irvine (1902–1924) had already reached the summit. However, neither returned from their expedition. In 1999, Mallory's body was found at an altitude of about 27,060 feet (8,248 meters). Experts disagree as to whether it is likely that he had previously reached the summit. One person certainly did not climb it: George Everest (1790–1866), the man after whom the peak is named. He was Surveyor General of India from 1830 till 1843, and was responsible for completing a large section of the Great Trigonometric Survey of India.

Reinhold Messner is the person who has climbed Everest most

Although the world-famous mountaineer Reinhold Messner (born 1944) was the first to climb Mount Everest without oxygen, and the first to go up the north face by himself, the record-holder for climbing the highest peak in the world is Appa Sherpa (born ca. 1962). As Climbing Sirdar, or Head Sherpa, he reached the peak for the 16th time in May 2006. He did four of these trips without supplemental oxygen. He made his first ascent of Everest in 1990, and earns enough to support his family by climbing the mountain. "Sherpa" is not a synonym for "porter," but the name of a tribe that originated in Tibet and now lives in the Everest region on the Tibetan-Nepalese border. Sherpa sometimes work as porters on Everest expeditions, but more often they are lead climbers and group managers (sirdars).

All the Himalayan mountains have been climbed

The major exception is Khumbi Yul Lha (Holy Mother of the Khumbu, also known as "the holy mountain"). That is not because the ascent to the peak is particularly difficult at 18,700 feet (5,700 meters), but because climbing it is an absolute religious taboo for the region's inhabitants. Up to now, European mountaineers have respected this, although previously, other holy mountains, such as Everest (in Nepalese, *Sagarmatha* — Goddess of Heaven), have been climbed.

The Cordillera lie in South America

The name "Cordillera" is often used as a synonym for the Andes Mountains. But *cordillera*, which means "mountain range" in Spanish, can refer to any mountain range. So it's not surprising to find that in addition to the many cordillera in the Andes, such as Cordillera de Venezuela and Cordillera Occidental, the name cordillera is attached to mountain ranges in Spain, the Philippines, Dominican Republic, Puerto Rico and Costa Rica.

Ayers Rock is the largest monolith on Earth

The largest is Mount Augustus (Burringurrah) in Western Australia, about 200 miles (320 kilometers) east of Carnarvon. Rising 2,352 feet (717 meters) and covering nearly 11,860 acres (4,800 hectares), it is more than twice the size of Ayers Rock (Uluru), which is 1,135 feet (346 meters) in height.

CANADA AND THE UNITED STATES

The United States is the largest country in North America

Canada is larger. It covers an area of approximately 3,854,083 square miles (9,984,690 square kilometers). The dry land includes some 55,000 islands — more than any other country in the world. After Russia, and ahead of China, Canada is the second largest country in the world.

Canada is a bilingual country

Officially Canada is bilingual, and all government documents and services are required to be available in French and English. But it's a different story when it comes to what people speak at home and work. According to the 2001 national census, barely 18 percent of Canada's 30 million citizens can speak both languages. The only exception is *la belle province* — Quebec — where of its five million residents, 64 percent speak French, but only 31 percent can communicate in English.

The worst volcanic eruption was that of Krakatoa

The eruption of Krakatoa (its Indonesian name is Krakatau) on August 27, 1883, is the greatest recorded volcanic eruption. It destroyed two-thirds of the south Asian island and blanketed the area for 22 days in a cloud of smoke and dust, which was visible more than 435 miles (700 kilometers) away. The seismic waves caused a tsunami that killed about 36,000 people on Java and Sumatra. However, the eruption of Sumbawa (also in Indonesia) in 1815 may have been smaller in size but as it continued for several months it had about three times as many victims, some dying from the blast and lava flows while others died of disease and starvation. The weather of the entire planet was affected by the ash that blanketed the area. The temperatures were so much cooler that 1816 was known as the "Year Without a Summer."

The Niagara Falls are the highest waterfalls in the world

With their longest fall just 188 feet (57 meters), Niagara Falls, on the border between United States and Canada, is one of the lowest of the world's spectacular waterfalls. What makes them so impressive is their width (3,600 feet/1,097 meters) and the volume of water passing over them: about 600,000 gallons (2,271,000 liters) per second. The highest waterfalls in the world are the Angel Falls in Venezuela at 3,212 feet (979 meters), followed by the Tugela Falls in South Africa at 3,110 feet (947 meters).

CITIES

The capital of Thailand is Bangkok

The official name for the capital of Thailand is Krung Thep Maha Nakhon (City of Angels Metropolis), or more commonly, Krung Thep. But even this is an abbreviation of the city's ceremonial name, which at 163 letters has won a place in the *Guinness Book of World Records* as the longest place name in the world. Bangkok was the old capital of Thailand, located across the river from present-day Krung Thep. In 1782 King Rama I (1737–89) established his capital on the other side of the river in a more defensible location. He named the city "Krung Thep Mahanakhon Amon Rattanakosin Mahinthara Ayuthaya Mahadilok Phop Noppharat Ratchathani Burirom Udomratchaniwet Mahasathan Amon Piman Awatan Sathit Sakkathattiya Witsanukam Prasit." Roughly translated, this means, "the city of angels, the great city, the residence of the Emerald Buddha, the impregnable city of God Indra, the grand capital of the world endowed with nine precious gems, the happy city, abounding in an enormous Royal Palace that resembles the heavenly abode where reigns the reincarnated god, a city given by Indra and built by Vishnukam." Children in Thailand memorize the name by singing a popular song that teaches them the city's title. But outside Thailand the old name of the original city has somehow stuck, and the city is best known by foreigners as Bangkok.

The capital of Israel is Jerusalem

The question of the capital of Israel is a highly charged political matter. Up until 1980, Tel Aviv was the capital, but in 1980 Jerusalem was annexed by Israel and declared to be its capital. Because Jerusalem is also claimed by the Palestinians, and no agreement over the status of the city has yet been reached, most countries do not recognize Jerusalem as the capital of Israel.

New York City is the capital of the State of New York

Although New York is the largest city in the State of New York, the capital is Albany, situated 125 miles (200 kilometers) to the north of the Big Apple on the Hudson River.

Hong Kong is a city

The former British Crown Colony of Hong Kong consists of the Kowloon peninsula, the two larger islands of Hong Kong and Lantau, and over 200 smaller islands. The urban center is made up of Kowloon on the southern part of the peninsula and the towns of Victoria and Aberdeen on the adjoining island of Hong Kong. However, Hong Kong is governed by one unified administration, with no separate government for the individual towns and local communities. Within its 425 square miles (1,100 square kilometers) live more than 6 million people, mostly Chinese.

The largest city in the world is Mexico City

If we consider only individual cities, not agglomerations (which consist of one or more central cities linked by a continuous built-up area), then currently Mumbai (Bombay) with 12,883,645 inhabitants is the largest city in the world. It is followed by Delhi (11,215,130), Karachi (11,969,284), Moscow (10,472,629) and Seoul (10,409,345). Mexico City (8,659,409) and New York (8,124,427) lag far behind. If, however, we consider what are known as agglomerations, then the highest is Tokyo with 32.4 million inhabitants. It is followed in close succession by the agglomerations of Mexico City, Seoul, New York and São Paulo. Size in terms of land area is a whole other discussion.

LONDON AND HOLLAND

It continuously rains in London

With an average of just about 24 inches (60 centimeters) of rain per year, London is one of the driest places in Europe. In fact, its municipal government is promoting water conservation because the city's growing population is stressing available water supplies. New York, on the other hand, gets almost double the amount of rainfall per year — an average of almost 43 inches (110 centimeters). However, the number of wet days can alter a person's perception of wet weather. New York has about 125 rainy days each year, but with an annual average of 153 rainy days, London is wet an additional 30 percent of the time.

Holland is another name for the Netherlands

Holland is just a portion of the Netherlands. North and South Holland are two of the 12 provinces that make up the kingdom. Equating the Netherlands with Holland has been going on for a long time, perhaps because ever since the 16th century, Holland has dominated the country. The cities of Leiden, The Hague, Amsterdam and Rotterdam all lie within either North or South Holland. Dutch is the official language of the Netherlands, and although it is common to refer to its inhabitants as "the Dutch," Netherlanders is a bit more accurate.

STORMY WEATHER

The influence of the weather on the preparation of food is superstition

In thundery weather, milk turns sour, gelatin doesn't set and yeast doesn't work properly. All fairy tales? In recent times, meteorologists have discovered "sferics" — extremely short-lived electromagnetic waves produced during a thunderstorm. Anyone who is sensitive to the weather can feel these atmospheric disturbances. Since sensitivity to the weather is not confined to human beings, but is also experienced by bacteria and fungi, it may be possible that the bacteria in various foods reacts differently under the influence of sferics.

Lightning never strikes the same place twice

Lightning can strike the same spot many times. Tall buildings provide good targets for lightning, and some skyscrapers are struck several times a year. The Empire State Building is hit by lightning approximately 100 times a year, and on one memorable occasion, 15 strikes of lightning were recorded during 15 minutes.

Lightning happens before thunder

They both occur at the same time. Because light travels almost a million times faster than sound, we see the flash of lightning before we hear the thunder. Light travels at a speed of about 186,000 miles (300,000 kilometers) per second, while sound travels at about 1,090 feet (332 meters) per second.

Ice is slippery

Ice is not in the slightest bit slippery, as can be experienced by opening a freezer and touching the white crusty ice that forms on the walls. Ice becomes slippery only when the surface layer thaws and a fine film of water forms over the top, making it slick.

Hail occurs when rain freezes in mid-air

The formation of hail requires two meteorological conditions: an air temperature below freezing (32°F/0°C), and extremely turbulent, windy conditions in which the raindrops do not fall but are instead carried high up into the atmosphere (usually several times up and down). The raindrops are supercooled by the cold air and layer by layer form into ice, becoming larger with each circuit until they eventually fall to the ground. The reason it can hail on a summer day is because the temperature higher in the atmosphere is cold enough to freeze the raindrops. In North America, as many as 20 hailstorms a year are experienced in "Hail Alley" — an area stretching from northern Alberta to Texas.

Polar regions have the highest snowfall

New snow is extremely rare in the polar regions. In the center of the Antarctic only about an inch (2.5 centimeters) falls in a year. The Antarctic is extremely dry, and water vapor is required for the formation of snow. The highest snowfalls occur in mountainous regions that are close to a coast. The record is held by the Southern Alps in New Zealand, with over 165 feet (50 meters) of new snow falling annually.

HEAT AND WIND

During the dog days, even dogs find it too hot

The dog days of summer were not named after man's best friend — at least not directly. The dog days mark the time when Sirius, the brightest star in Canis Major (the Great Dog), rises with the Sun. The dog days last for a full month, until the whole constellation is visible in the morning sky. Four thousand years ago, the start of the dog days fell in the middle of July, but now it has moved to a period beginning around August 19. However, over the years the expression "dog days of summer" has come to mean the hottest days of the summer.

Chinooks only happen in the Rockies

Chinook conditions occur when a cool, humid wind blows across mountains. The clouds that it carries produce rain. The air, now much drier, warms quickly as it descends into the valleys on the opposite side of the range, creating warm, dry winds that can raise temperatures by as much as 54 degrees Fahrenheit (30 degrees Celsius). This phenomenon occurs with almost all major mountain ranges: in the Alps it is know as the *föhn*; in the Andes as the *puelche* or *zonda*; and in Southern California as the Santa Ana winds.

The Inuit have more than a hundred terms for snow

Much like a snowball gathering more packing snow as it rolls down a hill, this is a myth that has grown exponentially over the years. In 1911, in *The Handbook of North American Indians*, ethnologist Franz Boas (1858–1942) stated that the Inuit (or Eskimos as he called them) had four words for snow: *aput* (snow on the ground), *gana* (falling snow), *piqsirpoq* (drifting snow) and *qimuqsuq* (snowdrift). Thirty years later, linguist Benjamin Whorf (1897–1941) helped create the Whorf-Sapir hypothesis of linguistic determinism, which suggested that a culture is both reflected and determined by the structure of its language. According to Whorf, the Inuit had seven words for snow. By 1978 there were 50 and by 1984 the *New York Times* put the number at 100. Since then even higher numbers have been cited. More recently, anthropologist Laura Martin and linguist Geoffrey K. Pullum were able to convincingly refute the "100 words" myth. The several different Inuit languages have varying numbers of words to describe snow, just as English does (e.g., blizzard, white-out, glacier, slush, flurry). But because the Inuit languages are polysynthetic (several words that might be a phrase or a sentence in another language are all joined together as one new word), there is limitless potential for words to describe snow — or hair, houses or toasters for that matter.

El Niño is a result of climate change

The El Niño phenomenon was recorded as early as the 16th century. The trade winds usually push warm surface water west, away from the South American coast. But every few years they falter and sometimes blow in the opposite direction, toward the east. At the same time, the cooling effects of the jet stream weaken. The result is that instead of cold, fish-rich waters and dry, high-pressure weather, the western coast of North America experiences warmer weather while its South American counterpart experiences warm tides and torrential rainfall. In southeast Asia meanwhile, they experience a considerably drier climate than usual. Since the intense El Niño event of 1982–83, however, climate researchers fear that climate change may be causing the phenomenon to strengthen. El Niño's sister, La Niña, is different and more destructive. Producing extremes of existing weather trends, it means that rainy regions can experience floods, drier areas, more drought, and so on.

TWILIGHT, DEW AND THE NORTHERN LIGHTS

When is becomes cold at night, dew falls from the sky

Dew does not fall. When nights are a lot colder than days, the water vapor in the air condenses on cold surfaces. This is how dew forms. If the temperature falls below freezing (32°F/0°C), then the dew freezes and becomes frost.

Twilight only happens just before dark

Twilight is the time when, although the sun is not visible above the horizon, light reflected from the upper atmosphere produces a dim half-light. Twilight occurs in the evening after sunset and in the morning before sunrise.

The northern lights are seen only in the north

Polar auroras (known in North America as northern lights) occur when large flares on the Sun eject electrically charged particles into space. If these eventually crash into molecules in the Earth's upper atmosphere, they create the ghostly glows and bands of light that often persist for hours. Because of their charge, the solar particles are attracted toward the Earth's magnetic poles, where auroras are most frequently seen. When the Sun is particularly active, auroras may occasionally be seen at lower latitudes, such as those of the United States and Central Europe.

THE SUN

The Sun is a glowing sphere

The Sun is an enormous, hot star, and its intense heat turns matter into energy. It is essentially a giant ball of spinning gases, primarily hydrogen and helium (with a bit of oxygen and carbon). It appears to us as a sphere because we cannot see through the dense gases. At its visible surface the Sun's temperature is slightly less than 9,900°F (5,500°C), but at its core this rises to about 28,000,000°F (15,000,000°C). The Sun's radiation is produced by nuclear fusion, in which hydrogen atoms fuse to become helium atoms, releasing a vast amount of energy that travels outward to the Sun's surface.

The Sun mainly emits yellow light

The Sun emits light at all wavelengths, but much of it is scattered by the Earth's atmosphere. Blue, green and violet radiation are the most strongly scattered because they have shorter wavelengths. The longer wavelengths of yellow, orange and red are scattered the least. For this reason, practically no violet, blue or green sunlight reaches the Earth's surface. Yellow forms the major part of the sunlight that we see, in part because our eyes are most sensitive to yellow light. When the Sun is close to the horizon, then much of the yellow light is also filtered out, and the orange and red portions appear much stronger.

Only the Sun produces a rainbow

On rare occasions a lunar rainbow can be formed, when the light from the full moon is bright enough be refracted by raindrops. Because moonlight is so much fainter than sunlight, a lunar rainbow is not very bright, and often appears to be white rather than different colors. They are sometimes called white rainbows, or "moonbows."

The Sun does not move

It actually moves in three different ways. First, it rotates around its own axis. Second, it orbits the center of the Milky Way galaxy. In doing so, it moves at about 137 miles (220 kilometers) per second, and takes 220 million to 225 million years to complete one orbit. Our whole solar system moves with it, so the position of the Earth relative to the Sun does not alter. Because the whole universe is expanding, the Milky Way galaxy is moving and our solar system with it, which is the third way that the Sun moves.

The Great Wall of China is visible from the Moon

The Great Wall can definitely not be seen from the Moon nor, according to NASA, even from low Earth orbit. This was confirmed by Chinese astronaut Yang Li Wei, who said he couldn't see the historic wall. In photographs taken by astronauts, the wall is impossible to discern because it is made of the same material as its surroundings. However it can be "seen" quite easily using radar imagery, as revealed in a photograph taken from the Space Shuttle *Endeavour*. The image shows the wall as an orange line in the desert 435 miles (700 kilometers) west of Beijing.

There is no danger of the Sun going out

This is precisely what will happen. The Sun is a star and all stars have a finite life. In the Sun's case, its duration will depend on how long it takes for its hydrogen supply to run out. Experts say this will take at least four billion years. In the course of time the Sun will expand, eventually becoming a giant, red, glowing ball and then it will collapse. That will naturally mean the end of all life on the Earth.

THE MOON

The Earth's atmosphere makes the Moon seem larger on the horizon

Contrary to popular belief, there are no magnification effects caused by the atmosphere of the Earth that make the Moon appear larger when it is low on the horizon. The Moon does sometimes look bigger on the horizon than directly overhead, but this is the result of what's known as "moon illusion" — a type of optical illusion.

The Moon does not rotate

It does, it just doesn't look like it to us. This is because we always see the same side of the Moon. Due to tidal forces, the Moon's rotation and revolution are synchronized: the time it takes for the Moon to make one rotation on its axis is equal to the time it takes for the Moon to make one revolution around the Earth. As it tracks its orbit, it always presents the same side to us. The "dark side of the Moon" is simply the side we never see.

Only half of the Moon is visible from Earth

It is true that a large portion of the Moon, the "dark" side, cannot be seen from Earth. But because the moon's velocity is variable, a phenomenon called "libration" allows us to see a bit more than half of the moon — as much as 59 percent of its surface is visible from Earth at times. However, 41 percent still remains hidden on the dark side.

It is bitterly cold on the Moon

At night the temperatures can go as low as –387°F (–233°C). But during the day on the side turned toward the sun, the moon's temperature can be as high as 253°F (123°C).

A blue moon is a rare event

It all depends on which definition of "blue moon" you are using. Usually the phrase "once in a blue moon" refers to an event that is very unlikely. But a blue moon is an astrological term, and as it is now understood, it happens approximately every 2.7 years. Before 1946, the accepted definition of a blue moon was when four full moons occurred within one season (usually each season has three full moons). But in 1946, *Sky & Telescope* magazine published an article that mistakenly defined a blue moon as occurring when two full moons happen in the same month. The Moon itself does appear blue sometimes, when smoke or dust in the atmosphere give it a bluish tinge.

THE PLANETS

Planets and their satellites are named after ancient gods

People tried to do this at first. The satellites of Jupiter have the names of the god's lovers, such as Io, Europa and Ganymede. Pluto, the god of the underworld, has Charon, the ferryman of the dead, as its companion; Neptune, the god of the sea, has Triton, a subordinate water deity; and Mars, the ancient god of war, is orbited by Phobos and Deimos ("Fear" and "Flight"), named after his sons. But because so many more satellites have been discovered in recent years, it has been necessary to be somewhat more flexible with names. Uranus is accompanied by Shakespearean characters — Puck, Ophelia, Desdemona and Portia. Saturn's satellite names have been taken from various world mythologies, including Celtic (Albiorix), Inuit (Kiviuq) and Norse (Ymir). Many of the most recently discovered satellites have been given numbers but are not yet named.

Only planets have satellites

In addition to the nine planets whirling around the Sun in our solar system, there are hundreds of thousands of minor planets, or asteroids. Most are found in the asteroid belt between the orbits of Jupiter and Mars. Many of these have their own satellites, but this was not confirmed until 1993, when the *Galileo* space probe discovered Dactyl orbiting the minor planet Ida (Dactyl was a mythical creature from Greek mythology that lived on Mount Ida). Ida is a cylindrical lump of rock 35 miles (56 kilometers) long that orbits the Sun at a distance of approximately 261 million miles (about 420 million kilometers). Since then at least 40 satellites of minor planets have been discovered.

Only Earth is surrounded by an atmosphere

An atmosphere is a shell of gases that surround a planet, held there by its gravitational force. Earth is not the only planet with an atmosphere: the other planets in our solar system also have them. However, each atmosphere has a different composition. Smaller planets with lower gravity than Earth have much thinner atmospheres. Mars has an atmosphere consisting of 95 percent carbon dioxide, with the remaining 5 percent made up of nitrogen, methane, argon and carbon monoxide, as well as traces of oxygen and water vapor. Scientists believe that the atmosphere on Mars was once significantly thicker, but has been "blown away" by the solar wind.

All the planets orbit the Sun from west to east

The solar system was formed from a single rotating cloud of gas. Consequently, almost all of the planets orbit the Sun in the same direction, east to west (or counterclockwise if you were looking down on the Sun's north pole), as do the moons. This is also the direction that the Sun itself rotates on its axis. Most of the planets also rotate on their axes in the same direction, but Venus rotates from west to east (clockwise). Venus rotates on its axis so slowly that it actually completes a full orbit around the Sun before it completes one rotation. This results in one Venus day lasting 243 Earth days, and one Venus year just 225 Earth days.

Seasons are only experienced on Earth

Several planets experience seasons, including Mars, Uranus, Pluto, Saturn and Neptune. On Mars, seasons last almost twice as long as they do on Earth, because Mars takes almost 687 days to orbit the Sun. Spring in Mars is marked by sandstorms, while one of the polar ice caps experiences melting in the summer. Frosts migrate across Pluto according to the season.

A flight to Mars would last two years

That is an old figure. More recently, it has been calculated that the flight alone would last between six and nine months. The prerequisite is that the distance between Earth and Mars be suitable for both the outward and the return flights. Depending on their orbit positions, the distance between Earth and Mars varies between about 35 million miles (56 million kilometers) and 63 million miles (101 million kilometers). The most recent best-case scenario for a trip to Mars occurred in 2003. The next possible date is 2020, when an entire expedition could be accomplished in just under three years.

The gas giants consist solely of gas

The inner planets — Mercury, Venus, Earth and Mars — are called the terrestrial or Earth-like planets. They are rocky planets with metal cores and solid surfaces. The outer planets — Jupiter, Saturn, Uranus and Neptune — are Jovian (or Jupiter-like). They have no solid surfaces and consist mostly of hydrogen and helium, which is why they are also known as the gas giants. However, they are composed of small fractions of heavier materials such as rock, metals and ice, and it is thought that each of the gas giants may have a rocky core at its center.

Only Saturn is surrounded by rings

No other planet exhibits such beautiful and distinct rings as Saturn, which mainly consist of ice. But weak rings have also formed around Neptune, Jupiter and Uranus. None of the rings consist of solid material, but rather of innumerable small fragments of rock. It has been suggested that in about 10 million to 100 million years, Triton and Phobos may be drawn close enough to Neptune and Mars, respectively, to break up and form ring systems that are equally as striking as that around Saturn.

Pluto is the outermost planet in the solar system

It all depends. Like all planets in the solar system, both Pluto and Neptune have elliptical orbits, meaning their distance from the Sun varies. Neptune's orbit gets as close as 2,771 million miles (4,460 million kilometers) to the Sun, while at its closest point Pluto is just 2,757 million miles (4,437 million kilometers) from the Sun. In galactic terms, that's not much difference. But it does mean that for 20 years of its 248-year orbit around the Sun, Pluto is not the most distant planet.

Mercury is the smallest and hottest planet in the solar system

With a diameter of 3,031 miles (4,878 kilometers), Mercury is the second smallest planet to orbit the Sun. The smallest is Pluto, with a diameter of approximately 1,413 miles (2,274 kilometers) — about half the size of Mercury. Despite being the closest to the Sun, Mercury is not the hottest planet, though it comes very close. Because it rotates very slowly and effectively has no atmosphere, its shadowed side cools down to about –274°F (–170°C), while the side warmed by the Sun hovers around 806°F (430°C). By contrast, the dense carbon dioxide atmosphere of Venus traps the Sun's heat, causing the planet to experience a stable temperature of about 896°F (480°C), making it the hottest planet in the solar system.

THE STARS

The Milky Way is a neighboring galaxy

The Milky Way is our home galaxy. Its shape is that of a large, flat, swirling spiral, and it has an end-to-end diameter of more than 100,000 light-years, roughly 600 million miles (966 million kilometers). In total, it contains approximately 100 billion stars or stellar systems. Our own Sun lies well out from the center on a spiral arm, which explains why the Milky Way appears to us as a narrow, distant band of stars.

We are only able to see stars that actually exist

Many of the stars we can see probably died long ago. The nearest star that we can observe, Proxima Centauri, lies at a distance of just over four light-years. That means that we see it as it was four years ago. When we look at stars that are millions of light-years away, we are seeing them as they were millions of years ago. By using improved technology and ever-stronger telescopes, scientists are able to see farther and farther into the past. At present, they can "look back" 15 billion years.

Between March 21 and April 21, the Sun is in the constellation of Aries

The locations of constellations relate to the period during which the Sun travels through that constellation. So we know that the Sun travels through the Aries constellation between March 21 and April 21. Or at least that was how it was when the constellations were first named 2,500 years ago. Since then, the wobble in the Earth's axis has resulted in a change in the position of the Earth relative to the North Pole. This has caused the location of various stars, including the ones that make up the constellations, to shift about 1° every 70 years or so. To track the change, astronomers use a specific reference point in the sky called the "First Point of Aries." Today the constellations are about 30° out of sync and the First Point of Aries lies in Pisces. It will take another 24,000 years for the whole circuit to be completed and the zodiacal signs to coincide again.

Time can be measured in light-years

Light-years measure distance, not time. A light-year is the distance a beam of light will travel in one year: approximately 5,865,696,000,000 miles (9,460,800,000,000 kilometers).

Shooting stars are falling stars

Shooting stars have nothing to do with stars. They are meteoroids, formed when small particles of dust and rock from space encounter the Earth's atmosphere and burn up. Many of these particles are no larger than a grain of sand. The friction between the particle and the atmosphere is so great that the particles immediately begin to heat up and glow. The trail of light the meteoroid produces is called a meteor. Meteors are particularly easy to see in August, when the Earth passes through a cloud of cosmic dust left by an orbiting comet. These annual events are called meteor showers.

The Evening Star is a star

Nope. What people refer to as the "Evening Star" is usually Venus. Venus is often the brightest object visible in the evening. It also appears as the Morning Star when visible in the early morning.

Stars are white

The color of stars depends on their temperature. Blue stars are hotter than red stars. When stars are very dim, their color appears as white, but most stars are really red. Some colorful stars: blue-white Vega, red Antares and blue Altair.

THE FINAL DELUSION

This book contains 1,000 delusions

By now the gentle reader will no doubt be alert to the

many common delusions held by an unsuspecting public.

Here's one more: contrary to its title, this book actually

contains 1,003 delusions.

1,000

784

329

95

2

INDEX

INDEX